T0271225

HOLLYWOOD
HATES!
HITLER!

CHRIS YOGERST

HOLLYWOOD HATES! HITLER.

JEW-BAITING, ANTI-NAZISM,

and the

Senate Investigation into Warmongering in Motion Pictures

University Press of Mississippi / Jackson

The University Press of Mississippi is the scholarly publishing agency of
the Mississippi Institutions of Higher Learning: Alcorn State University,
Delta State University, Jackson State University, Mississippi State University,
Mississippi University for Women, Mississippi Valley State University,
University of Mississippi, and University of Southern Mississippi.

www.upress.state.ms.us

The University Press of Mississippi is a member
of the Association of University Presses.

Sections throughout the first chapters have appeared in "Searching for Common
Ground: Hollywood Prior to the 1941 Senate Investigation into Motion Picture
Propaganda, 1935-1941" in the *Historic Journal of Film, Radio, and Television*.

First printing 2020

∞

Library of Congress Cataloging-in-Publication Data

Names: Yogerst, Chris, 1983– author.
Title: Hollywood hates Hitler!: Jew-baiting, anti-Nazism, and the Senate
investigation into warmongering in motion pictures / Chris Yogerst.
Description: Jackson: University Press of Mississippi, 2020. | Includes
bibliographical references and index.
Identifiers: LCCN 2020010607 (print) | LCCN 2020010608 (ebook) |
ISBN 9781496829757 (hardback) | ISBN 9781496829764 (trade paperback) |
ISBN 9781496829771 (epub) | ISBN 9781496829788 (epub) |
ISBN 9781496829795 (pdf) | ISBN 9781496829801 (pdf)
Subjects: LCSH: Motion pictures—United States—History. | Motion
pictures—Censorship—United States. | Motion pictures—Political
aspects—United States. | Anti-Nazi movement in motion pictures.
Classification: LCC PN1993.5.U6 Y68 2020 (print) | LCC PN1993.5.U6
(ebook) | DDC 384/.8097309044—dc23
LC record available at https://lccn.loc.gov/2020010607
LC ebook record available at https://lccn.loc.gov/2020010608

British Library Cataloging-in-Publication Data available

"The Name 'Hollywood' provokes either amusement or indignation in those whose conception of Hollywood has been formed by publicity and gossip."

—Leo Rosten, 1941

Contents

Acknowledgments

While every book has an author, any work of history is undoubtedly a group effort. This project began while I was researching for a different book at the Oviatt Library at California State University–Northridge. There, David Sigler and his team were incredibly accommodating and gracious. While in Northridge, I came across files full of press coverage from the 1941 Senate Investigation into Motion Picture Propaganda. My first reaction was that these findings could work for a journal article, which they did. I am grateful for the *Historical Journal of Film, Radio, and Television* for publishing my essay titled "Searching for Common Ground," which analyzes the history leading up to the Senate investigation. My editor at the journal, James Chapman, provided timely advice as I was preparing my book proposal.

When I flew to Toronto to present my work at an SCMS conference, University Press of Mississippi acquisitions editor Emily Bandy reached out to ask if this narrative could be turned into a book. Unsure, I dug into it further and also reached out to my mentor Thomas Doherty for advice. Tom felt there was certainly a book-length story here and offered timely advice and support about moving forward with this manuscript. Emily remained accessible and supportive throughout the entire process, providing useful suggestions along the way.

After getting a contract from UPM, I flew to Washington, DC, to inspect the Senate files at the National Archives. Katherine Mollan, Dorothy Alexander, and everyone else in the reading room was kind and enthusiastic. When I found myself with a little extra time, the staff at the Library of Congress quickly got me set up with a card and database access. In Southern California, Ned Comstock and Brett Service at USC were helpful as always. Warren Sherk, Louise Hilton, and everyone else at the Margaret Herrick Library worked quickly to get me necessary materials while this project evolved, as I flipped through documents in the reading room. This project also wouldn't be possible without Eric Hoyt at the University of Wisconsin, who has worked tirelessly to keep open source archival files available to the public through the Media History Digital Library.

I have many friends and colleagues who offered support and suggestions along the way, both regarding this manuscript and general advice about navigating this point in my career. I am thankful for the conversations with many of you, including Mark Peterson, Kirk Tyvela, Vanda Kreeft, Drew Casper, Michael Newman, and Andrew Patrick Nelson. Joel Berkowitz, Rachel Baum, and Lisa Silverman at the Stahl Center on campus at UW–Milwaukee also provided useful support, conversation, and collegiality while I finished this project amidst a university-system-wide merger.

Lastly, and most importantly, I would like to thank my family, who listened to my stories, put up with my absences during research trips, and provided encouragement over the years. To my wife, Caitlin, thank you for all of the support while I completed another book. It will be a joy to share our love of history and popular culture with the beautiful new addition to our family, June Rose.

Introduction

Competing Ideologies in Dangerous Times

1941 was a tumultuous period similar to the first decades of the twenty-first century, where aggressive rhetoric and staunch disagreements captured headlines, fueled debates, and tested friendships. Radical groups enjoyed increasing influence, while government officials provided cover. American culture was struggling economically and torn politically. Discussion about subversive propaganda would continue throughout the 1930s, and Hollywood would be implicated more than once. As clashes with organized labor exposed political allegiances in Hollywood, prewar production trends gave some government onlookers curiosity about the propagandistic power of cinema.

Interest in contemporary propaganda can be dated back to Gustave Le Bon's *The Crowd: A Study of the Popular Mind*, first published in 1895. Le Bon's study of mass behavior was a central influence on Walter Lippmann's work, *Public Opinion* (1922). Lippmann outlined the relationship between the "scene of action, the human picture of that scene, and the human response to that picture working itself out upon the scene of action."[1] Lippmann opened the door for Edward Bernays, author of *Propaganda* (1928), who became known as the Father of Public Relations. Bernays looked at public relations in terms of its potential to manipulate mass audiences by "invisible wirepullers" with the ability to "control the destinies of millions."[2] Bernays was a high-profile figure who organized a 1929 celebration of the fifty-year anniversary of Thomas Edison's lightbulb (furthering the myth that Edison was the sole inventor) and a campaign for Dixie Cup in the 1930s. The master manipulator also served as publicity director for the 1939 World's Fair in New York. During Bernays's lifetime, propaganda would become the central focus of many government investigations.

Bernays defined propaganda as "the conscious and intelligent manipulation of the organized habits and opinions of the masses," while those who operate the "unseen mechanism" held the "true ruling power of our country."[3] Those skeptical of motion pictures had long spread fear about the medium's ability to influence. The primary reason for Hollywood's self-imposed production code (i.e. censors) was to minimize the social outcry from moral crusaders afraid that movies caused social erosion. Henry James Forman's best-selling tome *Our Movie Made Children* (1933) served as strong propaganda against the film industry for anyone willing to believe movies turned youths into delinquent sinners. A similar fear of Hollywood's influential power would be picked up by a few United States senators in 1941.

The issue of the day, from the late 1930s into 1941, was the question of intervention into what was then referred to as the "European war." Isolationist support increased steadily as the war in Europe escalated. Some citizens carried buyer's remorse over World War I and were reluctant to get into another global conflict. Popular films like *All Quiet on the Western Front* (1929) and *The Dawn Patrol* (1930) serve as a reminder that antiwar sentiment continued long after the First World War concluded. Peace advocates encouraged the continued exhibition of such films throughout the 1930s so that new audiences could learn about the horrors of war. *All Quiet on the Western Front* was given special Armistice Day screenings every year from 1935 to 1937, with a special rerelease in 1939 that lasted until 1942.

After the Great Depression hit, citizens also became weary of the United States' own economic instability. Phrases like "the Forgotten Man" were used to describe a quarter of the population that was out of work. Those forced out into the streets were living in tent communities derisively named Hoovervilles after President Herbert Hoover, who was in office when the stock market crashed on October 29, 1929. On July 28, 1932, World War I veterans marched in protest to demand early payment of their earned benefits, which were set for redemption in 1945. Veterans would not get paid until 1936. As the country recovered from economic collapse, the public was understandably hesitant to join another expensive war.

Other groups supported America's isolation for much more sinister reasons. The rise of fascist and Nazi groups in the United States saw a terrifying rise in the 1930s. Nazi-influenced organizations expanded in the United States as Hitler was accumulating power and planning to take over Europe. The Friends of New Germany, a relatively small fascist group, operated in the early 1930s but disbanded in 1935. Shortly thereafter the Nazi-inspired German-American Bund, a much larger organization led by German immigrant Fritz Kuhn, founded training camps throughout the United States. Each camp was complete with uniformed children walking in goose step with the Hitler Youth. After taking up leadership in the Bund, Kuhn proclaimed, "Our goal here is to fight Jew-

Father Charles Coughlin. *Radio Mirror* (May–Oct 1935)

ish Marxism and Communism."[4] The association of far-left political ideology and Judaism would be a conflation that spread throughout the United States.

Another fascist group known as the Silver Shirts was organized by American William Dudley Pelley. The Silver Shirts were also modeled after the Brownshirts, Hitler's first stormtrooper paramilitary outfit. Like Kuhn, Pelley sought to quell two key threats: Jews and communists. The deranged Pelley planned to have all Jews rounded up and put into camps so that banking could be controlled by so-called real Americans. Any Jew who left these designated camps would be executed. Both the German-American Bund and the Silver Shirts had significant activity in Los Angeles near the Hollywood film studios. The flurry of fascism would not go unnoticed by the many Jewish moguls, performers, and below-the-line workers in the motion-picture industry. For the pro-Nazi camp, isolation was a key component of keeping the United States out of the war so Nazi Germany could steamroll through Europe.

Another major cultural and political influence in the 1930s was Detroit radio priest Father Charles Coughlin. The radio preacher gained prominence for his charismatic and accessible sermons. Coughlin was heard across the United States on over thirty stations with a complete listenership of forty million.[5] However, by the 1930s his rhetoric had turned entirely political. Particular attention was given to combating anti-Catholic animosity. One of Coughlin's key messages was to highlight "the steady erosion of the individual's ability to control his own destiny."[6] Coughlin's influence was peaking in the mid-1930s, but after the 1936 election Coughlin became increasingly unhinged. His radio broadcasts began to sympathize with fascist leaders in Europe. Coughlin's anti-Semitic magazine *Social Justice* began publication in 1936 and became infamous for its belief in *The Protocols of the Elders of Zion* (1903), a fictitious Jewish conspiracy to control the world. Coughlin would be removed from the radio in 1939. *Social Justice* would continue, with one issue published during the 1941 Senate investigation referring to movie studios as "Hollywood propaganda mills."[7]

With fascism on the rise in the United States, Senators John William McCormack (D-MA) and Samuel Dickstein (D-NY) founded a special House committee dedicated to investigating Nazi propaganda in what became the first Special Committee on Un-American Activities (later known as HUAC). From 1934 to 1937 the special committee heard testimony focusing on subversive propaganda. By the late 1930s, however, the focus shifted towards investigating communist subversion and propaganda, led by Texas Democrat Martin Dies. With the government's sights set on communism, the Nazi-sympathizers could comfortably work on infiltration and influence. As fascist sympathizers moved out of the shadows, anti-Semitic rhetoric became more commonplace on the national stage as major figures and politicians openly derided Jews without consequence. Oftentimes, as in the case of famed aviator Charles Lindbergh at American First rallies, anti-Semitic remarks would be rewarded with applause. What began as a movement to oppose war and connect Americans, the America First Committee was quickly co-opted by fascist sympathizers interested only in helping Germany by keeping the American military stateside.

By 1941, tensions were rising on Capitol Hill as John E. Rankin (D-MS), an open supporter of the Ku Klux Klan, accused a "group of our international Jewish brethren" of pushing the United States into war.[8] Heated over the prejudicial accusations, Morris Michael Edelstein gave a staunch denunciation of Rankin. Edelstein, a Jewish New York Democrat, explained how Hitler made similar statements to justify his own hateful views. Overwhelmingly agitated with the rise of anti-Semitism in America, Edelstein dropped dead of a heart attack shortly after his speech.[9] When the session closed shortly after Edelstein's death, Rankin refused to release the text of his speech and showed no signs of remorse for Edelstein.[10] Such mainstream prejudice against Jews would fuel that fascist sympathizers throughout the United States.

The Aviator and the Soldier

The cultural divide over intervention can be seen in the disparate support of two national heroes, aviator Charles Lindbergh and Sgt. Alvin York. Lindbergh was a celebrated pilot known for making the first solo transatlantic flight from North America to Europe. Serving in the US Army Air Corps Reserve, Lindbergh completed his flight in a monoplane famously named Spirit of St. Louis. The flight landed Lindbergh the Medal of Honor. The pilot also grabbed unwanted

Lindbergh Speaks Out Against Jews in Des Moines, Iowa, 1941

Alvin York, war hero, in 1941

media attention when his son was kidnapped and murdered in 1932. In the following years, Lindbergh became a strong antiwar advocate (like York), but his rhetoric led many to believe he was a fascist sympathizer or at least strongly anti-Semitic. Both York and Lindbergh became national heroes in their own right, though they would sit on opposing sides of the debate over intervention.

Born in Tennessee, York entered World War I as a conscientious objector. In 1918, York was one of seventeen soldiers fighting to take down a German machine gun. After suffering major losses, York took command of his unit, took down the machine gun, and also captured over a hundred prisoners. York was awarded the Medal of Honor for his heroism and forever after hailed as a war hero. While many theater and film producers wanted to immortalize York's story on stage and screen, the war hero refused and went home to find a quiet life. In the subsequent years, York became an ardent voice for the antiwar movement. Hollywood would eventually prevail when Warner Bros. produced *Sergeant York* (1941), based on York's life and war experience.

On September 11, 1941, Lindbergh addressed a crowd in Des Moines, Iowa, as part of his isolationist advocacy. Lindbergh went on to list three groups "who have been pressing this country toward war," which were "the British, the Jewish, and the Roosevelt administration."[11] While the aviator took time to attack each, he singled out the Jews because "their greatest danger to this country lies in their large ownership and influence in our motion pictures, our press, our radio and our government."[12] For Lindbergh, the conflict in Europe was only of interest to European immigrants. Expressing his prejudice in supposed sympathy for the Jews, Lindbergh continued, "We cannot blame them for looking out for what they believe to be their own interests [defending their faith and homeland], but we must also look out for ours." Assuming a desire to defend the United States was camouflage for a drive to defend a foreign homeland, Lindbergh's xenophobic sentiments, labeling the "foreign war" as "their problem," would drive many in the isolationist movement at America First rallies.

Three days after Lindbergh's Des Moines speech, the only comparable hero in American life spoke out against the increasing isolationist rhetoric that smeared Hollywood as a Jewish-run propaganda machine. Alvin York addressed fellow veterans at the national convention of the American Legion in Milwaukee, which was not far from the German-American Bund's Camp Hindenburg in nearby Grafton, Wisconsin. Sergeant York argued, "If the story of my life is propaganda, then so is this very convention, because the simple story of my life revolves around the same great experience as yours."[13] While not directly responding to Lindbergh, York used the widely seen image of Nazi book burnings to hammer his point home and attack another isolationist who would be a central figure in the 1941 Senate Investigation. Senator Gerald P.

Nye, a Wisconsin journalist turned North Dakota senator, was famous for taking down the Mammoth Oil Company in the Teapot Dome bribery scandal during the 1920s.[14] "If our lives are propaganda, Senator Nye should destroy all the history books, just as Hitler made bonfires of great literature in Germany," York continued, "because the histories of this country tell story after story about every generation's fight to keep alive in this nation's freedom of religion, freedom of speech, freedom of thought."[15]

◆ ◆ ◆

Speaking to a deeply divided United States, York and Lindbergh were fully engaged in opposite sides of the war debate. York would continue to see his celebrity status and influence grow while Lindbergh, an apologist for Nazism ever since he was awarded a medal from Nazi leader Hermann Goring, would continue receiving criticism for his Jew-baiting.[16] Despite the conflicting press, both would eventually see their lives immortalized in film. *Sergeant York* (1941) would come first at the peak of York's prominence, while Billy Wilder's *The Spirit of St. Louis* (1957), featuring James Stewart as Lindbergh, came years after memories of Lindbergh's rhetoric had faded. Representing disparate political camps, Lindbergh and York serve as useful examples of the dominant partisan divide in prewar 1941.

The Senate and Hollywood

The 1941 Senate Investigation into Motion Picture Propaganda would be born out of the cultural tensions that were exacerbated throughout the 1930s. Widespread economic struggle coupled with political tensions surrounding another world war led to a significant cultural divide. Seeds were planted in the 1930s that sprouted both jingoistic and paranoid politics throughout World War II and the Cold War years. What began with the Dies Committee investigating Hollywood subversion would be picked up in the 1941 Senate Investigation. However, the 1941 investigation would ultimately be overshadowed by the 1947 HUAC inquiry into Hollywood that would provoke the notorious blacklist.

The Senate Investigation into Motion Picture War Propaganda would serve as a culminating event in the prewar debate over intervention. After years of increasing Nazi activity in the United States, a handful of isolationist senators would punish Hollywood for a small number of anti-Nazi films released prior to entry into World War II. In the process, several senators would reveal their own prejudices and misguided assumptions about the film colony. The investigation would become a media circus that put the senators' ineptitude on the national stage, while the attack on Pearl Harbor ensured that Congress's focus moved from harassing Hollywood moguls to winning the war.

To the dismay of many isolationists, Hollywood had largely supported President Roosevelt's Lend-Lease bill, which approved the transfer of aid to Great Britain. The pro-intervention Fight for Freedom Committee saw involvement from prominent Hollywood figures such as Humphrey Bogart, Walt Disney, Howard Hawks, Edward G. Robinson, the Warner Brothers, William Wyler, Darryl Zanuck, and others.[17] Hollywood was also cranking out recruitment films that played in over seven thousand theaters in the spring of 1941.[18] Such interventionist rhetoric was accompanied by a number of anti-Nazi feature films that were produced by major studios. While not anywhere near representative of the majority of films released by Hollywood, isolationist senators feared the power of movies and saw them as a threat to their anti-interventionist cause.

The 1941 wave of congressional anti-Hollywood sentiment came from Senator Gerald P. Nye (R-ND), Senator Bennett Champ Clark (D-MO), and John T. Flynn, a journalist and America First organizer. The three would scheme against the American film industry for its alleged propagandizing in support of joining the European war. The result was Senate Resolution 152 in early August of 1941. The resolution was aimed at both radio and movies that "have been extensively used for propaganda purposes designed to influence the public mind in the direction of participation in the European war."[19] A separate set of hearings would be held for questions regarding radio propaganda. With the widespread political divide, Nye and Clark knew they must move quickly to get their resolution approved. The resolution found its way to Burton K. Wheeler's (D-MT) Interstate Commerce Committee. Wheeler then passed it to isolationist D. Worth Clark (D-ID), who put together a subcommittee and quickly scheduled hearings for the following month. As expected, Worth Clark's subcommittee would consist of Nye, Bennet Champ Clark (D-MO), Charles W. Tobey (R-NH), C. Wyland Brooks (R-IL), and Ernest W. McFarland (D-AZ). Homer T. Bone (D-WA) was scheduled to attend but fell ill and did not contribute.

After graduating from Harvard with a law degree, Worth Clark first served in the Idaho attorney general's office from 1933 to 1935 before winning a seat in the House of Representatives. Worth Clark served in the House from 1935 to 1939 before landing a position as senator of Idaho, where he served from 1939 to 1945. During his first years in the Senate, Worth Clark was a vocal critic of President Roosevelt's foreign policy, specifically the Lend-Lease bill. Worth Clark also became a fixture at America First rallies, including an impassioned speech delivered at the Hollywood Bowl in July 1941.

Gerald P. Nye was a Wisconsin journalist turned politician, serving in the United States Senate from 1925 to 1945. After working as an editor for the *Hortonville Review* in Wisconsin and *Creston Daily Plain Dealer* in Iowa, Nye purchased the *Fryburg Pioneer* in North Dakota. After gaining prominence for his political columns, Nye won a seat as a North Dakota senator. As a young senator, Nye would become involved in several committees. While serving as chair of the Public Lands committee, Nye assisted in uncovering Warren G. Harding's deal to cheaply lease land to the Mammoth Oil Company in return for kickbacks to the Republican National Committee. The event would become known as the Teapot Dome scandal. Nye also grabbed headlines while leading an investigation into the munitions industry, which examined a possible profit-based push into World War I. Interestingly, one of the government officials on the Nye munitions committee was soon to be accused Soviet spy Alger Hiss.

Bennet Champ Clark was destined to be in politics. His father was a Missouri congressman and eventually served as the Speaker of the House. Clark graduated from George Washington University Law School and served as the parliamentarian of the United States House of Representatives while completing his degree. Clark served in the United States Army during World War I before going back to Missouri to practice law. Clark would venture into politics again, serving as a Missouri senator from 1933 to 1945. During this time Clark was a loyal supporter of the America First organization and known as a staunch isolationist.

Charles W. Tobey had an interesting journey before his senatorial years. Tobey worked as a full-time farmer and school board member in Temple, New Hampshire. After being elected to the New Hampshire House of Representatives in 1914, Tobey would become known for being a progressive Republican, who would take on powerful business interests. Tobey became a state senator in 1924 and would eventually win the governorship in 1928. After serving only two years, Tobey would run for a seat in the United States House of Representatives and serve from 1933 to 1939. Tobey, who served in the Senate from 1939 to 1953, was a vocal critic of President Roosevelt on economic and foreign policy issues and would quickly align with the America First crowd as the war in Europe escalated.

C. Wyland Brooks had a much shorter political career than his colleagues working on Senate Resolution 152. Brooks served in World War I as a marine and would suffer several combat wounds. After the war, Brooks attended law school at Northwestern University, graduating in 1926. Brooks's first foray into politics was a losing campaign for governor of Illinois in 1936. When Illinois senator James Hamilton Lewis died suddenly, Brooks ran for the seat and won in 1940. Brooks would serve in the United States Senate until 1949.

Ernest W. McFarland was also a World War I veteran, serving stateside at the Great Lakes Naval Training Station. After the war, McFarland attended Stanford University Law School. The newly minted lawyer would start a legal practice in Arizona where he became involved in local and state political campaigns. While serving as the attorney for Pinal County, McFarland represented Eva Dugan, the first and only woman executed in Arizona. Because of the grisly scene at Dugan's execution, the state soon changed their capital punishment method to the gas chamber. McFarland also worked on the Winnie Ruth Judd case, winning her a sentence commuted from execution to life in a mental asylum. Judd was known for the infamous trunk murders. Remaining engaged in state politics, McFarland would land a seat in the United States Senate in 1941 and serve until 1953.

Many works of American film history only skim the surface of the 1941 investigation of Hollywood. Larry Ceplair and Steven Englund's five-hundred-page tome *The Inquisition in Hollywood: Politics in the Film Community, 1930–1960* (1979) dedicates a page and a half to the Senate inquiry. Bernard F. Dick's *The Star-Spangled Screen: The American World War II Film* (1985) provides a couple pages of analysis. Some attention is provided in Clayton R. Koppes and Gregory D. Black's *Hollywood Goes to War: How Politics, Profits and Propaganda Shaped World War II Movies* (1987). The hearings are noted in Donald T. Critchlow's *When Hollywood Was Right: How Movie Stars, Studio Moguls, and Big Business Remade American Politics* (2013).

A 2018 biography of Senator McFarland's Arizona years fails to even mention the hearings, even though his line of questioning established McFarland as a heroic maverick on the national stage.[20] The memoirs of the isolationist senators largely skip over the 1941 investigation, likely because the session did not paint them in a positive light. Like many often do in Hollywood, these senators decided to print their own legend by forgetting this embarrassing event.

Historians have given more attention to the hearings in recent years. Michael E. Birdwell's *Celluloid Soldiers: Warner Bros.' Campaign against Nazism* (1999) dedicated a chapter to the hearings, providing further detail of the influences leading up to the hearings. The isolationist anti-Semitism against Hollywood was further explained in Steven Carr's *Hollywood & Anti-Semitism: A Cultural History Up to World War II* (2001). Carr goes as far as to compare Senator Wheeler's political tactics of personal destruction as an important precursor to those of Senator Joseph McCarthy.[21] David Welky further considers the films that the Senate subcommittee claimed as dangerous, along with the political climate during the prewar years, in *The Moguls and The Dictators: Hollywood and the Coming of World War II* (2008). While each of the aforementioned books are worthwhile studies of important topics of Hollywood and its surrounding culture, the 1941 skirmish with the United States Senate was a piece of a larger story.

My own examination of the Senate investigation began at the end of my first book, *From the Headlines to Hollywood: The Birth and Boom of Warner Bros.* (2016), when I came across Harry Warner's staunch defense of the motion-picture industry. The other testimonies also deserve to be explored in depth. After seeing the current coverage of the Senate investigation, it is clear that the anti-Semitic slant of the isolationist senators was established. There are still many untouched primary documents and lengthy congressional records that provide a deeper explanation of how Senate Resolution 152 came to be and how it played out. This book details the senators' relationship with America First and paint a clearer picture of the investigation's daily events both on Capitol Hill and in the national press.

The years leading up to and through the Senate Investigation into Motion Picture War Propaganda can serve today as a reminder that the United States has lived through, and survived, contentious times. The investigation itself is a story worth telling. Readers will likely find connections and parallels to periods of political and popular-culture history that came after 1941. Xenophobic and myopic politicians are nothing new. Their tactics and arguments should be studied, as should the defenses against them. Fortunately for Hollywood, the senators and fellow isolationists were defeated before the United States' entry into World War II. Historians have pointed to the attack on Pearl Harbor as the reason investigations were halted, but it is important to show how the combination of Hollywood's defense and the senator's ill-considered reasoning set their defeat in motion months before December 7, 1941.

More importantly, this story shows that ignorance, no matter at what level of political power or at which point in history, will always find its rightful place as a punch line to those who manage to do their research.

HOLLYWOOD HATES! HITLER!

PART ONE

PREQUEL

to the

INVESTIGATION

CHAPTER ONE

Hollywood, Fascism, and Jew-Baiting Prior to 1939

Nazis, Hollywood, and Leon Lewis

Local attorney Leon Lewis helmed the Hollywood-funded underground battle against Nazis in Los Angeles. Lewis operated an espionage unit that infiltrated Friends of New Germany (FNG) and the German-American Bund, testified against Nazi conspirators, thwarted assassination plots on Hollywood elites, and kept Hollywood informed on fascist activity all while local authorities turned a blind eye. Lewis's spies kept tabs on resident Nazi organizers by tracking propaganda from the Aryan bookstore in downtown Los Angeles, to the San Pedro docks, and back to Berlin.[1] After exposing Nazi agents, the fascist American Nationalist Party issued an insert to be placed inside the *Los Angeles Times*. Readers in September 1935 would open their papers to find "The Proclamation," which called for the elimination of Jews.[2]

Nazi activity in Los Angeles dates back to early 1933, when the Friends of New Germany began dumping Nazi literature all around town.[3] Further investigation showed that the FNG headquarters was in the back of the Aryan Bookstore. FNG began outreach for US veterans miffed over the lack of postwar benefits promised to them. FNG hoped to fuel a sense of betrayal directed at the US Government that would open a clear path towards their pro-Nazi membership. The Jewish press simultaneously began publishing columns critical of the Nazi organization. Members of the Disabled Veterans of America (DAV), such as John Schmidt, Carl Sunderland, and Bert Allen, began to investigate FNG once the group began its national campaign.[4]

Schmidt, Sunderland, and Allen examined FNG on their own, but it was not long before they were reporting to Leon Lewis, who became known as "the most dangerous Jew in Los Angeles."[5] In addition, John Schmidt's wife, Alyce, was brought in to do clerical work at FNG headquarters. Alyce "typed key documents, overheard key conversations, and then went home and typed reports to Lewis on what she had observed."[6] The FNG was not publicly affiliated with Nazis, but once behind closed doors, their pro-Nazi agenda was unquestionable. Although finding dirt on these organizations was not difficult, the struggle was convincing government officials that the threat was real. Too often when Lewis shared his findings with local leaders, his concerns were not reciprocated.[7] While Lewis and his spies were working to uncover the truth of Nazi front groups like FNG, other factions were also taking a stand.

Knowing the Los Angeles fascists needed to be defeated, Lewis sought those he knew to have both money and a passionate hatred of Nazis—the Hollywood moguls. On March 13, 1934, Lewis organized a gathering at the Hillcrest Country Club in Beverly Hills. Among the attendees were powerful figures from MGM, Warner Bros., Columbia, RKO, Universal, and United Artists. The studios each chose one representative to help finance Lewis's operation through outreach. These representatives, including Irving Thalberg (MGM), Emanuel Cohen (Paramount), and Jack Warner (Warner Bros.), began with a personal donation before seeking money from their colleagues.[8]

Hosting its first public fundraiser in July 1936, the Hollywood Anti-Nazi League (HANL) united Popular Front activists in a communal stance against Hitler.[9] The rise of fascism in Europe brought together FDR Democrats, communists, and even conservative Catholics and Protestants who found Nazism to be "a triple threat against ethnicity, religion, and trade."[10] The HANL held influence through its own publication, organized events, and radio broadcasts from the Warner Bros. owned KFWB. After Nazi vandals trashed the HANL headquarters, organizers knew they were shaking the right tree.[11] While opposition to fascism in the United States had yet to take serious root, HANL was a vocal and visual aid drawing support to the cause.

Additional criticism came from prominent writer and failed politician Upton Sinclair. After losing his bid for governor of California, Sinclair wrote about how Hollywood, and MGM studio boss Louis B. Mayer in particular, used power for political purposes.[12] Mayer worked with Calvin Coolidge in 1924 and Herbert Hoover in 1928 and would eventually sit as the head of the California GOP from 1932 to 1934. Mayer worked with Ida Koverman, a top political strategist in California who operated major campaigns from 1924 to 1952. Mayer's most important resource was using MGM stars to glamorize the Republican Party.[13] Claudette Colbert, Walter Huston, and Frank Morgan all campaigned for Republicans in 1928. By the 1930s, the process of using Hollywood stars to secure votes was common practice—something Sinclair found problematic.

Sinclair's exposure to the movie industry's power came when the novel-ist reluctantly penned a defense of pioneering mogul William Fox in 1935.[14] Fox was integral in taking down Thomas Edison's notorious Trust (Motion Picture Patents Company) that kept exhibitors paralyzed with royalty fees and put many film companies out of business. By the late 1920s, however, Fox found himself in financial straits that resulted in the loss of his studio. As the work of an influential author, Sinclair's writing about the politics of Hollywood certainly brought more attention to the debates and tension within the industry. Another side effect was that Sinclair's political follow-ers got wind of the happenings in Hollywood. As Hollywood's interest in politics grew, so did the public's knowledge of the industry's influence in both local and national politics. The cultural and industrial prominence of movies inadvertently set them up to be the next medium investigated by special-interest crusaders.

Others, such as professor, rabbi, and future president of the National Council of Family Relations Sidney E. Goldstein, argued that movies had become a form of social control. Movies could be seen as another form of invisible wire-pulling. Goldstein contended that the growing ethical outrage over movies originated by the Payne Fund Studies "is not a sporadic and isolated outburst of public sentiment against a single evil; it is nothing less than one phase of a great wave of moral wrath that is sweeping wide and deep through every segment of life."[15] Goldstein was not alone in seeing movies as an indictment on morality.

Production Code Administration (PCA) hatchet man Joseph Breen was a staunch Catholic who had a nose for sniffing out morally objectionable mate-rial before scripts went into production. Since 1922, movies had imposed self-censorship as a means to avoid government regulation. It was clear by the late 1920s that the industry was not policing its product as promised. Breen and the National Legion of Decency were hired in 1934 to keep the movies from becoming the deplorable industry many feared it had already become. After years of organized protest from religious, parent, and education groups and the publication of Forman's *Our Movie Made Children*, the Production Code was rigorously enforced by June of 1934.[16] Hollywood decided that they either had to bring in someone to work with them or be forced to bend to the will of government regulation. For the next couple of decades, Breen would have more power over motion-picture content than anyone else in the industry. Through the next twenty years of government investigation into Hollywood, Breen would never be called to testify on behalf of the industry. Perhaps the lack of interest in Breen proves Hollywood's defenders correct—the govern-ment has no clue how the movie industry truly operates.

Defending Hollywood

Undeterred by the anti-movie detractors, some filmmakers began using cel-luloid as a primary weapon against fascism. Some examples include the anti-authoritarian themes in the Warner Bros. biopics directed by William Dieterle, such as *The Story of Louis Pasteur* (1936), *The Life of Emile Zola* (1937), and *Juarez* (1939).[17] Dieterle's work resonated with Hollywood progressives, who regularly fought for roles in the director's projects.[18] Biographical films gave Dieterle a platform to showcase simultaneously an influential figure and the impact of prejudice. The American public was still weary of war in the 1930s, as seen by the common view of the Great War as a misguided venture whose supporters had fallen victim to British propaganda.[19] A 1935 Gallup Poll showed that 71 percent of Americans saw World War I as a mistake for the United States. In addition, most discussions of fascism at this time were limited to the rise of domestic prejudice in national personalities like Louisiana senator Huey Long and radio priest Father Charles Coughlin.[20] Both leaders began wielding politi-cal influence without the infiltration of prejudice, but by 1938, Coughlin had certainly backed himself into a corner with the inclusion of hateful rhetoric.[21]

Amidst this culture, no studio was more eager than Warner Bros. to put their anti-Nazi politics on the big screen. Warner Bros. was the first studio to pull its product out of Germany after one of their European employees was assaulted by Hitler's Brownshirts in 1933.[22] In addition to Dieterle's series of allegorically anti-Nazi films, the studio began to make its passionate case against prejudice with films like *Black Legion* (1937), about the KKK outgrowth, and *They Won't Forget* (1937), about the false murder accusation and eventual lynching of Leo Frank. Before opening the floodgates with *Confessions of a Nazi Spy* (1939), Warner Bros. considered adapting Upton Sinclair's *It Can't Happen Here*. The studio also produced the technicolor swashbuckler *The Adventures of Robin Hood* (1938), which historians have read as an antifascist allegory.[23] While the studio was regularly tied to anti-Nazi films in the late 1930s, the Warner family was also active in fighting fascism from outside the studio gates.

The next round of trouble for Hollywood came from the United States House of Representatives. Martin Dies (D-TX) led an investigation that initiated the House Un-American Activities Committee. This House committee, or HUAC as it is better known, was the successor of another investigative body focused on outing fascism in America: the Dies Committee was made up of sub-groups that traveled to different parts of the country to conduct investigations on subversive activities. Representatives John Dempsey (D-NM), Harold Mosier (D-OH), and Joe Starnes (D-AL) headed west as part of a trip that included Seattle, San Francisco, and Hollywood.

Dies took aim at Hollywood in 1937 alongside another investigation proposal from Samuel Hobbs (D-AL). The focus of Hobbs's resolution was an accusation of monopolistic practices in Hollywood, a baton that would be picked up again during the 1941 Senate Investigation. Both Dies and Hobbs proposed resolutions that shared a trust-busting agenda. Dies's resolution, however, also noted the importance of investigating propagandistic practices within the motion-picture industry. One of Dies's loudest cheerleaders was Representative Samuel Dickstein (D-NY), who began his own committee in 1934 to investigate Nazi propaganda in the United States. Dickstein was such a staunch antifascist that he eventually became a Soviet informant, getting paid $1,250 per month between 1937 and 1940 to provide information on Nazi activity.[24] Another one of Dies's advocates was J. Parnell Thomas (R-NJ), who would become the notorious leader of the 1947 HUAC investigation into Hollywood subversion. On May 10, 1938, Dies submitted Resolution 282 to investigate un-American propaganda in the United States, which passed with a vote of 191 to 41.

By mid-August the investigations were grabbing national headlines thanks to the three-day testimony of John P. Frey, the president of the metal trades department of the American Federation of Labor. Frey made accusation after accusation about communist influence in the labor unions. With his testimony going without cross-examination, the Dies Committee bought the allegations, which spread like wildfire and set the paranoid tone for future hearings. Although Dies publicly stated that his investigation "would not become a three-ring circus," it was not long before the Dies Committee was defined by media spectacle.[25] *Variety* would soon throw Dies's words back in his face by calling the inconclusive probe a "one-ring circus."[26]

When HUAC came to Hollywood in August of 1938, a former Communist United Front leader named Dr. Joseph B. Matthews named a list of allegedly subversive Hollywood stars, including Clark Gable, Robert Taylor, James Cagney, Miriam Hopkins, Bette Davis, and Shirley Temple. The naming of Shirley Temple, who was then ten years old, became a punch line in the newspapers. However, naming the child star subversive came prior to Matthews's testimony. On February 26, 1938, the pro-Nazi American Nationalist Bulletin issued a statement alerting parents that Popeye and Shirley Temple clubs were "training points in Communism for the kiddies. The salute is the clenched fist of Communism. Just think that one over, folks."[27]

Literal Red flags were raised when Matthews spotted Shirley Temple's profiles in far-left-leaning publications such as *Ce Soir* in France. Matthews argued that communist publications rely on "dupes" who show "carelessness or indifference" when "lending their names [to far left publications] for its propaganda purposes."[28] After calling out the First Lady as a "dupe" for engaging with the Youth World Congress (an alleged front group), Mathews turned his testimony back to Hollywood: "Almost everybody in Hollywood except Mickey Mouse and Snow White has been signed up by the Communists at one time or another."[29] Representative Starnes interjected, "How about [comedian] Charlie McCarthy?" "The Communists have enough Charlie McCarthys of their own," Mathews replied.

Additional allegations about Hollywood Reds came from Margaret Kerr, a member of the Better American Federation of Los Angeles, who told the Dies Committee that members of Hollywood donated $6,600 to *The People's Work*, another communist outlet. Hollywood's power players were kept apprised of these accusations through Lewis's espionage operation, which was also eyeing the growing skepticism of motion pictures by a few politicians. Months later the *Hollywood Reporter* responded, continuing charges of communist sympathies in Hollywood, a skewed viewpoint aided by the pro-Nazi groups in Los Angeles who often equated Jews with communism. Even the law enforcement in Los Angeles showed indifference, if not support, for anti-Semitic sentiment.[30] One headline in the *Hollywood Reporter* asked, "The government and its investigators are now chugging this industry through more mud, in the hope of what?"[31] The prominent trade publication continued the following day by urging the industry to defend itself more effectively.[32]

With HUAC in the headlines, party politics in the late 1930s became increasingly focused on extremism. One reaction that would inform the 1941 Senate Investigation of Hollywood was that if Hollywood was largely anti-Nazi, then it must be pro-communist. Groups like HANL represented, for many, the Popular Front alliance of left-wing ideologies that ranged from New Deal democrats to dedicated communists, all connected by standing against Nazism. It did not help that HANL chairman Donald Ogden Stewart was a known communist, although the group was made up of a wide range of political allies. One of the most quoted lines from the 1938 investigations was from Dies Committee investigator Edward F. Sullivan, who referred to Hollywood as "a hotbed of Communism."[33] Sullivan would be fired as his connection to the German-American Bund and other anti-Semitic activities surfaced. In an attempt to defend the legitimacy of his investigation, Dies claimed that the firing of Sullivan and two other investigators was financial in nature and had nothing to do with the emerging allegations of anti-Semitism in his camp.[34]

HANL responded to Sullivan's claim that "certain groups within the film industry are rife with Communism" with an event at the Shrine Auditorium in Los Angeles.[35] W. S. Van Dyke, a director at MGM and vice president of the Screen Directors Guild, along with John W. Considine, producer at MGM, sent telegrams to the Dies Committee denying the accusations of communism in

Hollywood. "Sullivan evidently knows little about moving pictures people and probably less about communism."[36] Considine hoped the investigators would know that "we are busy making motion pictures here—we haven't time to act [on] any ism, Nazi, Fascist or Red."[37] To make matters more complicated for any outsider looking in, screenwriter Morrie Ryskind made statements regarding his refusal to join the HANL because of his suspicions about its political agenda.

As part of the ever-shifting political allegiances in the late 1930s, the communists in HANL would break away from the anti-Nazi messaging to embrace an isolationist stance after the Hitler-Stalin Pact on August 23, 1939. HANL would eventually change its name to the Hollywood League for Democratic Action, which would further purge any last dedicated leftists from its ranks. The back-and-forth political reversals would continue into 1941 when Hitler violated the pact and invaded the Soviet Union, forcing communists to once again join the battle against Nazism. From August 1938 to August 1939, however, HANL would continue to keep a keen eye on fascism.

Looking for Common Ground

One of the films noted by the Dies Committee, the Walter Wanger–produced *Blockade* (1938), dealt with the impact of totalitarian leaders. The cultural influence on *Blockade* was the Spanish Civil War, which allowed for an anti-authoritarian message complete with civilian defense of freedom, espionage, and a consciousness-raising call to action. While the film was nominated for Oscars (for story and score), sympathetic left-wing audiences found the film confusing.[38] Catholic conservatives reacted to the interventionist conclusion by picketing Radio City Music Hall, protesting to the Hays Office, and writing a string of criticisms in the press. Film bans were attempted in Boston and successful with the Fox West Coast theater chain. Wanger was also subjected to bullying "that included union sabotage, financial threats, and organized demonstrations."[39] Similar films would soon change to more direct criticism as the moguls became increasingly vocal about their attitudes towards the rise of fascism.

In July, Harry Warner invited a list of Hollywood big shots to his house in Santa Monica to discuss the mounting concern of prejudice both at home and abroad.[40] Warner also reached out to Leon Lewis in hopes he would invite his many anti-Nazi associates.[41] With the growth of special interest groups in Los Angeles all vying for funding and attention, Warner was careful to note his gathering was only a discussion and not a fundraiser. Warner's party included independent producer David O. Selznick, director Mervyn LeRoy, actor Paul

Muni, MGM producer Al Lichtman, writer/producer Jerry Wald, Warner Bros. producer Hal Wallis, MGM producer Harry Rapf, and exhibition executive Sam Katz, among others.

True to his word, Warner's discussion focused on the contents of Morris S. Lazaron's timely new book, *Common Ground: A Plea for Intelligent Americanism* (1938).[42] A World War I veteran and cofounder of the interfaith Military Chaplains Association, Lazaron was in a good position to comment on the religious challenges of the world. By 1938, Lazaron had been traveling the United States leading seminars on interreligious dialogue. It is no surprise that *Common Ground* would connect with Warner, whose studio had long been connecting audiences through accessible, culturally conscious films for many years. From the dismal reflection on World War I's impact on veterans, the effect of the Great Depression on hardworking Americans, concerns about urban crime, and the rise of fascism, Warner Bros. was a force of topical filmmaking in the 1930s.

Lazaron's trepidation, like Warner's, was the rise of "chauvinistic nationalisms and dictatorships" that forced the Jewish man to place "the duty of self-defense against the propaganda of misrepresentation and hate designed to destroy him. But they have done more than this. They have made him self-critical. They have created a crisis in Jewish life which will demand of the Jew that he make a decision about what he is and where he stands."[43] *Common Ground* served as a guide not only for concerned Jews but also Protestants and Catholics. As the title suggests, hammering prejudice was not simply a Jewish problem. For Warner and many others in Hollywood, it was an American obligation.

Arguing that the struggle of one is a challenge for the entire community, Lazaron concludes with a plea of collaboration to "preserve our democratic institutions" by making sure all "men of good will set our hands to the task of righting the wrongs that afflict our society today."[44] Lazaron's concerns for the future foreshadow what would be heard from Warner in the coming years. "A Jew or Catholic or Protestant citizen is an American," Lazaron writes, "and if he imports the hates of the Old World, he is lifting a banner other than the stars and stripes."[45] Like Lazaron, Warner would continue to be publicly weary of any idea that did not support the United States or appeared subversive in any way to the freedoms the immigrant mogul loved even more than the studio that bore his family name.

On Saturday, October 15, a German propaganda film titled *About the Right of Humanity* was shown at German House, a gathering place for Nazis and their sympathizers in Los Angeles. As described by one of Lewis's spies, one scene in the film featured a stereotyped Jew killing a steer. The scene was horrific. Many expressed disgust and a few walked out. One patron was heard saying, "Let's do the same thing to the Jews."[46] The film's purpose was to associate Jews with disturbing imagery, a juxtaposition that certainly worked on the audience at German House. The less graphic images in the film were often close-ups of Nazi leaders Hermann Goering and Adolf Hitler. The film's climax featured Nazis marching into Sudetenland, the areas of Czechoslovakia taken over by the Germany.

Events on the evening of November 9 would have ripple effects felt across the globe and would undoubtedly increase the desperation and anxiety felt for many in Europe. Known as Kristallnacht, or the Night of Broken Glass, the culmination of a growing pressure put on Jews in Europe that began as formal intimidation in the early 1930s and led to destruction of property, exile, and condemnations to concentration camps and ghettos by 1938.

The *New York Times* reported on Kristallnacht with a headline that read "JEWS ARE ORDERED TO LEAVE MUNICH" next to a large photo of a burned synagogue and another of a vandalized store owned by Jews.[47] The article details the initiative to boot Jews from the area and confiscate their belongings, homes, and vehicles. One of the events that lead to Kristallnacht, as reported in the *Times*, was the murder of Ernst vom Rath, a German diplomat in Paris who was gunned down by a Jewish teenager who sought retribution for undesirables exiled from Germany. Additional wires came to New York reporting that prominent Jewish doctors and professors were promptly arrested, while most Jews were left standing in the spoiled remains of their homes.

Following Kristallnacht, the attitude towards fascism from the moguls became more vocal as Hollywood expected a visit from Germany's most prominent fascist filmmaker. The previous year, Hollywood entertained a visit from the son of Italian fascist Benito Mussolini, which was strangely well received. German filmmaker Leni Riefenstahl came to town on November 29, a visit that was quite different for the Nazi. While Mussolini's visit turned into a swanky party, the HANL made sure the same would not occur with Riefenstahl. Though Warner Bros. was the first studio to cold-shoulder Hitler, the short time between the Mussolini and Riefenstahl visits became a major turning point in Hollywood's attitude towards Germany. The blithe ignorance of fascism in Europe that defined Mussolini's visit quickly turned into intolerance for the dangerous ideology before Riefenstahl came to town.

The HANL took out pages in the *Hollywood Reporter* and *Variety* to warn readers about the incoming Nazi representative.[48] Riefenstahl's stay was largely slighted by the film capitol with the exception of a party at the residence of German Consul Georg Gyssling. As the infamous director of *Triumph of the Will* (1935), the most notorious Nazi propaganda film, Riefenstahl was currently peddling *Olympia* (1938), a propaganda-through-sports venture about the 1936 Berlin Olympic Games. After refusing to meet with Louis B. Mayer (who would not bring her to the MGM lot) and following a tour of the Disney Lot, Riefenstahl was invited to screen *Olympia* at the California Club on December 18, 1938.[49] The German filmmaker brought three versions of the film with her and opted to screen the version with all references to Hitler removed. The result was positive press from the *Los Angeles Times* as well as from Henry McLemore, who would eventually blast the Senate investigation in the *Hollywood Citizen-News*.[50]

Rumors flew that Riefenstahl was turned down for representation in Hollywood. Hedda Hopper tried vaunting Riefenstahl as "the only woman who writes, directs, acts in and cuts her own pictures," but most of Hollywood was all too aware of the dangers caused by fascists in Europe to be impressed by Riefenstahl's filmmaking credentials. Aside from a few "tone deaf" actors and filmmakers who quietly met with Riefenstahl, the German filmmaker saw many of her events canceled and learned that former friends from Germany would no longer speak with her.[51] Being a good fascist, Riefenstahl revealed her true colors after returning to Europe when she blamed the lackluster visit to Hollywood on a predictable demographic—the Jews.[52]

Another adamant supporter of antifascist causes in the United States was Universal Studios founder Carl Laemmle. Before he died in September of 1939, Laemmle spent the last years of his life trying to save victims of the atrocities going on in Europe by bringing European citizens to the United States and employing them in Los Angeles. Sharing a similar concern, Lazaron had also noted the need for American Jews to find new homes for European refugees.[53] The situation in Germany was dire. As three thousand Jews applied for visas each day, a single consulate, such as the one in Stuttgart, could only issue 850 visas per month. Over a hundred thousand were already on a waiting list.[54] To make matters worse, when Congress introduced a bill to either amend the immigration restrictions to allow more refugees or simply to open our doors wider for children under the age of fourteen, the bill was quickly shot down.

After submitting as many affidavits as he could to bring Europeans to the United States, the American government limited Laemmle's requests to family members only. The United States was working in a quota system, which began in 1924 as the National Origins Act, and carried strong congressional allegiance to its policy of making no exceptions for those under religious or racial oppression. Undeterred, Laemmle began reaching out to everyone he knew, including Leon Lewis, hoping they would sponsor a desperate person or family overseas.[55]

In one such letter sent out on December 5, 1938, Laemmle stressed that the "Jewish situation in Germany has been getting on my nerves for a long, long time. I feel that these poor, unfortunate people need help in the worst way."[56] In a recent trip overseas, Laemmle had promised one hundred and fifty people that he "would move heaven and earth to find sponsors for them."[57] The letters came with instructions on how to file affidavits and assured potential supporters of the limited risk involved. Laemmle promised to waste no time sending names "of the persons who are so anxiously waiting for this valuable document."[58] While Warner Bros. often gets credit as the most aggressive anti-Nazi studio, Laemmle deserves praise as the Oskar Schindler of Hollywood for his work saving lives before the breakout of World War II.

CHAPTER TWO

Hollywood and Anti-Fascism, 1939–1940

University of Chicago professor Leo Rosten claimed that somewhere between fifty-three and fifty-five million people attended the movies each week in 1939. The United States housed over fifteen thousand theaters, which was considerably more than the number of banks in the country and twice the number of hotels. The assumption had always been that Hollywood was run by "an assortment of illiterates, 'geniuses,' divorcees, crackpots, and poltroons," but as Rosten found out, that cast of characters fell apart quickly under closer analysis.[1] Though the founding moguls originally came from what was considered "shabby zones of enterprise," the fact remains that these "movie pioneers were men of demoniacal energy and a striking variety of talents. They had brains, confidence, and a phenomenal capacity for work."[2] As will be seen, the movie moguls not only solidified the new mass medium, but wielded it powerfully, and defended it passionately.

By February of 1939, Motion Picture Producers and Distributors Association (MPPDA) President Will Hays argued that movies needed more realism connecting to the types of problems that face average Americans.[3] The movies saw at least thirty million unique viewers a week (one quarter of the population at the time), signaling the cinema as one of the most significant influences on society.[4] While these numbers would become inflated in the coming years, the social authority of Hollywood drew its share of critics who felt movies were a dangerous force in America. The previous ten years saw both local and national campaigns against movies, most prominently from the Payne Fund Studies and Legion of Decency. Hollywood was accustomed to defending itself from detractors and fearmongers.

Two months later Senator Gerald P. Nye reported to Congress examples of British propaganda, which he found in a book purportedly written by a propagandist from Great Britain. Nye's report was not surprising as the senator led an inquiry from 1934 to 1936 that questioned the United States' involvement in World War I. According to the investigation, foreign investors and weapons manufacturers, referred to as "merchants of death," motivated the US entry into the war. Nye's statement added fuel to the sentiment that this new war was following the same arc as the Great War, by alluring the United States into a war it should avoid. Taking Nye's lead, Boston educator Porter Sargent made ten thousand copies of Nye's statement and distributed them to teachers around the country.[5]

With growing anti-Nazi sentiment in Hollywood, the release of *Confessions of a Nazi Spy* on May 6 would become a watershed moment for an industry largely cautious of how it should approach the growing unrest in Europe. Knowing that Hitler and Goebbels took issue with the film, a *New York Times* headline above Bosley Crowther's column read, "The Warners Make Faces at Hitler."[6] However, critic Frank S. Nugent was not sure if the public would be as easily taken with the narrative as the studio was, musing that he "would have preferred to see them [Warner Bros.] pitch their battle on a higher plane."[7] The Warner Bros.' film was one of the most blatant anti-Nazi film to date, in addition to *Hitler, Beast of Berlin*, which served as an early depiction of concentration camps. While it may not have been the hit of the year, *Confessions of a Nazi Spy* certainly got under the skin of fascists and their sympathizers around the country.

On May 9, a local Los Angeles radical spoke about the new Warner Bros. film with Hermann Schwinn, the west-coast leader of the German-American Bund. The result was a leaflet urging a boycott of *Confessions of a Nazi Spy*. Twelve thousand handbills circulated with the headline "Suicide of the Hollywood Motion Picture Industry."[8] The main argument was that an employment problem existed in the film industry because the "JEWISH MONOPOLY of the motion picture industry, BRAZENLY DISCHARGES NON-JEWISH MEN AND WOMEN, and replaces them with refugee JEWS FROM EUROPE."[9] The handbill argued that the producers, publicity staffs, publications, writers, actors, and Hollywood Anti-Nazi League were all creating propaganda to "satisfy Jews who were thrown out of Europe."[10] Films such as *Blockade* (1938), *House of Rothschild* (1934), *The Life of Emile Zola* (1937), the RKO *March of Time* newsreels, and *Confessions of a Nazi Spy* (1939) were all targeted as "WAR-PROVOKING PROPAGANDA."[11]

Another argument was that the Jews in Hollywood were hurting foreign markets, which should concern the non-foreigners in the industry (and, of course, pit them against the Jewish immigrants). The handbill concluded with an overview of the production staff on *Confessions of a Nazi Spy*, which appeared as follows:

"CONFESSIONS OF A NAZI SPY"
Produced by **Jew** Jack Warner.
Story by **Jew** Milton Krims.
Acted by **Jew** Emannuel Goldenberg (Edward Robinson),
Communist supporter of Leon Trotsky.
Acted by **Jew** Fancis Lederer, Communist "peace" advocate.
Directed by **Jew** Anatole Litvak, sponsor of
Communist Hollywood Anti-Nazi League.
Technical Advisor **Jew** Rabbi Herman Lissauer,
founder of the Communist "Liberal Forum."
Historical Director **Jew** Leon Turrou, former employee of Jacob Stern.[12]

Noting the Jewish background of each member and the birth name of
Edward G. Robinson made no secret of anti-Semitism. The handbill ended
with a reminder that these films ruin the foreign market and hurt the jobs
of "real" Americans. The Bund's newspaper also reported on *Confessions of a
Nazi Spy* by highlighting that not only was the film propagandistic but that all
previous investigations of the Bund had failed.[13] Of course, at this time they
likely did not know of the extent of Lewis's infiltration of the Bund. By June,
the German embassy began protesting the Department of State with objections over the Warner Bros. film.[14] In addition, the film was protested in other
cities, such as Kansas City, where the German vice consul coerced citizens into
signing a petition of protest.[15]

At the same time, Hitler's Minister of Propaganda Joseph Goebbels discon-
tinued the shipment of official Nazi war films to the United States.[16] Goebbels
likely saw the negative influence such footage was having on the Nazi image. In
addition to newsreels about the war in Europe, Hollywood films like *Confessions
of a Nazi Spy* were using Nazi stock footage to drum up antifascist sentiment
that was certain to aid the Allies in Europe. Clearly sensing that Germany was
losing the battle over film propaganda in the United States, Goebbels formally
requested that the American newsreel managements be careful not to allow
editors to use imagery of Nazis that is "in any way detrimental or derogatory
to Hitler, his henchmen or the Nazi cause."[17]

In September, the New York Public Library found that a number of returned
books had been vandalized. Some of the books had "such annotations as 'the
British are liars.'"[18] In addition, other books had large sections torn out. Authorities eventually found the culprit, who turned out to be a local electrician. When
asked why he destroyed these books, his answer was "to help the next reader
read properly."[19] This sort of vitriol towards interventionists was not uncommon
and showcased the influence of agitators like Nye and Schwinn.

Pressure against anti-Nazi films grew as the ink dried on the Hitler-Stalin Pact of August 23, 1939. While leftists and communists in Hollywood were once aligned with New Deal liberals in support of anti-Nazi rhetoric, the Hitler-Stalin Pact lead many to change their tone in support of the two authoritarian nations. The issue was a subject of hot debate in filmland, as the Hollywood Anti-Nazi League changed their name to the Hollywood League for Democratic Actions. Industry leftists found commonality with isolationist Republicans to stand against FDR supporting anti-Nazi interventionists. It was a period of ideological cognitive dissonance for many and would add weight to the battle for isolationism in the United States.

Hollywood discussion continued about the purpose of the feature film during this pivotal and tense point in history. Industry insider and historian Terry Ramsaye told the *Motion Picture Herald*, "The motion picture is the first of the arts to be controlled by the whole people, an art of democracy, as contrasted with the other classic arts which have taken their authority from princes, potentates, cults, and the arrogances of scholarship."[20] Though boasting movies as a truly democratic art, Ramsaye derided filmmakers who want to put messages into their films by encouraging them to "hire a hall."[21] For Ramsaye, the stars should remain the most important attraction to a motion picture, not social or political messages.

Not all of the Hollywood reflection was negative, as seen by the observations of industry insider William C. DeMille. Besides being brother to one of the most prominent directors in the industry, Cecil B. DeMille, William was also a keen observer of how movies had evolved over the previous decades. "If the motion picture is to be the great art it should be," asserted DeMille, "it must be allowed to find truth through freedom, just as all democratic institutions can find truth only by being free to search it out."[22] DeMille's words track well with the growing populace interested in movies that were not just entertainment but socially engaging as well.

DeMille also went after those critical of movies, such as the Payne Fund, Legion of Decency, and other earlier investigations. DeMille observed that "there are those who consider it dangerous for the people to think for themselves, or to decide for themselves what they shall see, what they shall read, what they shall believe."[23] For DeMille, the potential of movies peaks when the medium is able to become "the voice of common humanity" by bringing ideas, fears, dreams, and desires to the screen for all to see.[24] The voice of humanity found in the anti-Nazi films would soon come to represent the bane of interventionism for several isolationist senators.

Another keen observer was Princeton professor Margaret Thorp, whose seminal 1939 study *America at the Movies* became an important barometer of how films influenced society. Thorp's study built on the claim that movies had eighty-five million viewers per week, an estimation considerably larger than Rosten's.[25] *Variety* discredited the claim, stating that the "number continues to be widely used in and out of the industry" and on "both sides at the Clark Senate subcommittee hearing on propaganda."[26] A Gallup poll showed the previous year's film attendance at closer to fifty-four million per week. *Variety* sought the origin of the eighty million figure and found that the Hays Office and Department of Commerce both cited it. When questioned, the Hays Office claimed the number came from the Department of Commerce. The Department of Commerce maintained it originated from the Hays Office. When the "who's on first" routine was over, both sides admitted the number was only a rough estimate.

Despite the inflated attendance estimation, Thorp contended that movies had evolved over the last decade from a more simplistic platform for entertainment to one of mature commentary on the world's affairs. Thorp knew what the Senate subcommittee also understood, that movies were becoming an important part of our cultural fabric. As audiences grew and evolved, so did the market for a wider range of films. Thorp pointed out the difference between Hays's 1938 and 1939 memorandums on the industry, which moved from a definition of movies as entertainment to one embracing new ideas about American life.[27]

Writing during the rise of anti-Nazi filmmaking, Thorp concluded her study with an analysis of film propaganda. In January 1939, Hollywood studios announced sixty-three patriotic shorts and twenty-nine full-length projects described as "Americanism features."[28] Thorp quickly moved her analysis to Warner Bros.' *Confessions of a Nazi Spy*, questioning if the film went too far beyond entertainment and into straightforward agitprop. Thorp also called attention to *Young Mr. Lincoln* (1939), which features Henry Fonda in the president's early years, and *Juarez* (1939), about Mexico's nationalist president Benito Juarez, as part of a growing trend of films that praised democratic heroes.[29] The rise of propaganda in Hollywood movies was multifold for Thorp, beginning with evolving audiences, socially conscious filmmakers, and intellectuals writing about movies.

The consciousness about the importance of democracy in the world of the late 1930s was not lost on the United States president. Franklin D. Roosevelt presented the United States declaration of neutrality on September 15, 1939. "This nation will remain a neutral nation, but I cannot ask that every American remain neutral in thought as well," said Roosevelt.[30] The president continued, "Even a neutral cannot be asked to close his mind or his conscience."[31] Despite large support for FDR, Hollywood was far from neutral in the lead up to World War II. The Hollywood Anti-Nazi League, mogul funded anti-Nazi espionage, and anti-Nazi films all showcased the clear interventionist stance of the American film industry during this period.[32] Of course, as we will see, intervention in Hollywood did not mean all-out war. For many, primary interest was in sending aid to Great Britain. The social and political origins of the 1941 Senate Investigation on Motion Picture War Propaganda would resume as Hollywood continued producing anti-Nazi fare into the next year.

◆ ◆ ◆

Tensions were also increasing between popular producer Walter Wanger and divisive Hollywood radio personality Jimmie Fidler, who would eventually testify against the film industry in the 1941 Senate hearings. While there had been smaller spats prior to Wanger's *Liberty* essay titled "The Stars Call Them Leeches," this article served as an excuse to make the battle public. Wanger fired shots about the "chiseling movie critics" by calling the Hollywood press the "worst of any major news source." Because stars were not as interesting as the press wanted them to be, Wanger accused journalists of taking to "retaliatory journalism, dripping malice toward any player or company failing to cater to the chiseler's vanity or pocketbook." In Wanger's opinion, both the fans and movie business suffered by the misinformation provided by journalists. The fault was not all the journalists', however, as Wanger explained how major studios had caved to outlandish press demands for years. Desperate for press coverage while movies were longing to become a legitimate medium in the early twentieth century, studios had granted journalists anything they wanted. Wanger feels that catering to journalists' demands grew into a regular malevolence from the press. A desire to paint Hollywood as a cesspool had become the norm, but Wanger countered, "I don't know a group of cleaner-living people than those who do Hollywood's work today." If one wants scandal, Wanger suggests readers to "glance around your own neighborhood!"

Wanger offered a long list of ways to improve the relationship between journalists and Hollywood, which included only working with well-trained professionals who practice with ethical standards. In addition, studios should work more closely with their publicity departments to ensure press coverage was coming from professionals and not "chiseling" journalists. Wanger also urged fans to write to their local editors when their favorite stars were maligned. Wanger noted the pressure he received when showing interest in producing a film on journalist Vincent Sheean's memoir—the film that would ultimately become *Foreign Correspondent* (1941), which would be discussed during the Senate investigation.

What really stoked the flames of this fire between Wanger and Fidler were the references to despicable radio personalities, even though he did not name anyone specifically. "When some honey-voiced heel comes on the air, calls all the stars by first names, and, with an I'm-sorry-to-have-to-do-this attitude, tears down reputations, he's making a sucker of you," Wanger expounded. Fidler had a distinctively high-pitched voice, so readers would immediately connect the reference. "If the stars answer the telephone when he calls, or chatter with him when he forces his company on them, that's the chatter of terror. He threatens *them* with *you*." Wanger concluded, "Why permit the dirtmongers to make a living by destroying such people—and our pleasure in them? Let's take the leeches off the stars!"[33]

Wanger's article struck a nerve with journalists across the country. Many expressed general respect for the producer but frustration with his current take on their profession. Others were confused and surprised by his anger, finding it coming seemingly out of nowhere. Fidler himself responded on the air. "Do you really know the chiseling reporters?" Fidler asked. "When you took your slap at what you term 'chiseling radio columnists' did you mean me?" Fidler slapped back across the airwaves: "If you did, perhaps it will interest you to know that neither you nor the entire film industry has enough money to buy my opinion, and I'm just as positive you couldn't buy Walter Winchell's." The radio personality may not have known that sometimes Winchell would invite Wanger to write a guest column, so that relationship was rosier than Fidler assumed. Fidler again asked for names and offered airtime on his show should Wanger be willing to show up.[34]

Wanger penned a seven-page response to Fidler, but was only given three minutes of air-time to respond. Wanger claimed his column was not personal. His goal was to distinguish between the professional journalists and the "chiselers." "One thing we should get clear right here," wrote Wanger, "when Mr. Fidler talks on the Procter and Gamble program to radio listeners he is not really a reporter, a columnist, or a critic. He is, in essence, a shampoo salesman." Wanger goes on to define what he meant by chiseling, which was "a person who tries to maintain a position of importance by hanging on the coat-tails of people who do things. A flea, so to speak, on the fringe of accomplishment. A person who chisels for his influence. A person who tries to impress his audience by taking chiseling angles on the news." Wanger argued that sponsors like Proctor and Gamble should soon take stock of how their products are being sold when it had to do with furthering shady gossip. Fidler was using "commercially sponsored time to cry," Wanger protested. Wanger shared a 1938 sworn testimony from Fidler, who was being sued by a Hollywood star. During the deposition he admitted to making up a story as part of what he called "newspaper license."

The spat between Wanger and Fidler led to a lawsuit.[35] Letters went back and forth between the two camps, and a case was eventually filed with the Superior Court of the State of California. Wanger claimed Fidler's rating system, which was based on a number of bells (like many critics today use stars), was hurting the industry. The issue was not just the ratings but how Fidler described underperforming films with vitriol. One example from Fidler's broadcast was shared where the radio host reviewed a film he was not officially given a screening of. In fact, the film had not yet been released. Wanger took issue with the following part of Fidler's recent broadcast:

> "The final picture is *Send Another Coffin*, a one bell picture. This one was advertised as a who-done-it mystery. Unluckily, it turned out to be a who-cares-who-done-it. The opening shot reveals a speeding automobile crashing over an embankment. But the plot of the picture must have been in the car, because nothing much happens from that point on."

Send Another Coffin would be released as *Slightly Honorable* (1939). In addition, Wanger argued that the film was not advertised as a who-done-it mystery. The claim for damages was $500,000 plus another $50,000 for punitive damages. Fidler's lawyer responded by arguing that any defamation or malice would be impossible to prove. After hearing Fidler's broadcast, Wanger got a letter from Mark N. Silver, a sales representative at United Artists, complaining about Fidler's tactics. "I am in the mood to telephone Fidler in Hollywood and call him names until he hangs up on me," wrote Silver.[36] Kosiner responded noting that Fidler and the *Hollywood Reporter* publisher Billy Wilkerson had had it out for Wanger for a few years—they trashed anything with Wanger's name on it. The battle between Wanger and Fidler was just one piece of the animosity growing against Hollywood. It is fitting that Fidler was one of Senator Nye's primary contacts in Hollywood.

Hollywood Doubles Down Against Fascism

In February 1940, MPPDA president Will Hays sent out a report commending the cultural importance of movies during the 1930s as "exposing the tragedy of war."[37] Sensing the isolationist pressure, Hays pointed out that many Hollywood films had been banned overseas because of their anti-military stance. Movies had shown the atrocities of war through feature films and newsreels, a perspective that was lost in Europe (according to Hays). Always working to keep politicians happy, Hays commended the US government in its ability to recognize movies as an important export.[38]

Some industry figures, however, were reluctant to push headlong into war films. An article in *The Forum* titled "Movies and Propaganda" addressed the discussion of engaging movies in the current European conflict.[39] While Screenwriters Guild president Dudley Nichols vocally opposed any controversial film, others such as Martin Quigley (publisher of the *Motion Picture Herald*), Paramount president Barney Balaban, former United Artists president A. H. Giannini, and Twentieth Century Fox president Joseph Schenck also showed opposition to propaganda films. RKO president George Schaefer saw motion pictures as a medium of entertainment. Shaefer would be pitched adaptations of the popular anti-Nazi novels *Address Unknown* and *The Mortal Storm*, but was weary of endorsing any side of an international conflict with his studio's films.[40] One studio that never equivocated on their attitude towards Nazism was Warner Bros.

On June 5, 1940, studio president Harry Warner spoke to thousands of his employees and their families about the increasing threat of global fascism.[41] Warner's speech was also printed as a pamphlet to be sent out to others who could not attend, including Leon Lewis. Warner's speech, titled "United We Survive, Divided We Fall," was intended to increase awareness of the realities of the prewar world. Warner shared his European travel experiences, where he learned how ignorant many leaders were to the threat across their borders. Leaders in Copenhagen, Oslo, and London all laughed at Warner's concern about invasion.[42] Many in the United States feared the rise of fascism; Warner wondered why those nations closest to the threat harbored a slipshod attitude.

For Warner, it was essential not to underestimate the enemies of freedom, some of whom might already be in the United States. Warner encouraged his audience to organize opposition to domestic fascism and introduced them to local FBI representative Arthur Cornelius Jr. As Warner and the other moguls already knew, Nazi subversion was always creeping around town. Warner shared excerpts from pro-Nazi meetings and rallies to remind them that fascists were always organizing. Reminding the audience that Europeans were living in constant danger, Warner argued that it did not have to happen here as long as America was awake to the true dangers in its midst.

Warner harbored disinterest in war but strong interest in intelligent defense. For the film industry, this included being conscious of extremist employees. "We don't want anyone employed by our company who belongs to any bunds! Communistic, fascistic, or any other un-American organization."[43] Warner knew how the German nationalist organizations (such as the German-American Bund and Friends of New Germany) were actually fascist front groups used to recruit radicals and distribute Nazi propaganda. Warner felt members of these organizations should be deported. Concluding with a prayer for peace, Warner channeled Lazaron and urged the audience to organize in defense of the possible invasion of the United States. Warner encouraged his listeners to stay alert, informed, and unified beyond politics and religion.[44]

Shortly after Warner's speech, MGM released a film that would rival any of Warner's anti-Nazi films. *The Mortal Storm* (1940) depicted the ripple effects of Nazism on a single family as the destructive ideology ripped across the country and divided friends and communities. The film takes place in a university town and is centered on Hollywood's everyman, Jimmy Stewart, but never once mentions the United States or the Jews. *The Mortal Storm* does not trade entertainment for propaganda, which was shown in the MGM press releases that made sure audiences knew the film included some romance.[45] Shortly after the film was released, Germany banned MGM pictures from the country.[46]

From his perch at the *New York Times*, Bosley Crowther described the film as "blistering anti-Nazi propaganda."[47] Such designations of propaganda certainly helped the isolationist senator's cause. Crowther wrote that the film "strikes out powerfully with both fists at the unmitigated brutality of a system which could turn a small and gemutlich [comfortable] university community into a hotbed of hatred and mortal vengeance." *The Hollywood Reporter* saw *The Mortal Storm* as "impossible to view dispassionately" but acknowledged the film "carefully avoids hysteria."[48] Reviews from *Variety, Los Angeles Times, Los Angeles Examiner, Film Daily*, and *Boxoffice* were also positive. *Los Angeles Herald-Express* labeled the film as "poignant, stark reality" while Walter Winchell called it an "anti-Nazi masterwork."[49]

Boxoffice gave the film the 1940 Blue Ribbon award in June for the "best picture of the month for the whole family."[50] The author of the novel, Phyllis Bottome, had high praise for the adaptation of her work. "The film will nevertheless live in my mind as the best possible medium for a message that the hour has made more pregnant now than ever," Bottome commented. "Without liberty there is no happy human life. Without the individual's complete acceptance of moral responsibility there is no such thing as human decency; there is only a shameful slavery enforced by inhuman cruelty."[51] Though *The Mortal Storm* is one of the most direct anti-Nazi films to be released prior to World War II, the film was not viewed as propaganda by everyone. For many the film remained an astute commentary on a dangerous political trend.

The film's gloomy, tragic, and timely narrative did not deter audiences or critics; however, in one case a negative review was supposedly pulled and the story was sent to the subcommittee on the first day of the 1941 hearings. At the State Theater in Salem, Oregon, *The Mortal Storm* was the most successful film of the year. A feature in the *Showman's Trade Review* detailed the film's popularity in an interview with the theater's manager, Alden Adolph. Using the growing patriotism to his advantage, Adolph customized the film's advertising by cutting the heads off of the film's stars and replacing the top of the ad with the American flag. Adolph added copy that read, "Beneath this flag live the freest people on earth—we Americans! Lest we forget . . . Here is a picture that will make the wild blood run cold in your veins."[52] The National Anthem was played before the film and audiences would sing along, which created a sense of patriotism over tragedy. After *The Mortal Storm* ended, the audience would give a standing ovation.[53]

The antifascist fare continued on June 14 with *Four Sons* (1940), produced by Darryl Zanuck at Twentieth Century Fox. Released shortly after *The Mortal Storm*, *Four Sons* was easily overshadowed by MGM's star-driven production. As one historian observed, moviegoers who already paid for one gloomy anti-Nazi picture probably would not be anxious to do it again a few days later.[54] Less preachy and propagandistic than the previous anti-Nazi films, the *New York Times* still described the film as "more sentimental melodrama than tragedy" and "lacking conviction and unity of attack."[55]

Released in August, a prewar message collided with an Alfred Hitchcock thriller in *Foreign Correspondent* (1940). The film was based on Vincent Sheean's memoir, *Personal History* (1935), which was updated to reflect the expanse of Hitler's surge across Europe. The film features an American reporter, John Jones (Joel McCrea), who outs Nazi spies in Britain. Audiences saw this film prior to hearing Edward R. Murrow's radio reports from London during the bombing raids. *Foreign Correspondent*'s final scene is an eerie precursor to Murrow as Jones reports during an invasion. With bombs exploding nearby, Jones shouts over the airwaves, "Hello America. Hang on to your lights. They're the only lights left in the world!" The timeliness of the film could not have been better coordinated.

Fully aware that filmgoers might tire of straightforward propaganda, *Foreign Correspondent* was meant to have a wartime message coupled with engaging entertainment. This sentiment was seen in a memorandum from the director of Walter Wanger Productions to Wanger himself: "re-dating and re-playing *Foreign Correspondent* in key cities would offer perfect springboard for newspaper and magazine editorials on *what could happen here*."[56] The growing concern over the invasions in Europe coming stateside continued gaining attention from both the US Senate and the pro-Nazi organizations in America.

Because conditions in Europe were changing at an alarming speed, *Foreign Correspondent* was finished and rewritten several times. When the adaptation of Sheean's novel was ordered, the times had changed. When the first draft was done, the Spanish Civil War had just broken out. The story needed to be amended as the conditions in Germany and France changed. Once the Nazis invaded Austria and Czechoslovakia, another script was needed. Finally, when Germany invaded Poland, Hitchcock presented Wanger with another angle, which ended up becoming the film that was shot.[57]

The *New York Times* review downplayed the film's wartime connection, instead describing Hitchcock's narrative as "oddly exciting [with] highly improbable shenanigans."[58] Being directed by the larger-than-life Alfred Hitchcock certainly drew audience and critic attention in and of itself, though the film did allow for timely war reflection. The *Motion Picture Herald* commended the wartime message and the film's specified setting, London and Amsterdam, unlike other prewar pictures that leave locations anonymous.[59]

Warner Bros. continued its war-conscious films with the anti-authoritarian swashbuckling adventure *The Sea Hawk* (1940). Germany's propaganda aficionado Joseph Goebbels admired both *The Sea Hawk* and *Foreign Correspondent*, another signal that could have tipped in the isolationists' favor, but these films were given minimal attention during the investigation.[60] *The Man I Married* (1940) carried a strong anti-Nazi theme at a time when it was not easy to pinpoint the fascist sympathizers unless they were involved in the organizations that Lewis's spies were infiltrating. In addition, Charlie Chaplin's powerful satire *The Great Dictator* was put into production, although it would not get a wide release until May of 1941.

On October 28, *The Film Daily* reported that University of Chicago professor Leo Rosten would be working with the Division of Information of the National Defense Commission. Rosten, who had been working on a sociological study of Hollywood, would be stationed in Los Angeles to advise the industry's national defense films.[61] Rosten's book would be published in three volumes and ultimately as the single manuscript titled *Hollywood: The Movie Colony, the Movie Makers* (1941). While those in the National Defense Commission were eager to work with the film industry, others in the United States government were not so happy with the product coming from the dream factories and presented on the nation's screens.

While Warner made a strong defense of Hollywood back in June, another lesser-known figure would also get his voice heard. Born in Germany, Joseph Roos moved to Chicago in 1927 as racial tensions grew across Europe. Roos worked numerous newspaper jobs and eventually published an anti-Nazi periodical with his uncle, Julius Klein.[62] Observations of anti-Nazi activity turned into espionage when Roos and Klein uncovered documents proving that Hitler had spies in the United States.[63] The two ultimately landed in Los Angeles, where Klein had been an assistant to Universal Studio founder Carl Laemmle. Roos took storyediting jobs with Laemmle, Jesse Lasky, and Mary Pickford. Still monitoring anti-Nazi activity, Roos connected with Leon Lewis and would eventually train new recruits in the principles of espionage.[64]

Connected to both the film industry and the anti-Nazi spy ring in Los Angeles, Roos was in a good position to comment on the growing discussion

AN OSCAR FOR DIES!

There should be an added Oscar in the awards by the Academy of Motion Picture Arts and Sciences this month, and it should be given to Representative Martin Dies, of Texas, chairman of the House committee on un-American activities. The classification should read: 'For Best Original Melodrama by a Non-Professional.'

In successive articles in Liberty, under the headings of 'The Reds in Hollywood' and 'Is Communism Invading the Movies?' the statesman shadow-boxes with the idea that the motion picture industry, unknowing and naive, is harboring vicious propagandists whose subversive manipulations are tainting the screen, and therefore the minds of the American public. And as a topper to his 'sensational disclosures,' he further alleges in a statement from Washington within the past week that certain producers (unnamed) have come into unauthorized possession of a report by committee investigators, who have made inquiries in California.

'There will be every effort to discredit the committee by the familiar methods of ridicule and slander,' Dies declares, adding that he understands Hollywood is about to produce a film satirizing the committee.

In a business which puts a high value on a vivid imagination, Dies qualifies in the field of fantasy. For instance, he sums up his impressions of Hollywood after a short trip to the Coast in May, 1938 (nearly two years ago), as follows:

'From what I saw and learned while in Los Angeles and from a mass of verbal and documentary evidence, I reached the conclusion that at least 42 or 43 prominent members of the Hollywood film colony either were full-fledged members of the Communist Party or active sympathizers, and fellow travelers, and that Hollywood contributed large sums of money to the Communist Party. I was also convinced that Communist influence was responsible for the subtle but very effective propaganda which appeared in such films as 'Juarez,' 'Blockade' and 'Fury.' It was also clear to me that the producers were completely deceived by Communist claims that Russia was a liberal and democratic country and served as a bulwark against the spread of Fascism and anti-Semitism. I also concluded that no cooperation could be expected from the management in exposing the Communist Party in Hollywood because large sums of money are tied up in publicity build-up of some of

these writers and actors who are Communist Party members.

'I knew from reliable sources the names of some of the actors and screen writers who belonged to the Communist Party or followed the Communist line or contributed to Communist organizations. This information has lately been corroborated by the sworn statements of former officials of the Communist Party of Los Angeles who sat in Party meetings with these actors and screen writers and who collected dues and contributions from them.

'While I have no doubt about this in my own mind, I realized the difficulty of proving it to the satisfaction of the country....'

There is a lot more of it along similar lines. Everything except facts.

Picture business has endured some rough tossing around by its enemies and publicity seekers who understand the magic lure of the name of Hollywood and the ease with which any mention of it can get their names in the newspapers. Films have been attacked, booted about and libeled for years. One more poke will be absorbed, and in time forgotten.

There is just this point of difference, however, between the usual type of jealous squawk and the kind of jolt which Dies is handing out in sweeping statements and generalities. He is indicting a whole industry, and when he writes about 'subversive activities' he is including all branches and not limiting his accusations against an insignificant few.

On its record for patriotic service and accountability to the public, the film industry does not have to make any excuses, apologies or explanations. The motion picture theatre occupies a useful place and performs a constructive function in every community where it operates.

If there is one note of helpful criticism in the issues raised by Dies it is that the picture business may be remiss in its duty to itself, too prone to take jabs from any source without cracking down on its maligners.

Whatever his status as statesman, Dies is a third-rate magazine writer which makes it difficult for the reader to understand exactly what he is beefing about. Innuendoes and implications are the tools of irresponsibles.

Until he is willing to step out into the open with facts, not fancies, his charges must be judged as unwarranted and untrue.

Dies: Oscar Candidate

of motion-picture propaganda. Because the government popularized a focus on Hollywood's connection to communism by way of the Dies Committee, it was all the more important to redirect legislative focus to the threat of Nazism. By this point Dies claimed there were six million communist and fascist sympathizers in the country.[65] Roos wanted to make sure the true Nazi threat on the ground was noticed as a primary enemy, but attention was hard to turn from the spectacle that the congressman was creating. Dies was still a punch line in Hollywood. *Variety* went as far as to call for the Academy of Motion Picture Arts and Sciences to award an Oscar to Dies for "best original melodrama by a non-professional."[66] Dies had continued his allegations of a communist-influenced Hollywood through a series of articles in *Liberty* magazine, but these articles included fabricated meetings with the Hollywood moguls. Writing about his investigation before a new session could be called ultimately hurt Dies's reputation with his colleagues, including Los Angeles congressman Jerry Voorhis, who berated Dies on the House floor.[67] Dies made a public promise to pick back up the investigation, stating, "We are determined to expose Hollywood."[68] His anticommunism was becoming so unhinged and defamatory that the Screen Writers Guild wrote to William Bankhead (D-AL), Speaker of the House of Representatives, asking for Dies to be removed from the committee because of his "prejudice and bias," as revealed in his essays for *Liberty* magazine.[69]

Closely following the Dies examination and the allegations of anti-Semitism within its ranks, Roos sent a memo regarding his anti-Nazi dossier to the United States Senate in 1940 and administered a defense of the film industry a year before the formal Senate investigation began. The timing of Roos's submission shows that the Senate had ample time to review the long list of pro-Nazi organizations. Roos's memo provided in-depth detail on the extent of Nazi propaganda in the United States. Roos advised the Senate that Joseph Goebbels, Germany's Minister of Propaganda, provided orders from Berlin "to Nazis and Nazi agents in this country, to concentrate their attack on the American Motion Picture industry."[70] By this time, Goebbels's interest and use of German films for propaganda was widely known. Roos continued, "If films cannot be used as outlets of the German Propaganda machinery because they are beyond his reach, Goebbels reasons, only one alternative remains; discrediting such films."[71] The previous years of anti-motion-picture propaganda coming from the Nazis in Los Angeles should have been enough evidence to convince the Senate that the real warmongering was coming from the German Nationalist groups.

Providing the sort of verifiable information that Dies never could, Roos provided a list of Nazi leaders in Los Angeles and throughout the United States. The names included Hermann Schwinn, Arno Risse (leader of the Los

CHARGE WEALTHY PASADENA WOMEN FINANCE ALLEN, ACCUSED NAZI LEAFLET CIRCULATOR

Report Based on Action By Allen's Attorney To Secure Fees

Has Criminal Record Ranging Over 25 Years, "Ken" Alleges

By IVAN SPEAR

HOLLYWOOD—Several Pasadena women allegedly wealthy, are accused by the Hollywood Anti-Nazi League of financing the pro-Nazi campaign of Henry D. Allen who the League continues to assert, is responsible for distributing the vicious anti-Semitic, anti-industry "Boycott the Movies" throwaway.

New, official organ of the League, bases its latest accusations on suits filed in the Superior Court by Henry K. Elder, Allen's attorney, against the women named, alleging they had retained the lawyer to defend Allen and subsequently failed to pay the agreed upon retainers.

SAYS RETAINED BY WOMEN

The League asserts the complaint sets forth Allen was hired by Mrs. W. K. Jewett, Mrs. de Shishmareff, alias Mrs. Leslie Fry, Mrs. Faith McCullough and ten Jane Does to "promote the interests of the Gentile race and combat subversive Communistic and other racial activities."

Mrs. Jewett's address is given as 1201 Arden Road in Pasadena's "millionaire section." She is described as a widow. Mrs. McCullough's address is given as 3460 Grayburn Road, an exclusive district of Lamanda Park. *New* asserts she is the wife of William B. McCullough, a salesman. Mrs. Fry's address is given as 328 N. Louise Glen in Glendale. The League publication also claims she "has long been known as one of Allen's backers."

Elder's complaint contends the defendants in the suit which seeks recovery of $5,000 formed the American League of Christian Patriots and the Militant Christian Patriots and, further, that they served notice on Elder August 8, their agreement to retain him as attorney was off.

CITES TRIO OF INSTANCES

Elder's complaint goes on to cite three instances in which he alleges he was called upon to act for Allen when the latter presumably became involved with the law. One circumstance is claimed to concern an occasion when Allen allegedly was sent to San Diego by the defendants to distribute anti-Communist literature. A second is claimed to concern an incident in Fresno over an allegedly broken lease on an auditorium in which Allen was to have delivered an anti-Semitic address. The third concerns legal representation for Allen on a charge of fraudulent registration for voting. This is slated to be heard on November 3.

New, currently, has this to say:

A split had obviously occurred between the stooge Allen and his wealthy backers because Allen refused to let Elder with-

(Continued on page 28)

16

CHICAGO—Henry D. Allen, acknowledged author of pro-Nazi, anti-Semitic literature, but disavower of the "Boycott the Movies" pamphlet which the Hollywood Anti-Nazi League maintains is his, has a criminal record extending over a period of 25 years, according to *Ken*.

"Fascist Coordinator Allen, once No. 25835, San Quentin" was a central character of "Exposing Native U. S. Plotters," charges an article which appeared in *Ken* for September 8 with this foreword:

"The real inside job for the Bunds is not mere propaganda and conversion to Nazi ideology, but a military organization for sabotage and espionage in the United States in the event of European war, whether we are neutral or not. For this ticklish work, the leaders are too smart to use suspected aliens, but rely on native Americans."

As a prelude, *Ken* has this to say:

"Within the past few months native Americans, working with Nazi agents in this country, completed plans to organize a secret army in the United States with the ultimate object of seizing control of the government by force. ... The liaison man is Henry D. Allen, 2860 Nina St., Pasadena, Calif., the same man, who, with Herman Schwinn, leader of the Nazi propaganda and espionage organization on the west coast, helped organize the Mexican Gold Shirts headed by Nicholas Rodriguez, now in exile in the U. S.

Allen is at the present moment not only involved in the plot to organize a secret army in the United States, but also active in efforts to overthrow the Cardenas government."

Ivan Spear, western manager for BOXOFFICE, a few days ago had it readily admitted to him by Henry K. Elder, Los Angeles attorney who will represent Allen on November 3 on charges of fraudulent registration for voting, that Allen had served time in San Quentin and Folsom prisons. *Ken*, however, goes considerably deeper and, in substantiation of its allegation that this man's "criminal record extends over a period of 25 years," publishes the following:

"May 17, 1910: Arrested in Los Angeles charged with uttering fictitious checks. In simple language this means just a little bit of forgery. To those who have been accepting him as the great exponent of good government and honest citizenship, it is suggested that they look up the Los Angeles Police Department file No. 7,613.

"June 10, 1910: Sentenced to three years' imprisonment, sentence suspended upon tearful assurances of good behavior.

"May 12, 1912: Picked up in Phila-

—Courtesy of Ken
HENRY D. ALLEN

delphia charged with being a fugitive and brought back to Los Angeles.

"July 1, 1912: Committed to San Quentin. Guest No. 25,835.

"April 21, 1915: Committed to Folsom from Santa Barbara on a forgery charge. Guest No. 9,542.

"Feb. 1, 1919: Arrested in Los Angeles County charged with suspicion of a felony. Los Angeles County No. 14,554.

"June 31, 1924: Arrested in San Francisco, charged with uttering fictitious checks. No. 35,570.

"Oct. 5, 1925: Los Angeles police department issued Bulletin No. 233; Allen wanted for uttering fictitious checks."

BOXOFFICE :: October 22, 1938

Henry Allen, responsible for distributing racist propaganda

Angeles German-American Bund, who regularly went to Germany for marching orders), Michael Drey (leader of the uniformed Stormtroop of the Los Angeles German-American Bund), Henry Allen (Silver Shirt Legion member and author and distributor of prominent Nazi literature), along with their assistants and affiliates in other states, such as Nazi pamphleteer, US senatorial candidate, and

POISON GUNS ARE BARKING

Christian

Vigilantes

Arise!

BUY
GENTILE

EMPLOY
GENTILE

VOTE
GENTILE

Boycott the Movies!

HOLLYWOOD is the Sodom and Gomorrha
WHERE
INTERNATIONAL JEWRY
CONTROLS
VICE · DOPE · GAMBLING
where
YOUNG GENTILE GIRLS ARE RAPED
by
JEWISH PRODUCERS, DIRECTORS, CASTING DIRECTORS
WHO GO UNPUNISHED

THE JEWISH HOLLYWOOD ANTI-NAZI LEAGUE CONTROLS
COMMUNISM
IN THE MOTION PICTURE INDUSTRY
STARS, WRITERS AND ARTISTS ARE COMPELLED TO PAY FOR COMMUNISTIC
ACTIVITIES

Reproduction, slightly reduced, of a pamphlet discovered in circulation in the vicinity of theatres in the Middle West. See page 3 for "Bigotry Stalks the Boxoffice," an Editorial.

BOXOFFICE :: October 1, 1938

5

Example of flyer leafletted in the United States

prominent evangelist Gerald Winrod of Kansas.[72] Another name on the list, Leslie Fry, was the editor of the anti-Semitic *Christian Free Press* who fled to Europe when subpoenaed by the Dies Committee.[73] Roos supplied the home addresses for many of the radicals in the document, showcasing the detail of the ongoing investigation of Lewis's operation.

Roos also brought attention to an incident from August 19, 1938, when Stormtroopers tossed handbills from the roofs on buildings in downtown Los Angeles. The handbills were distributed by Arno Risse and drawn by Max Egen, member and shooting instructor of the Bund in Los Angeles.[74] The leaflet boasted that everyone should "Boycott the Movies!"[75] As the handbill asserted, "Hollywood is the Sodom and Gomorrah where international Jewry controls vice—dope—gambling; where young Gentile girls are raped by Jewish producers, Directors, [and] Casting Directors who go unpunished."[76] Even the leader of the national German-American Bund, Fritz Kuhn, knew this pamphlet could be prosecutable and pulled the leaflets from circulation.

In addition, Lewis and Roos got wind of a sabotage plot that would occur on Memorial Day weekend of 1940.[77] Roos had compiled a master list of foreign-born employees of aircraft factories, which was checked against the list of pro-Nazi memberships around the area. The FBI was alerted and factories were shut down, and security was increased over the weekend. After years of espionage sabotaging German plots, Hermann Schwinn was certain someone had infiltrated his ranks and promised, "The offender would be ferreted out and dealt with according to the rules of the Gestapo."[78] While the government began to crack down on Nazi activities, that same government would continue their suspicion of the motion-picture industry.

CHAPTER THREE

Isolationists Push Back

Two Competing Pamphlets

On March 31, 1941, MPPDA president Will Hays released his annual report, titled *Motion Pictures and National Defense*. Although most of the thirty-eight-page document would be ignored by the Senate investigation of Hollywood, Hays outlined Hollywood's response to the turmoil in Europe. Hays describes 1940 "as a period of supreme crisis in the history of the world."[1] Profits were the only true ideology in Hollywood, and the war was clearly affecting foreign sales. Hays listed fourteen countries that no longer bought Hollywood films and thirteen that were nearing the same position. The isolationist senators used this economic change as an explanation for why Hollywood made anti-Nazi films, but Hays also explained that the industry had simply shifted its export focus elsewhere.

The MPPDA president also gave an overview of the kinds of films released over the past year. Hays categorized them in terms of drama, comedy, and music and singled out films that portrayed the "somber and satirical aspects of the tragedy of Europe."[2] Several films that would be discussed during the Senate investigation were listed, such as *The Mortal Storm*, *The Great Dictator*, *Night Train to Munich*, *Foreign Correspondent*, *The Man I Married*, and *Pastor Hall*. For Hays, the war in Europe was a natural topic for movies, but the small number of such films "spoke most emphatically against any charge that the screen was a breeder of hate."[3] Only 5 percent of films released in 1940 dealt with the European conflict in any capacity.

While critics of Hollywood would soon refer to film primarily as a means of amusement, Hays defined film as "a medium of information, education, and entertainment."[4] Hays also stated that movies were an important force for national morale, which was proven by the Naval leaders who testified before the House Appropriations Committee two weeks prior to Hays's report. After describing the industry's growth in terms of exhibition policy and technology, Hays noted how Hollywood was leading the nation with its community service. The film industry raised millions of dollars for the Red Cross and donated thousands of films to health facilities, which was a testament to its civic responsibility.

Hays's conclusion argued that "the screen is too prominent a medium for criticism, right or wrong, not to be constantly levelled at it. Wholesome criticism allows for constant self-examination and stimulates our progress; baseless criticism gives us the opportunity to establish the facts about the industry."[5] The industry would certainly be providing facts countering ill-informed criticism, as the isolationist senators would grasp strongly to Hays's final paragraph that describes cinema as "an instrument of universal entertainment," but would ignore the rest of the sentence that describes film as an instrument of "widespread information and common inspiration."[6] Much of Hollywood's defense would be based on the medium's purpose of spreading information and, when necessary, inspiration.

The pamphlet that likely informed the Senate investigation on a more significant scale was G. Allison Phelps's dossier *An American's History of Hollywood: The Tower of Babel.* Phelps's arguments and accusations throughout the thirty-four-page document would regularly find their way into the comments made by the isolationist senators. *An American's History of Hollywood* opens with the claim that Hollywood is largely informed by its many Russian immigrant employees, and therefore is an industry led by communists. Phelps's evidence, without listing specific productions, was that "the Hollywood leaders, in selecting 'literature' from which to produce pictures, reached far back into Russia to bring forth the embryo of atheism, the oriental germ of eroticism, [and] the seeds of lust and hatred."[7] The films coming from Hollywood were described as "a constant stream of sexy, underworld pictures, propaganda pictures, European tales of hate, greed, and brutality, which do not furnish entertainment but which do serve to corrupt, warp, or to horrify the minds of not only America's growing boys and girls, but the minds of America's men and women, as well."[8] Phelps also pointed out Hollywood corruption in terms of its cavalier approach to marriage and divorce, noting that most industry couples do not make it past five years.

After arguing that Hollywood was abusing stockholders' money, a point that would come up in the coming Senate hearings, Phelps included a xenophobic satire of Louella Parsons's annual "All-American" Hollywood team. Phelps's team was called the "Indispensables" and was coached by Nicholas Schenck, who Phelps argued was the one truly running Hollywood. It would be no surprise when Schenck got subpoenaed by the Senate subcommittee. Assistant coaches included Bob Rubin, Eddie Mannix, Darryl Zanuck, and Adolph Zukor. The team consisted of a majority of other Hollywood moguls, including Harry Warner, Harry Cohn, Samuel Goldywn, and Louis B. Mayer. Each name included the foreign countries in which they were born and the lofty salaries each executive earned. In addition to a list of substitutes and cheerleaders, Jack Warner was humorously relegated to the status of water boy. Phelps referred to this team as "the shiftiest, fastest-blocking team of industrialists in America. Even the Government Team has not been able, yet, to make a clean tackle of this line-up."[9]

Additional chapters focused on nepotism, monopoly, and blacklist. Phelps argued that "motion pictures are connected by a link of cousins, uncles, brothers, wives, in-laws and out-laws."[10] The monopoly charges, Phelps observed correctly, were regularly being fought by Hollywood. Phelps added that "the stockholders will pay the expenses of this fight of the Hollywood leaders of the industry to control picture production through a Hitler cartel system in defiance to all decent American business systems."[11] The blacklist concern was based on claims that isolationists had a difficult time getting work once their opinions were known. Phelps added that many players found periods of unemployment after pressuring studios about their contracts.

Phelps concluded, ignoring the Dies Committee reports that gave Hollywood a clean record on communist infiltration, that "the most prominent figures in the business have communistic leanings."[12] The end of the document referred to Hollywood as "an influence of evil" and demanded a congressional investigation into the American film industry.[13] The last page of the pamphlet featured a headline that read, "Attention! Sam Goldwyn," with an acronym of "what's wrong with Hollywood" that included words like "Aliens," "Warped Judgement," "Refugees," "Nepotism," "Hate," "Propaganda," "Communist Ideology," but also surprisingly featured "Geniuses."[14] Phelps's isolationist and nationalistic ideology can also be seen in another pamphlet, "America for Americans." The xenophobic agenda is clear from the title alone.

Ideological Competition at the Hollywood Bowl

The summer of 1941 saw two competing events in Los Angeles that would serve as a primer for coming debates. Two rallies were held at the Hollywood Bowl, the first on June 20, 1941, in support of the America First Committee. The featured speakers at this isolationist rally were famous aviator Charles Lindbergh and Senator D. Worth Clark (D-ID), who on June 19 told the press, "Our business is to make ourselves strong and our further business is to let them, the Germans, the English and all the rest, settle their own business."[15] Clark further warned that if the United States did go to war, "We are going to wind up with some sort of state control. Capitalism as we know it will be through."[16] Lindbergh would echo Clark's fearmongering to a packed house of twenty thousand.

Receiving a wild ovation, Lindbergh shyly walked onto the stage to present his prepared speech. Lindbergh gained his composure while photographers' flashbulbs illuminated the bowl. "We fight with the blade of truth as our greatest weapon," the aviator proclaimed. "They use the bludgeon of propaganda."[17] Lindbergh's concern was that the United States was not ready for war, and the only way to prepare would be to turn the country "into a military nation that exceeds Germany in regimentation."[18] Confident that no country could invade the United States, Lindbergh argued that the United States should keep out of the European conflict to ensure foreign trade relationships. If we refuse to negotiate peace, argued Lindbergh, the result will be "either a Hitler victory or a prostrate Europe, and possibly a prostrate America as well."[19] Lindbergh also showed his animosity towards Europe by saying, "The only way European civilization can be saved is by ending it quickly," which sounds more like a talking point from Hitler than one from a patriotic American.[20] Showing great concern for the lives of young men who would be shipped into deadly conflict if sent to war, Lindbergh displayed no sympathy for the genocidal conditions growing in Europe.

On July 23, the Hollywood Bowl saw an interventionist gathering, hosted by the immensely popular actor Bob Hope, with former presidential candidate Wendell Willkie as the keynote speaker. Willkie was flanked by a list of Hollywood celebrities. Many of the industry's top actors and actresses spoke at the event, including Clark Gable, Carole Lombard, Robert Taylor, Barbara Stanwyck, Robert Montgomery, Myrna Loy, Spencer Tracy, Douglas Fairbanks, Lew Ayres, Bette Davis, John Garfield, Edward G. Robinson, Fredric March, Walter Pidgeon, Marlene Dietrich, Madelene Carroll, Hedy Lamar, Charles Boyer, Joel McCrea, Tyrone Power, Don Ameche, Harold Lloyd, and Joan Bennett.[21] The star-studded crowd filled the venue, with a crowd of nineteen thousand, slightly less than the Lindbergh event.

Willkie spoke after receiving a three-minute ovation complete with chants of "we want Willkie!"[22] Declaring the current interventionist-isolationist debate one of the greatest in history, Willkie argued that looking at the division as simply war versus peace was a misconception. The real debate was about peacekeeping and not warmongering. Willkie took aim at the argument that a European war was Europe's problem alone. "It is sophistry to try to define this danger in purely territorial terms."[23] The future security of the United States was

Willkie's primary concern, which did not mean a declaration of war but instead an increase in defense awareness. "Hitler was able to attack the unprepared," added Willkie. "We should have begun to prepare the moment the rise of Hitler revealed our danger."[24] Willkie's speech made it clear that his intention was not for the country to jump into war, as his detractors had claimed, but instead to push for a more focused plan of defense that considered the growing threats posed by strong fascist power in Europe.

Because the film industry czar Will Hays would likely be too cordial and accommodating going up against the attack dogs in Washington, Hollywood made its interest in Willkie clear.[25] As a political insider himself, Willkie was able to push the impending Senate investigation into September so he could meet Nye and prepare a defense.

Congressional Opposition Grows

In a radio address delivered from St. Louis on August 1, Senator Nye drew his line in the sand against the motion-picture industry.[26] Nye opened with a plea to fight for America and specified "but for America only." Arguing that America was wrongly lured into World War I thanks to effective propaganda, Nye asserted that the United States was being primed for another war. The cause, Nye argued, was the film companies that had "been operating as war propaganda machines almost as if they were being directed from a single central bureau."[27] Nye derided Hollywood for making films "designed to rouse us to a state of war hysteria." Specific films named were *Convoy* (RKO 1941), *Escape* (Metro-Goldwyn-Mayer 1940), *Flight Command* (Metro-Goldwyn-Mayer 1940), *That Hamilton Woman* (United Artists 1941), *Man Hunt* (Twentieth Century Fox 1941), *Sergeant York* (Warner Bros. 1941), *The Great Dictator* (United Artists 1940), and *I Married a Nazi* (which was released by Twentieth Century Fox as *The Man I Married*). Ignorant of Hitler's horrors, Nye scoffed that each of these films were "designed to drug the reason of the American people, set aflame their emotions, turn their hatred into a blaze, fill them with fear that Hitler will come over here and capture them, that he will steal their trade, that America must go into this war—to rouse them to a war hysteria."[28]

Sergeant York (1941) was particularly offensive to Nye because the film was praised by President Roosevelt, who invited the real Alvin York to the White House. Nye also called attention to Will Hays's recent statement that movies were primarily entertainment. After a spineless qualifier along the lines of "with all due respect," Nye argued that because Hollywood is made up largely of European immigrants, the industry's concern is not that of the United States. Nye's infamous line, that the film studios are "gigantic engines of propaganda," was based on the assertion that Hollywood needs European markets to survive.[29] Additional accusations were hurled at (Jewish) Leo Rosten and Major General Charles S. Richardson, who were working as liaisons between Hollywood and the US government.

Wondering if Hollywood had become something akin to Germany, Italy, or Russia's propaganda wings, Nye argued that the US government was to blame for recruiting filmmakers. Nye called motion-picture propaganda in Hollywood "insidious" because it undermined moviegoers.[30] "Eighty million people will go to the movies this week," Nye claimed, using the inflated attendance number to his advantage. "Seventy-five percent of those people are against going into war. But those seventy-five percent will pay three-fourths of the bill for this propaganda designed to get them into a war they don't want to go into."[31] After criticizing both newsreels and feature films, Nye stated that this "propaganda is moving us into a dance of death."[32] No in-depth analysis was made of Hollywood or its films and the speech remained a series of headline-grabbing quips followed by reminders that a large percentage of Americans are against intervention.

Senators Nye and Wheeler continued their attack on the *March of Time* newsreel series. Wheeler had complained to Will Hays years prior about unfair depiction of the Lend-Lease bill in the newsreels.[33] *Variety* noted that "the Senate isolationist group is grasping at every available material to sustain charges . . . that the film industry is propagandizing for war."[34] Louis De Rochemont, *March of Time* representative, responded with a letter: "The Hitler peace offensive is on and lots of well-meaning people will be taken in by it. We at *March of Time* are not. We know the record of Nazi Germany and know that Hitler means war, not peace, and war against America at the end of it all."[35] *March of Time* was putting together a new short newsreel titled *Peace—by Adolf Hitler*, which was to outline Hitler's history of deceit and make a case against believing any peace initiative from a totalitarian state. Larchmont's letter encouraged viewers to spread the word and discuss the contents of the film, signing off with the question, "Can I count on you?"[36] *Variety* concurred, stating that discussion of the film is "brutal to American thinking," presumably to the isolationist wave in the United States Government. An op-ed in *U.S. Week* was even more blunt with Wheeler, claiming that the senator simply had accepted that "Hitler has won the battle for the world" and felt that the country needed to be friendly with him.[37]

The day after Nye took his on-air shots against the film industry, Walter Wanger, now president of the Motion Picture Academy of Arts & Sciences, read a letter to Franklin Roosevelt on the KFWB airwaves. Wanger endorsed the president's leadership in the crisis period before America joined the war. As a supporter of war-conscious studio films and a producer of them himself,

Wanger wrote Roosevelt, "When we hear some of these politicians talk and tell us [Hollywood] to play safe and try to get along with these world aggressors, we wonder if this is the same America in which we were born and brought up."[38] Wanger was referring to senators like Burton K. Wheeler and Gerald P. Nye, who were stirring up suspicion of Hollywood. "There are a few men in our Senate, Mr. President, who have been hypnotized by *Mein Kampf* and believe that they can imitate him successfully in this country."[39] Without naming names, Wanger argued that these senators "should join Hitler and leave those of us who cherish our liberties the right to fight for them, unhampered by their fears and un-American influences."[40]

Wanger was ready to not only help defend the United States, but had already established a record of defending Hollywood as isolationist voices grew. In May, Wanger addressed the Variety Clubs of America convention in Atlantic City, New Jersey, by focusing on the increased importance of films as part of our culture. "Our duty is to entertain," Wanger emphasized, "but great entertainment can also be enlightening." Wanger felt that movies should help Americans wake up to the happenings of the word, that movies can help people face reality. Part of his frustration was that less than ten out of 350 Hollywood films focused on something beyond variations of romance. "I say motion pictures can aid in National Defense by giving us many, many more that 10 out of 350 pictures which deal with democracy in the world crisis," argued Wanger.

Even though anti-Nazi or interventionist filmmaking was a minority of Hollywood's output, Wanger was well aware of the increased pushback. He lived it with *Blockade* and *Foreign Correspondent*. Wanger made the understandable argument that while critics may take shots at a film they see as propaganda, they say nothing about the best-selling book or popular play the film was based on. Wanger pointed out that the *Saturday Evening Post*, a publication that opposed the president's Lend-Lease Bill, was the same magazine that published the serialized anti-Nazi story *Escape*. The book became a best-seller, but when the film was made, "It was barbarism. The cry went up [that] Hollywood is going in for propaganda," explained Wanger. The producer went on to specify that the main problem was a group of United States senators pushing isolationism with false data in support. Wanger encouraged the Variety Clubs to use their local theaters as "lighthouses of the community" to centralize "strength in the interests of freedom."[41]

America First, and Second, and Third

Another major player in the isolationist movement was the America First Committee, which was built around the neutrality legislation of 1939–1940. The committee was a mixture of truly isolationist supporters still upset over the Great War, but also served as a hideout for both Nazis and communists who had different motivations to oppose war in Europe. Although the committee had rules against extremists, the fact that each chapter was independently organized made it impossible to police the membership nationwide. Each chapter was also self-sustaining, which created an imbalance of funding across chapters. America First spokespeople included aviator Charles Lindbergh, senators Burton Wheeler and Gerald Nye, journalist and FDR opponent John T. Flynn, and former Wisconsin governor Philip La Follette.

America First historian Wayne S. Cole admits that the committee attracted a wide range of political views. The meetings and rallies had supporters who included both economic liberals and conservatives. Cole notes that while the conservative *Saturday Evening Post* called out the isolationist movement as inherently socialist, the committee had many progressive supporters such as Senator Wheeler, labor leader John L. Lewis, socialist minister Norman Thomas, and writer and economist Stuart Chase.[42] While Cole works to establish the bipartisan nature of the America First Committee, the author acknowledges that one of its central problems was its susceptibility to becoming a "transmission belt" for extremism.[43] In fact, radical rhetoric was heard from Senator Wheeler, who had been known to refer to the Hollywood moguls as "Hollywood Hitlers."[44]

Speaking at Masonic Hall in Los Angeles on August 27, America First chairman William Hunt praised *Los Angeles Times* publisher Harry Chandler for allowing a column critical of the Hollywood studios.[45] Jimmy Fidler had recently defended the anti-Hollywood stance in the *Los Angeles Times*, which led Louis B. Mayer and Harry Warner to call a meeting with Chandler. According to Hunt, "Chandler said that the *Times* would not yield to pressure and that as long as Fidler wrote the truth he would be allowed to put in his column what he wished."[46] A syndicated columnist, radio personality and rival to Louella Parsons, Fidler certainly had a reach that could concern the Hollywood moguls. Defending their industry from the outside was expected, but having to deal with a local detractor was maddening.

Hunt continued by attacking the prospect of war. "I do not want to see our boys in this thing. I do not want to see their blood shed for Europe's quarrels again."[47] This statement is a telling foreshadow of the kind of commentary that would be hurled at Hollywood during the Senate hearings. The notion that the battle of fascism was simply a European problem was a key argument for the isolationists. Hunt continued to vaguely attack recent attempts at war propaganda, stating, "We are only in danger if we allow those few who have an interest in war to scare us into submission."[48] Going further, Hunt offered funding to send back across the pond anyone who had come to America to push foreign interests.[49]

While Roosevelt was gearing up for an inevitable war effort, United States senators would not accept American intervention and blamed its growing acceptance on Hollywood films. Wayne Cole's friendly biography of Nye posits that the senator was just building off of what began with antiwar groups throughout the previous years. For Cole, Nye's focus was simply on "more democratic control of foreign affairs."[50] As early as 1934, Nye pushed for legislation that would install government control of radio so that all political parties could have equal access to reach voters. The motion-picture industry certainly opposed government intervention in any capacity, which is one of the reasons the Production Code was implemented (though not immediately enforced) in 1922. Hollywood had fought off the government for two decades and they were not about to back down now.

With support of the America First movement, journalist John T. Flynn helped secure financing for an investigation of Hollywood war propaganda led by Senator Nye. Flynn sent a letter to Burton K. Wheeler on August 6, 1941, that told the senator he was putting together "a full analysis of the propaganda in the movies, names of the pictures, the manner in which the various war clichés are exploited" and "the cost of producing these pictures—25 or 30 million dollars' worth of propaganda in the last six months."[51] Flynn also promised to present the subcommittee with the names of companies and producers involved in propaganda films, as well as anything else that will support the argument that Hollywood was full of warmongers. Flynn asked to communicate with whoever would be the chairman as soon as possible and concluded his letter, "It begins to look as if our dear President was running into a little resistance. May his woes increase."[52]

On August 28, subcommittee chairman D. Worth Clark (D-ID) wrote a preliminary draft of questions for the subpoenaed film producers. They included a series of leading questions:

1. You are in the amusement and entertainment business, are you not?

2. The dissemination of propaganda is something that is foreign to entertainment, is it not?

3. When you produce propaganda pictures, you do so with the use of stockholder's money, do you not?

Such questions provide insight into the senator's intentions with the subcommittee. Each question has a built-in accusation. The first question is a set up for the producer to answer in the affirmative so the senator can declare the undesirable films as something other than entertainment. The second question is another trap, with the aim of the senator comparing films to other entertainment mediums that do not engage in the "dissemination of propaganda." The final question is geared to make both the public and the stockholders angry, and to raise the question of who was actually funding the movies. The senators may have felt this would be an easy case, but they certainly underestimated Hollywood's ability to defend itself.

The Week Prior to the Hearings

Support for America Firsters and their fellow travelers continued to surface, as the *New York Times* published a letter to the editor titled "Promoting Unity behind Defense" on August 31, 1941. The letter, by Arthur Glasgow, stated, "We put America first—and the rest somewhere—when we cooperate only sufficiently to ensure their success, with the vast Forces now combating Aggression at its Sources—and thus immunize our own Hemisphere from any and all acts or threats of Alien domination over our chosen ways of life."[53] Glasgow concluded, "As a loyal American citizen in [a] time of unrestricted emergency, I advocate this brutally selfish national policy of America first, last and all the time!"[54]

Will Hays sent a letter to Worth Clark at the end of August, castigating the senator for the "false and shameless" charges of Senate Resolution 152.[55] Hays told Worth Clark that he was ready to personally testify on behalf of the motion-picture industry and was offended that the committee's claims of Hollywood propaganda question both the "quality and extent" of the industry's patriotism.[56] The letter clearly outlined Hollywood's position and promised to challenge the isolationist senators on the values of freedom of expression. "No freedom is secure," Hays continued, "if the motion picture may not dramatize what the press prints, what the air carries, what the magazines serve to their readers, what the book publishers present in current literature or what the living stage portrays of the world scene today."[57] The purpose and quality of Hollywood's self-regulation was highlighted, and would be a major blind spot for the isolationist senators. Hays would not be called to testify, and the self-censoring protocols would not be discussed during the investigation.

Senator Wheeler received a letter on September 1, 1941, from D. C. Phelps of Hollywood, who sent a stack of press clippings and a list of names of industry players he found suspicious. The names listed were all either Jewish or sympathetic to causes; Irving Pichel, Edward G. Robinson, Errol Flynn, Eddie Cantor, Edward Arnold, Frank Capra, Douglas Fairbanks Jr., Fredric March, King Vidor, William Dieterle, Jack Tenney, Lionel Stander, Sylvia Sidney, John

Carradine, Melvyn Douglas, Frances Farmer, John Ford, Kenneth Thomson, Bette Davis, W. S. Van Dyke, Dudley Nichols, and P. M. Connoly (of the News Guild). Phelps concluded his letter, "But of course the big fish are right there in Washington, holding government positions. You wouldn't try to kill a snake by cutting off his tail, the head is there under your axe, muster a powerful force and strike while you can."[58] Solidifying the anti-Semitic sentiments, the back of this letter had an image of the Communist hammer and sickle inside the Star of David (five sides), with the inscription that read "Jew-Deal" in reference to the president's New Deal programs.[59]

On September 3, the subcommittee was furnished with a hundred pages worth of press from Hollywood about their war films. Periodicals included were *Motion Picture Herald*, *Motion Picture Daily*, *Film Daily*, and *Variety*.[60] That same day, Senator Wheeler received a letter from the National Legion of Mothers of America. Headquartered in Hollywood, the Legion advised Wheeler to bring the hearing to "the scene of the crime" and investigate in Hollywood where the films and publicity were created. Was it not reputable jurisprudence that the investigation be carried on near the scene of the crime?[61]

Samuel Dickstein (D-NY), still looking for fascist scalps, telegrammed Martin Dies (D-TX) on September 4 and urged him (as head of HUAC) to investigate the America First Committee. Albert E. Furlow, executive secretary of America First, wrote to General Robert E. Wood in Chicago to tell him of this finding. Wood was a primary financier of the America First Committee who had served in the United States Army and was a former executive for Sears-Roebuck. In his letter to Dies, Dickstein assumed that America First should cooperate and recommend that UNION NOW and other British propaganda agencies be investigated as well.[62] The communication was forwarded to Senator Wheeler, but the Dies Committee would not stand in the growing divide between America First and Hollywood. Dies already investigated Hollywood for extremism in 1940, which included testimonies from James Cagney, Fredric March, Philip Dorn, and Humphrey Bogart, all of which proved to be a nonevent. Dies did legislate a ban for both communist and fascist groups from America, which he estimated totaled around six million people in the United States.[63]

However, Dies planted belief in Hollywood propaganda in a series of articles for *Liberty* magazine in 1940. Hollywood not only saw the articles, but feared a backlash because Dies drew attention to the Jews in the film industry whose "natural resentment against the Nazis has led them to tolerate Communists."[64] Industry attorney Mendel Silberberg would write a memo to Will Hays regarding Dies's rehash of the "Coughlin line" of reasoning, echoing the hate-fueled rhetoric of radio preacher Charles Coughlin.[65] The growing anticommunist sentiment was a threat because of the prevailing assumption that Jews were predominantly of the extreme political left, although most studio moguls were either Republicans or Roosevelt Democrats.

In addition to Dies, Wheeler also received communication from Edward Kendrick, a self-proclaimed Hollywood insider. Kendrick asked his name be kept a secret and provided a list of industry personalities that should be subpoenaed. Kendrick advised Wheeler to investigate the writers of the films in question and provided a list. None of Kendrick's choices, which included the Warner Bros. screenwriters for *Confessions of a Nazi Spy* and *Underground*, would be brought in for questioning. Though hearing from the writers of the content in question would be useful. Kendrick fingered Milton Krims, the *Confessions of a Nazi Spy* scribe, as "Jewish and an ardent Roosevelt man."[66] Charles Grayson, screenwriter of *Underground*, was both an isolationist and Republican. Given this stance, Kendrick wanted to find out why Grayson wrote such a film. Kendrick listed several other names, such as screenwriters Richard Macaulay, James Edward Grant, Norman Raine, Arthur T. Horman, John Wexley, Leonard Spigelgass, and Dudley Nichols.

Senator Clark had also been receiving a great deal of mail from supporters of the investigation. One letter was from a Chicago professor who was chagrined that producer Darryl Zanuck referred to Lindbergh supporters as "bums" and stated that "the President's approval of the movie showing *Sergeant York* is to be deplored."[67] A Beverly Hills man claimed that Christians had been pushed out of powerful positions in Hollywood and attached a news article about Warner Bros. contract player George Raft refusing to act in an anti-Nazi film, *All Through the Night* (the role eventually went to Humphrey Bogart).[68] Another letter asked Clark to include Henry Luce, the publisher of *Time* and *Life* magazines, in the subpoenas.[69] A Los Angeles woman urged for an investigation of the movies and also attached a list of names she wanted investigated.[70] Another letter of support came on September 4, from a Mrs. H. Ladd McLinden, who accused the film industry of "most diligently trying to suppress freedom of speech by any means whatsoever, including propaganda and terrorism."[71] McLinden concluded, "Please continue to fight with all your might the attempt of the Administration and a minority faction to plunge us into war."

The most virulently anti-Semitic letter came from Helen Connell of Chicago. Not only did Connell support the investigation, she openly supported how the anti-Hollywood sentiment would help take care of what she called "the Jewish situation."[72] Connell attached excerpts from what she thought was a speech from the 1789 Constitutional Convention in which Benjamin Franklin supposedly made several anti-Jewish remarks. Franklin allegedly had tried to argue that the "vampire" Jews be written out of the Constitution, telling the audience that "In every land in which the Jews have settled, they have depressed the moral level and lowered the degree of commercial honesty.["73] The quotes she attributed to Franklin were of similar ilk and were based on a speech that was found in 1934 and wrongly connected to the founding father. The reality is that the speech was unknown until it was uncovered in the documents of William Dudley Pelley, leader of the pro-Nazi Silver Legion of America (i.e. Silver Shirts). Known today as the "Franklin Prophecy," the speech has been widely discredited but is still used throughout the world to justify anti-Semitic rhetoric. The subcommittee would open their investigation with the ammunition of hundreds of such supportive letters.

On September 8, a memo went around Hollywood about anti-Semitic radio personality George Allison Phelps's commentary regarding the Senate investigation. Phelps had delivered at least two anti-Hollywood rants over the air, one titled "The Great Hollywood Puzzle or What'll We Do with the Body," and the other "Terrorism in Hollywood."[74] The memo noted that many isolationists were really, knowingly or unknowingly, hocks for Hitler. The "Nazi regime spends years of careful work softening the enemy from within," reads the memo, "by creating political disunity, and by forming connections with the people in the government of the intended victim and getting them to support the Nazi political program in their own country."[75] Phelps had admitted over the air that he was aiding unnamed senators in Washington. The names of Phelps's allies in Washington would eventually make it into the press. By this time it was clear the investigation would come down hard, but Hollywood was prepared.

Senate Resolution 152, which authorized an "investigation of war propaganda by the motion picture and radio industries tending to influence participation of the United States in the present European war."[76] This resolution also stated that the subcommittee would investigate the film industry for the presence of a monopoly in terms of production, distribution, and exhibition. Between September 3 and September 5, the studios were told to submit advertising materials for specific films that would be discussed in the coming weeks. The hearings, led by D. Worth Clark and Nye, opened on the morning of September 9 and lasted until September 26. The investigation was a catastrophe for the isolationists, after the Hollywood trade press hammered the investigations and industry attorney Wendell Willkie exposed the anti-Semitic nature of the committee's arguments.[77] Willkie was a perfect fit to defend Hollywood with his history of activism against prejudice, including a bid to get Ku Klux Klan members booted from the school board in Akron, Ohio in 1925.

PART TWO
SENATORS
on the
ATTACK

CHAPTER FOUR

Senator Nye "Unloosed" on Hollywood

Day One: September 9, 1941

The morning of September 9 was a melee in the press. A headline in the *Hollywood Reporter* read, "Willkie Hurls New Bombshell."[1] The magazine referred to a statement sent to Senators Clark and Nye in hopes they would be convinced to end the investigation. Knowing that the senators were unlikely to budge, Willkie allowed his statement to run in the press. The full text of Willkie's declaration was published in the *Hollywood Reporter* and quoted around the country. "Willkie Questions Probe, Questions Legal Authority," read the *Motion Picture Daily*; "Propaganda Probe blasted" reported the *Film Daily*; "Film Blasting Starts Today" was a seen in *Variety*.[2]

Willkie made it clear that Hollywood opposed Nazism. Regarding the industry's opinion towards Germany, Willkie explained, "We make no pretense of friendliness to Nazi Germany and the ruthless invasions of other countries by Nazis . . . we abhor everything which Hitler represents."[3] Willkie argued that if the Senate hoped to investigate the motion-picture industry's stance on Hitler, no investigation was necessary. Hollywood was composed of "sincere patriotic citizens."[4] Nye pointed to Hollywood's work with the National Administration on matters of National Defense, but Willkie reminded Nye that the film industry found this a point of pride.

Willkie also responded to Nye's thinly veiled xenophobia, arguing that foreigners were "trying to make America punch-drunk with propaganda to push her into war."[5] Nye had assumed that Hollywood's interest was in defending Britain to ensure their exhibition profits overseas. Willkie pointed out that if economics were the industry's only interest, it would be beneficial to work with the Nazis instead of opposing them. Nye's race-based arguments would circle back to the senator throughout the investigation.

Since the war began, only 50 out of 1,100 feature films included themes dealing with the European conflict. Willkie argued that films with war-related premises presented them truthfully and honestly. If accuracy was a prime concern of the committee, Willkie assured the accusers that stories would be presented from citizens who had left the war-torn countries and could attest to the truthfulness of Hollywood's depiction of the war culture overseas.

Nye had also called attention to films like *Escape* (1940), a concentration camp drama, which he felt should never have been released. Willkie noted that the film was based on Ethel Vance's story, which was first serialized in the *Saturday Evening Post*, and made into a book by Little, Brown, and Company before being included as a selection in the Book of the Month Club. If Nye found the film problematic, reasoned Willkie, the senator should also investigate the author of the best-selling book, the editors at *Saturday Evening Post* (who previously attacked the America First Committee), the publishers at Little, Brown, and Company, and the editors at the Book of the Month Club.

Willkie also highlighted the freedom of expression that movies had been permitted. This, of course, was a bit of a contradiction because movies had freedoms only within the allowances of the Production Code. Nevertheless, Willkie noted that if the United States allowed the motion-picture industry to crack under the pressure of this subcommittee, it would not be long before other media industries fell under attack as well. Echoing the sentiments of Hays, Willkie explained, "The motion picture screen is an instrument of entertainment, education, and information."[6]

Willkie concluded by questioning the legality of the investigation and reminding readers of the "harassment of free speech" that Senator Nye had instituted through his personal comments.[7] Regardless of Roos's findings and Willkie's pushback against the Senate investigation, Senators Nye and Clark helped ensure there was enough skepticism of Hollywood to investigate the industry beginning September 9, 1941.

The Senate subcommittee, as part of the Committee on Interstate Commerce, convened at 10:15 a.m. in the Senate Office Building in Washington, DC. Present were Senators D. Worth Clark (Idaho, chairman of the committee), Ernest W. McFarland (Arizona), Charles W. Tobey (New Hampshire), C. Wyland Brooks (Illinois), Bennet Champ Clark (Missouri), and Gerald P. Nye (North Dakota). Most of the subcommittee members were staunch isolationists, but Wheeler appointed McFarland without inquiring about his stance on Hollywood or the European conflict. McFarland's cordial, noncombative attitude was taken for granted, and the Arizona senator's legal background would soon be driving his actions. Film industry representative Wendell Willkie sat next to other industry lawyers such as Robert Rubin (MGM), Austin Keough (Paramount), Joseph Hazen (Warner Bros.), and Charles Pettijohn from the Willkie office.

Senator Worth Clark of Idaho called the committee to order with his first breath and immediately took shots at the press with his next. Worth Clark argued that the heavy press coverage leading up to this day was presenting a misguided view of the purpose and legality of the investigations. Although the senator was trying to stifle the mounting criticism before the inquiry began, no words would be able to squelch commentary after the day's testimonies. Worth Clark continued to read Resolution 152, which officially set in motion the subcommittee of the Committee on Interstate Commerce that would focus on motion-picture propaganda.

> Whereas the motion-picture screen and radio are the most potent instruments of ideas; and Whereas numerous charges have been made that the motion picture and the radio have been extensively used for propaganda purposes designed to influence the public mind in the direction of participation in the European war; and Whereas all of this propaganda has been directed to one side of the important debate now being held, not only in Congress, but throughout the country; and Whereas this propaganda reaches weekly the eyes and ears of one hundred million people and is in the hands of groups interested in involving the United States in war.[8]

Note that the estimations between Thorp, Rosten, and Clark ranged from fifty million to one-hundred million film viewers per week. Either side of this range of numbers was large and justified interest in the medium's influence, but Clark established the blanket assumption here that Hollywood was warmongering—a claim that would soon be met with staunch defense. Clark continued:

> Therefore, be it resolved that the Committee on Interstate Commerce, or any duly authorized subcommittee thereof, is authorized and directed to make, and to report to the Senate the results of, a thorough and complete investigation of any propaganda disseminated by motion pictures and radio or any other activity of the motion-picture industry to influence public sentiment in the direction of participation by the United States in the present European war.

In addition to the original resolution, Nye proposed an amendment including investigation of monopolistic practices in the production, distribution, or exhibition of motion pictures. If Nye could not rid Hollywood of the so-called propaganda, he would draw attention to their presumably overextended control of the industry's business practices. To ensure nothing would be missed, Nye's amendment concluded with a call to report "all matters relevant, pertinent, or incidental to the production, distribution, or exhibition of motion pictures." Nye's resolution was unanimously adopted.

Wendell Willkie, Hollywood Counsel

Clark explained the procedure of the hearings and reminded everyone that cross-examination of speakers would not be allowed because the committee was not judicial in nature. This declaration, to be certain, was meant as a reminder to Wendell Willkie that he could not treat this session as a courtroom trial. Willkie's statements in the press undoubtedly gave the committee a clear idea of his arguments, so the isolationist senators prepared to combat them with the investigation's procedural strictures. Although Senator McFarland supported Willkie's request to cross-examine speakers, the motion was overruled by Senator Clark. All parties were allowed to have counsel present, but time would not be given for long objections and questions beyond those raised by the committee.

Testimony of Gerald P. Nye

Senator Nye was the first to be sworn in and opened his testimony by stating his hopes to accomplish "a degree of legislation that will give the American people a defense against what I consider to be the most vicious propaganda that has ever been unloosed upon a civilized people." After being pressed by McFarland on such a bold claim, Nye backed up and admitted that formal legislation was a last resort. Nye also took time to point out that any accusations of him on the grounds of bigotry were false and that his interest in the investigation was not to impose censorship or infringe on the freedom of the press. Doing his homework, Nye looked back to the 1915 case of *Mutual Film Corp. v. Ohio Industrial Commission* that declared movies ineligible to benefit from freedom of speech rights granted to the press. The most damning line Nye quoted was that movies "are mere representations of events" but as a form of entertainment, also "capable of evil, having power for it, the greater because of their attractiveness and manner of exhibition." The Mutual Decision, similar to the Senate's current investigation, was based on a fear that movies, as a growing force of socialization, were controlled by outsiders.[9]

Nye once again reminded the room he was not in favor of formal censorship of movies any more than he would be for censorship of the press. Contradicting himself, Nye pressed the film industry to take on responsibility for its freedoms before stating that any industry could endure censorship to keep it in line. After complaining about the charges of anti-Semitism inherent in his accusations against Hollywood, McFarland confronted Nye with, "Do you contend that the pictures you complain of do not portray real facts that exist on the other side?" "Yes, I do," Nye responded, maintaining that anti-Nazi movie propaganda is biased and a blatant appeal to fears and hatreds. Willkie leaned to his collages and acerbically asked if that meant there should be a pro-Hitler film for every anti-Nazi picture.[10] McFarland called attention to Willkie's letter that defended the accuracy of Hollywood's prewar films, to which Nye admitted to only a "casual reading" of the letter. Nye dismissively contended that he did not have time to research Willkie's claims.

With sharp prose, Jack Moffitt of the *Hollywood Reporter* observed, "Nye arrived wearing white flannels, a chip on his shoulder, and a bandage on his chin. He said he'd cut his chin giving himself a close shave. He hadn't felt any-thing up to that point. With a razor-edged wit, kept honed upon Nye's silver tongue, McFarland of Arizona proceeded to shave him once over and twice under."[11] The first morning session had barely begun and Senator McFarland had already proven he was not going to be the easy-going junior senator. Other members of the press were largely surprised by this snubbing of Willkie. Drew Pearson of the *Hollywood Reporter* called Nye's accusations "reckless and unsupported."[12] Particularly frustrating for Pearson was the committee's disregard for Willkie's formal letter to the senators. In addition, Pearson noted that the crowd in attendance was very vocal from the start, but it was difficult to decipher allegiance based on their responses.

Nye also drew attention to a news release from Dr. John H. Sherman, presi-dent of Webber College in Florida, who responded to Nye's August address. Dr. Sherman compared Nye and his rhetoric to that of Adolf Hitler. "His principal effort of the evening was a Hitleresque attack upon the American Jews," wrote Sherman. Nye's racist implications, for Sherman, came when Nye "called off a list of Jewish names associated with the motion-picture industry, amusingly exaggerating their most Hebraic sounding syllables, with pauses to encourage his inflamed hearers to shout and hiss." Nye contends that Sherman was not in attendance at his talk, and therefore such accusations on the grounds of race and bigotry are an ungrounded means to discredit the isolationist cause.

Film Industry on the Defense

Speaking out of both sides of his mouth, Nye continued to argue that motion-picture propaganda is the result of Euro-centric immigrants while also claiming to sympathize with their concern. "They came to our land," argued Nye, "and took citizenship here entertaining violent animosities toward certain causes abroad." The constant attention drawn to "otherness" and phrases like "our land" would be something Willkie and the Hollywood press would continue to use as examples of the senator's prejudice. Nye continued to defend his character by rolling out instances of how he had helped Jews attend medical school in his state, followed by the claim that only those accusing Nye of anti-Semitism were Jewish, which, he argued, made the issue nothing more than a distraction.

Nye attacked the film-industry trade press for smearing the Senate committee in their pages throughout the previous weeks. A headline in *Film Bulletin* read, "A Patriotic Industry Is Being Smeared," while an article in *Boxoffice* maintained that approval of the Senate investigation was an endorsement of the Nazis. Nye showed frustration with new collaborations between Hollywood and Washington, as the trade press began reporting a collaboration between Hollywood and a national defense effort to prepare for a potential war.

Senator Clark offered his own dirt on a paper called "The Hollywood Weekly," which he thought was published by "a man named Wilkerson." Clark, of course, was talking about the *Hollywood Reporter* published by Billy Wilkerson, a man whom G. Allison Phelps had once compared to Hitler's chief propagandist, Joseph Goebbels.[13] Clark proclaimed that "The Hollywood Weekly" sent ten agents to Washington to get information on the committee and advised them to subpoena Wilkerson. Nye agreed that Wilkerson should be brought in but called attention to the purposeful slurring of the *Hollywood Reporter*'s name—likely a gesture to gain some points back, as Wilkerson certainly had reporters in the audience.

Any gain was lost when Nye pointed to recent columns that accused the Senate Committee of being un-American and sympathetic to Nazis or, at the very least, anti-Roosevelt. For Nye, discussions of anti-Semitism were simply diversions set up to prevent the investigation from finding evidence of war propaganda. Nye pointed to the *Sentinel*, a weekly Chicago publication with a primarily Jewish readership, as an example of purposeful promulgation against the isolationists. The *Sentinel*'s primary devotion, according to Nye, was "Jew-baiting," a term Nye used because it appeared in the publication's pages as well. Jew-baiting is, in short, aggressively flaunted anti-Semitism. The sort of bigotry made out in the open to illicit a response. Though the *Sentinel* was largely focused on the movements of actual Nazis, the publication would cover the subcommittee hearings and call out Nye for referring to the allegedly Jewish-controlled movies as evidence of an "inferiority complex."[14]

Nye listed a few columns from the *Sentinel* that he claimed ignite hatred. Nye was particularly perturbed by a piece by Dr. G. George Fox titled "From the Watch Tower." In it, Fox claims Nye sounded off like a demagogue, makes comparisons to Hitler and Goebbels, and argues that Nye has "said things which every respectable bundist and Nazi accepts as being anti-Jewish." Fox's article was published on August 14, 1941, and opens with a clear sentiment that "no one objects to Nye's being an isolationist."[15] The issue, for Fox, was that Nye was using the Jews as "scape-goats" by listing Hollywood Jews name-by-name in his St. Louis speech as a means to incite prejudice. The Hollywood executives Nye approved of, predictably, were those born in the United States. Fox actually went as far as to defend Nye, assuming the senator might not actually be anti-Semitic and might simply need to learn how his words could be interpreted along Nazi lines.

Nye called attention to radio addresses that attack the senator with accusations of prejudice. Nye dismissed one such program from Dr. Frank Kingdon because he is a newly minted American citizen (read: not a "true" American), "there are so many like him parading our land these days so sure of their theory of what is best for America in this hour." Nye defended his racial impartiality by claiming he had Jewish friends who he hoped to maintain friendships with after the Senate investigation. Moving forward, Nye encouraged all talk of anti-Semitism to be "tossed into the ashcan so that we can proceed unmolested by such red herring in an honest search for the facts."

Getting farther away from the question of motion-picture propaganda, Nye compared the United States' current situation to that of the First World War, where, Nye claimed, Great Britain spent 165 million dollars "for propaganda in the United States to get us into Britain's war." The buyer's remorse regarding World War I was not unique to Nye and certainly had a strong foothold amongst isolationists of all stripes. Even many in Hollywood would agree with Nye. After the Great Depression hit and veterans lost their benefits, movies regularly took note of this "forgotten man." Most famously, Warner Bros.' backstage musical *Gold Diggers of 1933* (1933) ended with a number calling attention to all of the forgotten men after World War I.

Nye's problem with prewar films in Hollywood was that they did not focus on the pain and suffering of soldiers and their families, a sentiment well-known and not forgotten by many United States communities in 1941. New war-related films "are not revealing the sons of mothers writhing in agony in the trench, in mud, on barbed wire, amid scenes of battle, or sons of mothers living legless or lungless or brainless or sightless." Nye continued with more gruesome description, complaining that new films whitewash the realities that would truly make them antiwar films. Of course, audiences who had seen *The Mortal Storm*, *The Man I Married*, or *Escape* would have no questions about the evils that lurked in contemporary totalitarianism.

Nye quoted former celluloid superstar Lillian Gish about her experiences falling for propaganda in the silent era. Nye found that Gish had recently spoke of her experiences of being approached by the British and French propaganda departments to encourage director D. W. Griffith to make a propaganda film for the Allies. Gish remembered that "such stories were sent out for propaganda purposes—propaganda that made our people talk and think like idiots." For Gish, those who cared more about another country than the United States should go to that country and serve it in some capacity. Gish's love-it-or-leave-it attitude towards the United States did not do her any favors in Hollywood. An August 22 issue of the *Hollywood Reporter* claimed that Gish could not get film work because of her connection to the America First Committee.[16]

Nye argued that joining the current European war was simply an invitation to revisit the frustrations that followed the previous war. Nye claimed that motion-picture propaganda was painfully obvious, although he provided no specifics. The only instance he cited was a story about a film in preproduction, though he was also vague on those details. Arguments based on hearsay and assumptions would be a continuing battle plan for Nye and would soon erupt in his face.

Nye was adamant that discussion of propaganda in motion pictures was different from the war coverage found in the newspapers. Nye gave newsprint propaganda a pass as he felt readers were aware of the political positions of individual publishers, which Nye did not see as dangerous. Nye feared that films could attach a key moment or speech to a beloved actor or actress. Coupling an idea with an icon on the big screen added layers of influence not found in the popular press. Nye was not incorrect, as Hollywood had a history of connecting their stars with political and sociological trends.[17] The content of newspapers was determined by a large number of editors and publishers, while, according to Nye, the content of movies was dictated by a handful of foreign-born men, pointing to those who had been subpoenaed for this investigation. Apparently ignorant of the history of yellow journalism between publishing magnates like William Randolph Hearst and Joseph Pulitzer, Nye failed to see that the editors and writers in the newspaper industry were not dissimilar to the writers and directors in the film industry. Movies, like newspapers, have many levels of editing before the final product hits the screen. Of course, calling too much attention to screenwriters would undermine the notion that Hollywood was controlled by a handful of moguls.

The next major accusation thrown at the film industry was one of monopolistic practice. Nye charged that Hollywood's power and control was "a weapon of incalculable power designed to drag this country into the holocaust of the European war." The discussion regarding monopoly stemmed from charges filed against eight major film studies by the federal government beginning in 1938 and amended as late as 1941 as violations of the Sherman Act. Nye rolled out the names of the Big Eight—Paramount, Loew's, Fox, Warner's, RKO, Columbia, Universal, and United Artists—and stated the income and profits of each company. The seven charges against the film industry can be summarized as monopolistic control over the production, distribution, and exhibition of feature films, newsreels, and short films, which forced independent production companies (with the exception of United Artists) out of the industry. Nye cited that Fox, Loew's, Paramount, RKO, and Warner Bros. landed 70 percent of the film profits over the previous five years. In addition, 80 percent of the first-run theaters were owned by the major studios.

Senator Clark jumped in, stating that a monopoly may or may not exist in the film industry, and perhaps all discussion regarding the European war is propaganda on some level—including the committee's isolationist chatter. "You would not admit that, would you?" asked Senator McFarland, followed by a round of laughter and applause. Nye's point was that American citizens could choose to accept or reject any propaganda they see in the papers or hear on the radio. However, viewers are not afforded the same option in movie theaters where they expect entertainment and are blindsided by propaganda. According to Nye, theatergoers sit down unguarded and are more susceptible to being taken advantage of. Naturally, such an opinion assumes average Americans are not able to distinguish film from reality.

Interjecting again, Senator McFarland asked Nye to clarify what kind of legislation would fix the outlined problems. Nye was unable to answer adequately, to which McFarland responded, "You mean that we should conduct this inquiry just for the purpose of publicity?" The audience again burst into laughter and applause as Nye bit back calling McFarland's question unfair. Having trouble understanding Nye's arguments, McFarland stated clearly, "I want to know what we are trying to do here." Nye reminded his colleagues that the Senate has a history of investigations without specific legislation in mind, which should serve as a guide for this particular hearing.

Nye finally turned to the specific films he felt were particularly problematic. The senator named *Convoy, Flight Command, Escape, I Married a Nazi, That Hamilton Woman, Man Hunt, The Great Dictator*, and *Sergeant York*. Each of these films features a war theme with varying focal points. For example, *I Married a Nazi* and *Escape* are stories dealing directly with Nazis in Europe. *That Hamilton Woman* is a British love story that takes place during the Napoleonic wars; something anti-British isolationists might see as propaganda in 1941. *The Great Dictator* is a satire of dictators in the twentieth century and a passionate call for equality amongst people of various backgrounds. Nye equated all of these films, without providing specifics as to why they were guilty of warmongering.

After assuring additional films would be brought up as the testimonies continued, Nye admitted to not having seen most of these films that he listed as dangerous propaganda. Undeterred by his own ignorance, Nye reaffirmed to the committee that he received his information from unnamed but trusted sources, suggesting the committee watch all of the films mentioned. Willkie agreed by offering screenings of any or all films in question. "I think as time goes on possibly we can have a moving-picture show here in the committee room," interjects Senator Clark. "I guarantee it will be a good one, Senator," promised Willkie.

After the noon recess, Nye opened the afternoon session charging that it was time to "ascertain what perhaps [is] going on to destroy straight thinking, honest thinking, American thinking?" Summarizing his previous arguments, Nye drew attention to the massive profits reaped by Hollywood studios and their reliance on European sales to boost profits. Nye shared a report prepared by New York financial firm Goodbody & Co. that featured a specific section on the motion-picture industry. Reading directly from the report, Nye explained how studios often broke even with domestic sales, meaning their foreign sales constitute almost all of the profits.

McFarland questioned Nye's claim about financial influence, wondering whether foreign interest drove studio investment decisions. Nye agreed, but predictably described war propaganda as coming from anyone with a "direct interest" in the European conflict. McFarland needed more clarification. "What do you call 'direct interest?'"

SENATOR NYE: "I think the moving-picture industry has a very direct interest at the moment."

MCFARLAND: "Do you think that protection of American life is a direct interest?"

NYE: "Is of direct interest?

MCFARLAND: "Yes."

NYE: "Certainly it is."

MCFARLAND: "Then those that believe if England falls the lives of the people of the United States are in danger entertain a view that is in conflict with yours on the subject?"

Nye answered by sticking to his previous talking point about sympathizing with concern for Great Britain but animosity towards anyone who pushes intervention. McFarland allowed Nye to express his opinion and continue his analysis of the Goodbody & Co. report. Nye conjectured that theater owners complain because propaganda films do not make any money, which clearly clashes with box-office demand. Questions were raised about fictitious allocation costs reported by the studios. Nye cited an expert who he refused to name, while Willkie assured the chamber that cost sheets would be provided. Both Willkie and McFarland pressed Nye to cite his expert so that the previous claims could be founded. Nye continuously dodged by vaguely assuring the reliability of his trusted contact. Senator Clark moved the proceedings along affirming that the unnamed person would be called to the stand in due time.

The discussion moved on to the recent rallies at the Hollywood Bowl in Los Angeles. Charles Lindbergh, along with Senator D. Worth Clark, led a noninterventionist rally with the America First Committee, which filled the Hollywood Bowl to capacity. Nye may not have been aware of, or was turning a blind eye to, the large population of anti-Semites in the area who would have been excited to get a glimpse of the prejudiced aviator. In comparison to the America First rally, Nye overstated the smaller attendance for Willkie and

the Hollywood entourage to argue that there was less support for intervention. Even though studios like Twentieth Century Fox let their employees out
early to attend the event, the turnout was only slightly less for Willkie than
for Lindbergh. Harry Warner made a bold comment of his own: "We'd rather
march to hear Willkie on National Unity than be marched to a concentration
camp."[18] Nye claimed to have confirmed that over half of the attendance for the
Willkie event was mandated by the studio, inciting laughter in the chamber.
However, such accusations were also made by Wheeler, who received a letter
from a Samuel Goldwyn employee who claimed that nobody in the industry
was forced to attend Willkie's talk.[19]

Another frustration for Nye was that Harry Warner, as president of Warner
Bros., sent around a petition urging Congress to give Great Britain aid in the
form of a large number of battleships. An irritated Nye asked, "If there is individual spirit like this dictating moving-picture policy, is it unfair to assume that
such spirit might enter into the production of motion pictures with propaganda
to be flashed upon an unsuspecting audience gathering at theaters to be entertained?" Answering his own question, Nye spoke of the "prejudicial influence"
of producers like Warner, who "entertain hatreds" from the old world that did
not line up with those of, presumably, real Americans. The constant reference
to immigrants versus Americans continued to showcase Nye's xenophobia.

Going further, Nye accused Hollywood of aiding America's enemies by billing
the industry as "the most potent and dangerous 'fifth column' in our country."
Nye explained differing opinions on Hollywood war films through a series of
articles that he read to the committee. One article from a Washington reporter
quoted Jack Warner and Darryl Zanuck's impartial attitude towards war films.
Meanwhile, former Production Code enforcer and current RKO studio boss
Joseph Breen and director Cecil B. DeMille were cited to support the idea that
tragic stories should be watered down to improve potential box office results.

Nye continued to attack Harry Warner for rallying against a possible replace-
ment for Joseph Breen because the candidate was in the House of Representatives
and voted against the Warner-supported Lend-Lease bill. Nye also reported
that Warner had recently told his employees that leaders overseas were overly
optimistic about the possibility of invasion across Europe. Nye's reference
was, of course, to Warner's "United We Survive, Divided We Fall" speech that
was distributed around Los Angeles. To counter Warner and show a Hollywood divided, Nye cited a letter from the president of Cathedral Pictures,
a largely unknown Christian production company, who emphatically agreed
with Nye's criticisms of movie propaganda. Comparing Warner Bros., one of
the industry's largest studios, to Cathedral Pictures, a newly established small
production facility, shows Nye's inability to differentiate between major and

minor studios. Cathedral's largest claim to fame was a film titled *The Great Commandment* (1939), which was purchased by Twentieth Century Fox but given a near nonexistent theatrical run.

Nye pointed his finger at Victor Saville, who Nye argued was a British propagandist now working in Hollywood. Saville had worked during the silent era and directed several films before eventually landing a position with the prestigious Alexander Korda production company in 1936. Nye explained that Saville was in Hollywood, working for MGM, and had a major influence on *The Mortal Storm* directed by Frank Borzage. According to Nye, "Borzage was not satisfactory, or sufficiently brutal in directing the production, it seems, and Saville took over the task." Saville did work on the film in an unofficial capacity, but his control over Borzage's direction is unlikely. Borzage quickly wired Willkie a reply to Nye's claim, "Senator Nye's statement is incorrect. I started and finished direction of *The Mortal Storm* and was at no time removed from my directorial duties."[20] Nye continued, "There is a rumor, and it is persistent in the colony [Hollywood], that Saville is a British agent operating here on motion-picture lots." Nye's claims regarding Saville went unquestioned as Nye moved on to provide additional anecdotes about the dangers of propaganda.

The Mortal Storm remained on the subcommittee's list of propaganda films for the duration of the hearings. If anything solidified the film's place in the eyes of the subcommittee, it was a letter from film critic Ada Hanifin, whose less than enthusiastic review of the film was allegedly pulled from the *San Francisco Examiner*. Hanifin's letter came in during the first day of the investigation and included a copy of her blacklisted review from June 1940. According to Hanifin, the review ran in the early editions and was pulled before the remaining papers were printed. The repercussions were as follows. Hanifin was berated by the editor and was warned against writing anything else that would lean towards the isolationists. Over the next few months, Hanifin's work was regularly excluded from the paper, her by-line was removed, and she was fired in January 1941. Her husband was simultaneously canned from his job in an advertising agency owned by the same company. Hanifin concluded her lengthy letter by saying, "We hope this evidence will provide the bombshell you need."[21]

However wrongful her firing may have been, Hanifin's review was not much of a review at all. The piece was more of an isolationist rant with a brief mention of *The Mortal Storm* and *Four Sons*. Hanifin used her post as a film critic to dive into a political lecture, something that became more common in future generations of film critics but was a minority of criticism in 1941. "America's viewpoint and Europe's don't meet on the same ground," wrote Hanifin.[22] "The two continents don't speak with the same accent. To force European Fascism, Communism, despotism, or any ism but AMERICANISM on the consciousness

The Mortal Storm advertisement, July 10, 1940.

of the American People in negative or in positive form through any channel whatsoever, is contributing to UNAMERICANISM," she wrote before briefly mentioning that *The Mortal Storm* "leaves nothing to be desired."[23] Though most reviews of the day provided an overview of the film, brief mention of any merits or faults, and a recommendation as to which audiences would like the film, the isolationists senators would only see Hanafin's blacklisting as another example of interventionist overreach.

After many hours of lecturing from Nye, the formal questioning began with McFarland setting up a series of inquiries about the films Nye had seen in preparation for the day. Nye affirmed that he had viewed some of the films in question, to which McFarland asked, "Which of those pictures was the most objectionable that you saw, from your point of view?" Nye stumbled through a response claiming he could never remember the titles of films he watched and mentioned *I Married a Nazi*, again not knowing the film was released as *The Man I Married*. When asked to provide an example from the film that represented the propaganda in question, Nye gave the ambiguous reply, "Why, primarily it was the injection of scenes that could only have the effect of making us hate not only a fictional individual but an entire race of people." When pressed for more specifics, Nye claimed it had been too long since he saw the film and suggested the committee view all of the films in question, to which Senator Tobey jokingly replied, "I am afraid the committee would become punch drunk."

McFarland continued to push Nye, hoping to get some factual detail out of him. Nye diverted to what other people had told him as well as the reviews he had read in the newspaper, claiming the films he had heard about had a "spirit of hate that was engendered toward a race of people." A frustrated McFarland sought more evidence beyond Nye's generalities. "But that is a conclusion. How was that spirit of hate shown? What was it in the picture that showed this spirit of hate? Pardon me if I try to apply the rule of evidence so that it would be admissible in court." Growing increasingly annoyed by Nye's inability to support his claims, the subsequent conversation followed.

> MCFARLAND: "What is another picture that you think of that you saw, that was objectionable to you?"
> NYE: "Oh, Senator, I have seen three or four or five of them."
> MCFARLAND: "Let me see if I can help you a little bit. Did you see *Escape*?"
> NYE: "Perhaps if you can tell me part of the story I could tell you better whether I had seen *Escape* or not."

McFarland had previously stated he was not an avid moviegoer, so he was relying on Nye, the one backing the investigation of Hollywood most emphatically, to be prepared with evidence to support his history of accusations. McFarland called attention to the fact that only about twenty out of several hundred films produced in the previous years had any war-related theme. Their conversation continued:

MCFARLAND: "Senator, I might pick some of the names that you enumerated in your speech at St. Louis: *Convoy*. Did you see that picture?
NYE: "I think I did, Senator."
MCFARLAND: "Do you remember anything in that picture that was particularly objectionable?"
NYE: "I am at a loss to call to my mind any particular feature about it that led me to draw the conclusion which I have drawn."
MCFARLAND: "I see *Escape* here. We just discussed that. *Flight Command?*"
NYE: "I do not believe I did, Senator."
MCFARLAND: "*That Hamilton Woman?*"
NYE: "I did not see that."
MCFARLAND: "*Man Hunt?*"
NYE: "I think not."
MCFARLAND: "*Sergeant York?*"
NYE: "I think not."
MCFARLAND: "You mean, you have not seen it?"
NYE: "I did not."

McFarland then went back through them all again to get a definitive answer, which showed Nye had not seen any of the films he claimed were dangerous. When asked about *The Great Dictator*, Nye finally answered affirmatively. McFarland asked Nye to detail the problems with that film, to which Nye called the film a "portrayal by a great artist" but could not avoid pointing out that the film's star was "not a citizen of our country, though he has resided here a long, long while." Willkie pointed out to the senators that the man in question was Charlie Chaplin. Regarding Nye's concern over an unfair depiction of the war, Willkie would later quip to the press, "This, I presume, means that since Chaplin made a laughable caricature of Hitler, the industry should employ Charles Laughton to do the same on Winston Churchill."[24]

McFarland brought up *Confessions of a Nazi Spy*, and once again, Nye could not tell it apart from *The Man I Married*. "I take it then, Senator," McFarland concluded, "that you base most of your objections to those pictures upon what others told you?" While the investigation would continue, Nye's ignorance and lack of research of his claims would be the death knell for many in the press.

Unimpressed with Nye's day on the floor, *Variety* called out the senator for his "foggy memory" and for asserting "a great amount of hearsay information and suspicion."[25] Additional coverage in *Variety* questioned Nye's emphasis on the foreign-born, forgetting that most of those immigrants mentioned were US citizens and had been for some time. Within hours of the session's closing, *Variety* featured the headline, "NYE BRANDS FILMS 5TH COLUMN."[26] The article stated that Nye declared Hollywood a place "where selfish, scheming, foreign-born Nazi-haters are doing their utmost to plunge the United States into the European war to protect their pocketbooks."[27]

McFarland's tough questioning was the highlight of the day, as *Variety* staff correspondent Herb Golden wrote that the Arizona senator was the "answer to the film industry's prayer" and a "knight in Hollywood armor."[28] McFarland had shown he would not sit by idly as a muzzled junior senator. Instead, McFarland asserted himself, asked difficult questions without backing down. At the day's close, it was clear that not only would this investigation provide plenty of drama for the media, but it would make sport out of reading the audience. As *Variety* reported, the packed caucus room saw a range of responses, "applause and hisses, both sides."[29] As the investigation continued, the gallery would become increasingly pro-Hollywood.

Other members of the industry press panned the investigation right out of the gate. Jack Moffitt of the *Hollywood Reporter* wrote under the headline "SENATE INVESTIGATION A JOKE: Nye Holds Floor All Day—Talks Lot, Proves Nothing; Can't Point Out Propaganda."[30] Moffitt also chastised the Senate committee for gagging Willkie and other industry attorneys but praised McFarland's challenges to Nye.

Shortly after the session closed, Willkie dismissed Nye by claiming that his "long and tedious statement gives not one valid reason for investigation of industry. He does, however, give every reason why no investigation should be held."[31] Clearly aggravated over the lack of substantial findings from the long session, Willkie called Nye "a star witness for the film industry" who "demonstrates without a doubt why this foolish show should be ended. Even he is convinced there is no necessity for censorship or Government control of the industry." After all of the aggressive confidence from Nye over the previous months, it was clear that the senator opened the proceedings by quickly working himself into a corner.

Before Wednesday's hearings, Willkie would get in one more statement digging at the Senate investigation. "I am extremely reluctant to dignify further the reckless and unsupported charges made by Senator Gerald Nye," said Willkie. "The hearings hour by hour are proving my point that there is no justification for an inquiry into the motion picture industry."[32] Attendees on Wednesday would find another lengthy testimony, one that would not only rehash the same arguments heard on the first day but also showcase grand envy for the motion-picture audiences.

CHAPTER FIVE

Champ Clark Doubles Down

Day Two: Wednesday, September 10, 1941

The subcommittee came to order at 10:15 a.m., Wednesday morning, with Senator Worth Clark of Idaho, McFarland, Tobey, Brooks, and a few other senators observing the day's session. The courtroom was packed with five hundred, many of them reporters and photographers, equally interested in catching acerbic words from Willkie and the sweeping statements from the senators.[1] Worth Clark opened with a word of caution to the audience, based on the previous day's responses from the crowd, that "undue applause and demonstrations by spectators have a tendency to interrupt and bring disorder in these very serious proceedings." After making note of the expectations of the audience, Worth Clark swore in Senator Bennett Champ Clark of Missouri.

Testimony of Senator Champ Clark of Missouri

Senator Champ Clark of Missouri opened with a history of his participation in propaganda investigations. Champ Clark was involved with a special session of Congress, called by President Roosevelt on September 28, 1939, to discuss the option of revising the Neutrality Act. One major point of discussion was about backing out of the arms restriction within the Neutrality Act. During this session, Champ Clark presented a resolution allowing the Senate to investigate any foreign government for propagandistic actions. Champ Clark's interest was to open the possibility of investigating any side of the conflict. Because the special session was too short, Champ Clark's resolution was not considered in 1939 but was reviewed in 1940 by the Foreign Relations Committee and unanimously passed on March 4. The resolution ultimately went to the Audit and Control

66

Committee, where it was never voted on. Champ Clark contended his continual push for such a resolution. Senator McFarland asked if he thought this current subcommittee should be investigated. Champ Clark declined, trusting that the Arizona senator would keep everyone in line.

Focusing the lens of this new committee, Champ Clark explained that he and Nye narrowed their consideration to the "two most deadly and insidious of all propaganda agencies." The deadly organizations were, of course, film and radio. Up to this point radio had only received minimal attention in these hearings as there was a separate session held for radio earlier in the year under Resolution 111. For the Missouri senator, movies paraded as entertainment but worked as propaganda. The industry was organized as a monopoly, which was a grand wrongdoing that needed correction. Because Willkie questioned the committee's legality, Champ Clark expressed confidence (without legal citation) in the proceeding's legal merit.

Champ Clark also addressed Willkie's claims of anti-Semitism on the committee and promptly denied the accusation. Hoping to sweep the issue under the congressional rug, Champ Clark dismissed all such allegations as nothing more than an attempt by the film industry to distract and derail the subcommittee. Like Nye on the previous day, Champ Clark rolled out his resume and called attention to his history of opposing the Ku Klux Klan. The only true issue at hand for the subcommittee, of course, was the focus on Hollywood and its infringement on "the great problem of free discussion." Champ Clark attacked both Willkie and MPPDA president Will Hays as two men who did not stand on the side of free expression. When Champ Clark spoke of wanting a detailed client list from Willkie, the Hollywood counsel offered it up immediately. Willkie reminded the senators of his interest in being sworn in. Senator Worth Clark stopped the discussion quickly to remind Willkie of the no-interruption policy, which seems to have been enforced selectively.

Champ Clark provided his vision of what free speech meant in the United States. This right should not be granted to any group that holds a monopoly on a means of communication such as motion pictures. Free speech, Champ Clark contended, only applied to someone speaking to their neighbor, publishing an article, or standing on a soap box in a field. This definition clearly did not include any form of mass communication except the newspaper, which the committee made sure not to single out. Champ Clark followed with a history lesson about the purpose of free speech, which originally applied to a speaker reaching an audience through an oratory platform—without the aid of a mass mediated technology. Citing Abraham Lincoln's presidential campaign and the lengthy speaking tours of William Jennings Bryan, Champ Clark argued that in order to reach the masses one once had to work hard to find an audience in the thousands. Such was the culture free speech was intended to serve.

Someone could now get on the radio and reach millions in a matter of seconds, which called for new perspective on the details of free speech. Champ Clark complained that movies and radio exerted an unjustified influence over the government, marking them a threat to those who truly deserved to represent the people. The most powerful form of communication, not surprisingly coming from a senator, should have been that of elected officials. Frustrated that the movie moguls were out-influencing the senators, Champ Clark opined that the radio producer was "not a public official; he is not elected to office; he is not an authorized public censor; he is not chosen by the people. He is just a businessman who by virtue of his acquisitive talents has gotten possession of this little microphone." In other words, the movie mogul was the same type of greedy capitalist with a reach of eighty million. As Champ Clark continued, his frustrations were obviously rooted in the inability to outshine Hollywood. Claims that media producers were not authorized figures of public discourse displayed serious envy for Hollywood's platform. Politicians, according to Champ Clark and others on the committee, deserved the top seat, while anyone else with an opinion should hire a hall.

Seriously underestimating the number of producers in Hollywood, Champ Clark claimed that while the seventeen thousand theaters in the United States might be operated by thousands of people, only a few people produced the films that graced those screens. Theaters, in turn, served as a megaphone for "the idea of war, to the glorification of war, to the glorification of England's imperialism, to the creation of hatred of the people of Germany and now France, to the hatred of those in America who disagree with them." Strangely, Champ Clark protested that audiences were not given an accurate view of life in Russia. Willkie's question from the previous day held lingering applicability: does this mean we should have one pro-Stalin film for every anti-Stalin picture?

For Champ Clark, newspapers were not nearly as problematic because the news-gathering medium does not suffer from the monopolistic tendencies of the film industry. Also important for the anti-intervention members of the committee was the fact that the majority of American newspapers were against the United States' involvement in the war. The 1,900 newspapers in the United States, Champ Clark argued, featured a balance of publishers with a wide range of viewpoints. Champ Clark reasoned that in any city one can find multiple angles in the newspaper. For example, while the *New York Times* and *New York Herald Tribune* were interventionist papers, they would also print speeches given by isolationists. Because newspapers provide news, Champ Clark believed these mediums were inherently more balanced that the film or radio industries. Senators Tobey and Worth Clark of Idaho both commended Champ Clark on his arguments, both citing they had been given a fair shake in the radio and in the newspapers.

Champ Clark then brought the gauntlet down on Hollywood once again. Champ Clark complained about the lack of politicians featured in films and newsreels. "In the motion-picture industry we do not get a foot of film or a syllable of sound anywhere, any day in any of the 17,000 theaters in this country." Because isolationists were not represented adequately, movies "infect the minds of their audiences with hatred" and "make them clamor for war." Champ Clark called out the moguls he felt were imposing the most animosity on audiences. First, he named Nicholas Schenck of Loew's, Inc., owner of MGM, who "made one propaganda film after another to rouse the hatreds of the people of America." Warner Bros. was also highlighted as the studio "who probably have made more of these hate-producing films than any other company in America." Champ Clark then mentioned Joseph Schenck, whom the Missouri senator wrongfully claimed was in jail. Also noted was Twentieth Century Fox executive Darryl Zanuck, British producer Alexander Korda, and comedian Charlie Chaplin.[2]

Xenophobic frustrations surfaced once again as Champ Clark declared that Chaplin "has lived in this country for thirty years and made a great fortune here, and never though well enough of the United States to become a citizen." Chaplin's national loyalty was a recurring question with detractors of the film industry. The regular reminders that the comedian was not an American citizen had the usual ring of prejudice.[3] Coupled with mounting legal trouble and soaring political tensions, Chaplin would eventually live in exile in Europe during the Blacklist era.

Champ Clark turned back to the discussion of Hollywood as monopoly, acknowledging that there were many producers in the industry but declared all content decisions were made by a handful of bosses. Citing a session of the 76th Congress, Champ Clark stated that "the virtual elimination of competition" had been seen in the motion-picture industry. The senator pointed to the difficulty of making and distributing a profitable feature film for anyone outside the industry, who did not own theaters or have contracts with stars. Thus, the industry had set up the market to provide itself with maximum profits while deterring outside competition. While studios owned a minority of the approximately 17,000 theaters in the country, they did own a number of the most important venues. The numbers at the time, according to Champ Clark, were as follows: Paramount (1,270), Warner Bros. (557), Twentieth Century Fox (553), RKO (132), Loew's (122).

Champ Clark qualified his claims by noting that the major studios did compete with each other and had created impressive art, unsurpassed globally.

The problem however, he said, was that "the greater their art, the greater their efficiency and effectiveness," pointing once again to war propaganda. Champ Clark argued the industry was colluding in their propaganda efforts, aided by the Lend-Lease bill resented by isolationists. As Champ Clark discussed the dangers of a movie monopoly and the industry's propaganda, and presented counter-comparisons to the free press and complaints that the movies used to be entertainment, the crowd began to get vocal as people responded to any one of the many blanket accusations hurled at Hollywood. The disorder in the room began to overcome the testimony, and Senator Champ Clark of Idaho had to step in and ask the crowd for order and respect.

Once the room fell quiet, the Missouri senator unleashed a tirade on the immorality of the big screen. Falling victim to the misleading accusations of the Payne Fund studies that were completed in the early 1930s, Champ Clark described the film industry as having once entered "fully into the practice of putting filth and immorality and ideas subversive to decency and the decent way of life upon the screen, and the public rose up in great indignation." The public that rose up was the Catholic Legion of Decency, which had its own rating system and had been lobbying against the film industry for its inability to enforce the production code of ethics that had been in place since 1922.[4] Champ Clark showed gratitude that films no longer appeared as they were fifteen to twenty years prior and hoped that Hollywood could once again "purge itself in the eyes of the people as to this filth and immorality which [are] being foisted on the people of the United States." Champ Clark was upset that movies became "an instrument of social philosophy."

Hot off of his emphatic series of questions from the previous day, Senator McFarland asked the subcommittee to allow Willkie to cross-examine Champ Clark. Acknowledging that the senator was a tough lawyer and could handle anything Willkie dished, McFarland asked the committee to entertain Hollywood's counsel. Senator Worth Clark shut down the proposal immediately, reminding McFarland that this hearing was not akin to a court trial and that Senate subcommittees had never allowed cross-examination. McFarland pushed further, arguing that because Champ Clark noted Willkie several times, it would only be fair to allow both sides an opportunity to speak. "You know I am a pretty good Democrat and I did not want to have to defend a Republican [Champ Clark]," jested McFarland, drawing laughter from the audience. "I just preferred to let him defend himself by asking his own questions."

Willkie then asked Worth Clark for clarification. "Mr. Willkie, I would be perfectly happy to enter into a controversy with you, but," said the senator, before Willkie interjected, "I just want to ask a question in reference to the procedure." The question was in regard to the order of the witnesses, which

Willkie would like to question. Again, Worth Clark shut down any possibility of cross-examination. Citing the history of Senate proceedings, Worth Clark responded to Willkie's proposal, "Consequently, the answer to your question, Mr. Willkie, is no." Members of the audience erupted into applause, egging on the banter.

After a weak refutation of Willkie's claim that the committee's complaints were based on racial prejudice, McFarland opened up a line of questioning. McFarland asked for clarification on Champ Clark's claim that Warner Bros. made a majority of the hate films, as they were called. Champ Clark backed off: "I am not an expert on motion pictures. . . . I very seldom attend a motion picture show." Clark, like Nye, had taken the word of others that the aforementioned films were dangerous. McFarland mounted pressure:

MCFARLAND: "I take it these films have not influenced you very much."
CHAMP CLARK: "They have influenced me to stay away."
MCFARLAND: "On information and belief or from whatever source you want to give the information, what pictures did you have in mind?"

Champ Clark noted *Confessions of a Nazi Spy, Dive Bomber,* and *Underground* (1941), which was released the previous June. Of course, Champ Clark had not actually seen these movies but pointed to the "extremely inflammatory" films as productions of Warner Bros. When asked if he would watch any of the films to see if they actually served up propaganda, Champ Clark would not.

MCFARLAND: "After all, you have made some charges here. You are just making those charges on information and belief, I take it?"
CHAMP CLARK: "So far as having seen any of those pictures is concerned, that is absolutely true."
MCFARLAND: "You don't know, as a matter of fact, then, as to whether these pictures really portray actual facts or not?"

Champ Clark continued to duck and weave his ignorance of movies by restating how they were clearly propaganda films, based on his supposed reliable sources. After a lengthy deviation into previous Senate committees, Worth Clark brought the group back on point, stating that exposing propaganda will do American citizens a great service. "He that doeth evil hateth the light," said Senator Tobey. "A very pertinent quotation," responded the senator from Missouri, assuming the movie moguls chose dark subjects because they detest the lighthearted fare. Using the Bible quote against the isolationists who were using the quote affirmatively, McFarland asked if all previous religious films were propaganda for Christianity. Champ Clark quickly folded: "I do not know." McFarland commended the quality of religious pictures from Hollywood, but once again noted their bias that could be read as propaganda. Unsurprisingly, Champ Clark denied any comparison between religious films and the war-related films of recent years. Clearly put off by McFarland's parallel, Champ Clark responded, "I would not curtail the production of any [films] except the pictures gotten out by a monopolistic combination for deliberate propaganda purposes. I do not believe that any picture of any scene from the Bible would be considered propaganda by anybody." It is ironic that Champ Clark, who would never see a Biblical adaptation as propaganda, did not acknowledge that these Jewish or Jewish-sympathetic moguls were the ones who had produced these Bible films.

Moving back to the possibility of legislation, McFarland queried the options of the Senate to legislate against the film industry. Champ Clark pushed back noting that he was not in favor of government control of Hollywood, to which McFarland pointed out that the committee could not actually do anything to affect the film industry in the immediate future. Frustrated about the committee's lack of confidence in moviegoers, McFarland stated, "I have confidence in the American public to be able to distinguish between propaganda and facts." Champ Clark objected, drawing attention to the lack of facts leading into World War I as a reason to be weary of contemporary information about another war.

McFarland's last point of the day was to call back the comparisons made between film and radio. Of course, someone could simply turn off the radio if they did not like what they heard. Movies, according to the accusers on the subcommittee, could not ask audiences to walk blindly into propaganda. McFarland pointed out that one could tell the subject of these war films by the titles, which meant that audiences *knew* what they were getting into. Champ Clark remembered the one film he saw, *That Hamilton Woman*, as a counterexample, before admitting that he did not even stay for the duration. McFarland moved on to the previous day's accusation of collusion between Hollywood and the government; however, no one would take a definitive stand on the matter. Champ Clark observed that Lowell Mellett, who was an intermediary between Hollywood and Washington, had mentioned such collaboration in the press.

The day's shorter session adjourned at 11:55 a.m. as the afternoon was reserved for unrelated issues having to do with a tax bill. Taking the afternoon off, the subcommittee would reconvene the following morning at 10:30 a.m. The short day allowed more time for the press to reflect and react to the ongoing investigation, which lead to substantial coverage in the national papers. Although the coverage included those in favor and opposition to the investigation, it was clear the tide was not in the subcommittee's favor.

The Press Reacts to "Rump Subcommittee"

"Investigation in Deeper Bog," observed Jack Moffitt of the *Hollywood Reporter,* "Sen. Clark as Ignorant of Subject as Nye."[5] Moffitt picked up on how Champ Clark did not fall into the same trap as Nye by "beating the tom-toms of racial prejudice" but did show overt jealousy that movies had a larger impact on the masses than do elected officials. Reporting that Champ Clark was more focused than Nye, Moffitt explained that neither senator could pin down a definition of propaganda that applied to their accusations. Commenting on one of Champ Clark's long deviations, Moffitt described Champ Clark as he "went on a detour that took him back to the Napoleonic wars." Moffitt also spoke with Senator McFarland, the film industry's hero of the day (again), who claimed he was enjoying the sporting manner at which he is taking on the entire subcommittee. Responding to Chairman Worth Clark's demand that the investigation not turn into a circus, Moffitt added, "It's too late for that. The hearing began as a circus for Clark and Nye. But then came Willkie and McFarland. Now it is a circus that's been struck by a hurricane and of course the ring master doesn't like it."

Unable to speak freely during the session, Willkie opened up to reporters that afternoon. The industry counsel's complaints were threefold. First, "Senator Nye desires to foster and create prejudices against the motion-picture industry, and thus attempt to high pressure it to stop producing accurate and factual pictures on Nazism."[6] Second, that Nye did not approve of accurate portrayals of national defense, and third, that Nye was trying to divide the United States on racial and religious lines. Chairman Worth Clark was not happy with Mr. Willkie's interjections during the day. Clearly still jealous of the attention given to the industry's counsel in the press, Worth Clark stated that "obviously Mr. Willkie is not the attorney but the press agent for the movie industry."[7] Considering the restraint it must have taken to remain largely quiet during a day of slander against his clients, one can understand how speaking to the press was a necessary exercise in catharsis for Willkie. The counsel continued, "Destroying reputations by whim and fancy, on the part of Senators, is not a fitting role for elected representatives of the people."[8]

"To all my requests to protect the motion picture industry from slander," Willkie noted, "I get one answer—it is not the custom to permit [cross-examination]."[9] Willkie continued to let loose: "The power to make rules on these hearings lies with the rump subcommittee." For Willkie, the senators were pushing unsupported and contradictory information, which was ultimately "destroying reputations by whim and fancy."[10] Willkie's repeated requests, many of which were eliminated from the congressional record, to stop the investigation and have the senators actually watch the aforementioned films, were all denied.[11] Such approval of ignorance was not lost on commentators in the press, who leapt onto the subcommittee for its refusal to get fully informed. On Wednesday evening, Willkie gave an additional statement that called out Senator Clark, that "lacking proof of his original cry of propaganda, [he] has now drawn the usual red herring to cover up. He is now crying monopoly."[12]

An opinion piece by Charles Glenn in the *People's World* went after the Hearst press, particularly the *San Francisco Examiner*, which led with the senator's arguments but did give space for Willkie's comments. Glenn called the film inquiry "stupid" because the large control of the film industry by the major studios was "common knowledge and not a trade secret."[13] If the senators wanted to truly investigate why certain movies would be made, Glenn reasoned, they should reach out to Hollywood censor and former representative to the Legion of Decency, Joseph Breen. As someone who spent years with final approval for Hollywood's films, Breen should have been the first person called to testify. Responding to Champ Clark's dismissal of films without having seen them, Glenn mused, "Wonderful guy to be heading such a subcommittee."[14]

Echoing Willkie's allegations against the senators, Glenn wrote that "the [sub]committee is attempting to establish that the Jews are responsible for American foreign policy. This is the deeper aspect, the aspect of phony racism, of Nazism, of filthy reaction."[15] Glenn hammered the senators for not only taking orders from publishing plutocrat William Randolph Hearst (a claim never fully explored), but also for their misleading rhetoric. "The movie industry is not being investigated because it is the movie industry or because the investigators are interested sincerely in peace," argued Glenn, "it is being investigated because the Nye-Wheeler-Clark gang see here a vulnerable spot for their anti-Semitism, a spot which will get their filthy lies before the American people."[16] Glenn's viewpoint was echoed from both inside and outside the Hollywood press.

The Hearst-owned *Los Angeles Examiner* reported that attendees "urged on" Senator Champ Clark as he "snapped ferociously at the movie industry's heels charging monopoly, abuse of power, and collaboration with the Roosevelt administration to fan American hatred of dictatorship into a consuming flame of total war."[17] The *Los Angeles Examiner* also painted the day's events as "frequently interrupted by spectators, the asides of Wendell Willkie," as well as the committee's confusion over the fairness of the investigation. Champ Clark told the press he would entertain questioning from Willkie but reiterated that the traditions of such hearings did not allow it. The paper concluded its Wednesday coverage giving Champ Clark the last word, who claimed Willkie was "difficult to analyze" because "no one knows whether he is speaking as a private citizen or an attorney earning a large fee from very lucrative clients."[18]

An editorial in the *Washington Post* by John T. McManus theorized the motivations behind the subcommittee and called out its rhetoric as "the anti-Hollywood line of Goebbels, the Coughlinites, the Bundists and 100 Percenters, and Senator Nye is now trying to disclaim it."[19] After two days of testimony, it was not difficult to see the commonality of focus on foreign-born versus "pure" Americans that was found in the prominent supremacist groups. McManus offers one theory behind the subcommittee, which was that its true purpose was to damage the film industry so that Hollywood could be taken over by Hearst with the infamous and influential Joseph Kennedy hired to replace Will Hays. A fascinating theory for sure, but McManus argued the more likely purpose was to show off "phony isolationist muscle."[20] For McManus, the subcommittee should instead investigate the domestic banks that fund the movie studios.

Another editorial in the *Washington Post* worked to define propaganda—something overlooked throughout the investigation. Barnet Nover wrote, "It is obvious that we shall learn very little from this latest witch hunt on Capitol Hill. Yet propaganda, what it is and how it operates, is a subject worth looking into."[21] Nover covered the historical use of the word, such as the seventeenth century origins of the college of propaganda for educating priests (referring to the Sacred Congregation for the Propagation of the Faith). The definition of propaganda, which Nover found in *Webster's Dictionary*, was reported as "any organized or concerted group, effort or movement to spread a particular doctrine or system of doctrines or principles," and could also be seen as the "secret or clandestine dissemination of ideas, information, gossip, or the like, for the purpose of helping or injuring a person, an institution, a cause, etc."[22] Nover argued that movies had not propagandized the country into support of war. Instead, intervention support had grown because Americans "have become aware of the realities which can be ignored only to their destruction and the destruction of all that we hold most precious."[23]

An opinion piece in the *New York Daily News* followed a similar path by defining anti-Semitism as found in two primary groups. The first was the "Ku Klux Klan and the Social Justice front" that believed the Jews "should be harassed and restricted."[24] The second group was the "enthusiastic war mongers" who wish to "avenge upon Hitler the wrongs which he has inflicted on the Jews in Europe."[25] The essay notes that there are about five million Jews in a United States population of one hundred and thirty million. Observing that two million of them lived in the Greater New York City area, the article detailed the success and wide support of two prominent New York Jews, Governor Herbert H. Lehman and New York City mayor Fiorello LaGuardia, who served as an example of bi-racial acceptance. The piece cited Israel Zangwill's Melting Pot theory, that the country should continue accepting domestic Jews as Americans as a means to "eliminate the hyphen in the America of the future."[26]

Two op-eds in the *Los Angeles Times* took aim at the isolationist senators. Referring to a series of American battleships that were torpedoed or shelled while assisting the British since the previous November, Ed Ainswroth mused that the "seething senator says the films are propagandizing us into war, he probably thinks those United States ships were sunk by a director for Warner Bros."[27] Ainsworth continued to mock the investigation: "When you get to the point where you see the foul hand of the British conspiracy in Mickey Mouse and the terrible plots of Churchill in *Gone with the Wind*, it's about time to go out and fumigate your brain."[28] Not letting up, Ainsworth persisted, "And speaking of wind, the hot air from the desert that the weatherman promised didn't get here, it all stayed in Washington with the Nye committee."[29] The article concluded with a message encouraging readers to see whatever films they want and come to their own conclusions on the European conflict.

The second op-ed in the *Los Angeles Times*, by Westbrook Pegler, argued that while Hollywood made anti-Nazi propaganda films, they were no worse than what Hitler himself had done. "The most powerful propaganda against Nazi Germany," Pegler wrote, "is to be found in the daily record of events in Germany since Hitler began to rise."[30] Pegler called attention to the concentration camps, arguing that they were not the invention of Hollywood. In addition, Pegler called Chaplin's *The Great Dictator* "one of the worst films of all time" because it did not go far enough in calling out "the horrors that have been recorded in the news and verified and not merely admitted by the Nazi government but defended."[31] More than the other coverage up to this point, Pegler specified Hitler's rise to power in great detail. "The real reason there is no balanced account of Nazi Germany," Pegler argued, is that "there isn't enough favorable material to make a short."[32]

The *New York Herald Tribune* also mocked the hearings as an "isolationist boomerang," an investigation to see if there should be an investigation.[33] The *New York Times* reminded readers that it was not the film industry that had everyone worked up, as "Hitler tends to make people dislike Hitler."[34] While an investigation of propaganda could be useful, the *Christian Science Monitor* observed that "the main value" of this subcommittee was "to disclose what a world of fantasy isolationism lives in."[35] In addition, the *San Francisco Chronicle* noted that producer Jesse Lasky "dared" Senator Nye to investigate *Sergeant York*.[36] The senators, however, would remain vigilant in their decision not to watch the films in question for another week.

PART THREE
DISGRUNTLED
JOURNALISTS

CHAPTER SIX

John T. Flynn, "Nasty Man"

Day Three: Thursday, September 11, 1941

While the Senate subcommittee continued questioning Hollywood on September 11, aviator Charles Lindbergh addressed an America First rally in Des Moines, Iowa. Lindbergh was a regular fixture at America First events but was also a notorious anti-Semite who called out Jews as a major war promoter in the United States.[1] Lindbergh saw Jewish concern over the events in Europe as "agitating for war," when they should be "opposing it in every possible way." Calling these concerned citizens "short-sighted" and "dangerous" because of their controlling interest in movies, radio, and press, as well as "not American" in consecutive breaths, Lindbergh solidified his stance as an enemy of Hollywood.[2] Willkie labeled Lindbergh's speech "race prejudice" and described it as "the most un-American talk made in my time by any person of national reputation."[3]

Calling to order at 10:30 a.m., the subcommittee reconvened with Senators Champ Clark of Missouri, Nye, Maloney, Wiley, and Worth Clark of Idaho. Before the next testimony would begin, Senator McFarland requested that time be made to screen the films in question. McFarland pointed to the last two days of testimony where both Senators Nye and Champ Clark admitted their complaints were based "almost entirely upon hearsay." McFarland did not want to waste time on secondary evidence and felt that the only evidence on the table should be the motion pictures. Using *Sergeant York* as an example, McFarland said he felt it was a good film. Senator Tobey agreed. Always candid, McFarland concluded that maybe "we are wasting a lot of time here for nothing." Willkie assured the subcommittee that screenings could begin on the following day, but Worth Clark argued that they should only be screened without an audience. After two days of sessions it was clear that the investigation was becoming a media spectacle, and film screenings would certainly have drawn additional, unwanted vocal responses. Senators Tobey and Brooks agreed to meet in an executive session to discuss the issue further.

Testimony of John T. Flynn

John T. Flynn was the testimony of the day. Flynn opened by introducing himself to the three hundred attendees as a journalist who primarily wrote on economic and social issues.[4] Flynn also worked as an associate editor for *Collier's* and served as contributing editor for the *New Republic*, in addition to being an author of several books. Senator Worth Clark inquired about relevant background for this investigation, but Flynn had nothing new to add. When McFarland asked Flynn's purpose in testifying, Flynn stated his role as New York chairman of the America First Committee. However, Flynn was not appearing as a representative of America First and made clear he was not an expert in motion pictures. "I appear here as a complainant," Flynn said, "against what I believe to be the propaganda abuses of the moving-picture industry." McFarland held up one of Flynn's books and asked if the volume had any propaganda.

> FLYNN: "I have written a lot of propaganda. I have no objection to propaganda, but—"
> MCFARLAND: "(interposing) It is just the propaganda you do not agree with that you object to, is that it?"
> FLYNN: "Oh, no, no, no. I think if you will let me tell you what kind of propaganda I do agree with, and what kind I do not agree with, and what kind of propaganda is in the movies, then you could ask me some questions in a more intelligent way."

As the conversation continued heating up, McFarland worked to find out why Flynn was there and what, exactly, he was an expert on. Flynn assured McFarland his testimony would not be based on hearsay, though he did not have a clear familiarity with Hollywood. McFarland pointed to Flynn's America First Committee chapter and asked, "Is that the organization the bund paper advocated their members join?" Flynn punched back, stating that McFarland was "grossly misinformed," a line that was rewarded with raucous applause. Senator Worth Clark interjected, but Flynn continued to denounce the Bund and its interest in America First. As the two continued to spar, McFarland asked if Flynn was friendly towards the Bund. "No. I am not friendly toward the bund, and I think you must know that," responded Flynn amidst additional laughter and applause. McFarland stated that he simply did not know enough about Flynn. "That is your fault, senator," Flynn responded acerbically. "You cannot be forced to read."

McFarland and Flynn continued jabbing each other. "Do you mean that you are such a prominent man that everyone ought to know about you? Is that your idea?" McFarland inquired. "No. But I imagine my name gets in the papers as much as that of Senator McFarland, and the people who read know about me," answered Flynn. "I am not trying to get my name in the newspapers," said McFarland, playing along. Flynn hit back, "How did you get to the Senate? By hiding behind the bushes of Arizona?" As the room filled with laughter and applause, McFarland lost his composure. "You might come out to Arizona and find out." The room erupted into applause, but Senator Worth Clark stepped in to remind both those on the floor and the audience that outbursts of emotion would not be tolerated. Flynn and McFarland continued their banter, questioning each other's background. Eventually, Flynn brought the discussion back to that of motion-picture propaganda. No doubt the display of rhetorical posturing was both amusing and showcased the increasing tensions in the room.

Flynn continued on to the question of monopoly, noting that while the Senate had investigated several cases of monopoly, there had been little attention given to the film industry. Turning to another interventionist, Flynn began to cite influential public relations expert Walter Lippmann, who once spoke of the motion-picture industry by criticizing its alleged monopoly. Lippman felt movies were low culture at best: "The remedy for the undeniably low condition of the movies is not to impose standards on the existing monopolistic corporations but by invoking the anti-trust laws and perhaps new legislation to break their power." Lippman's key line, quoted by Flynn and then read again for emphasis, was, "For the evils of the movies come not from too much liberty for the giants, but from the destruction of real liberty by the giants." Flynn reiterated that it was not his goal to impose censorship but to crack the control of the movie industry that he felt was in the controlling hands of only a few men.

Flynn quoted director Frank Capra for support, who told the *New York Times* in 1939 that "six producers today pass upon 90 percent of the scripts and get out and edit 90 percent of the pictures." Flynn also paraphrased a 1918 statement from Paramount's Adolph Zukor who warned the industry that "the evils of producing and exhibiting are one of the gravest perils that have ever confronted the moving-picture industry." In addition, Flynn recited a line from an unnamed industry executive who told the *Film Daily* in 1940 that "we are no longer fighting each other, but simply establishing solidarity or perishing." The unnamed executive was Spyros Skouras, who would soon be president of Twentieth Century Fox. Skouras also noted a desire for a "moral merger" of film content because of concern over executives becoming "battered and punch-drunk with worry" over the situation in Europe.⁵

The journalist cited additional lines from prominent isolationist Thurman Arnold, who was currently an Assistant Attorney General at the US Department of Justice, and Robert Jackson, Justice of the US Supreme Court. Flynn made clear he wanted to show similar opinions from a range of sources that supported his complaints about the film industry. In 1940, Jackson had called the film industry in violation of sections one and two of the 1890 Sherman Act, which Jackson described as an "act to protect trade and commerce against unlawful restraints and monopolies." Flynn elaborated by highlighting the 2,800 first-run theaters that were owned by the major companies, which exerted great influence when taken together as a single platform for any given film.

The next argument would be directed at Willkie, who had been heard during a previous testimony telling reporters that "they [the isolationists] want to have the Nazi side presented as sure as you were born." Flynn took issue with the statement and argued that one could take the side of the United States without standing with the Nazis. It was evident that while Hollywood felt there was simply two sides, pro- or anti-Nazi, Flynn saw that there was pro-British, pro-Nazi, or pro-United States. Flynn overlooked the potential overlap between the outlined views as well as the possibility of one being both anti-Nazi and pro-United States.

Turning to censorship, Flynn presented opposition. "If this Government ever undertakes to censor the movies I will be opposed to it and will do whatever I can, and I will be over there alongside of Mr. Willkie opposing it—that is, if Mr. Willkie is still on that side," Flynn said, rousing laughter from the audience. "I could not shift as fast as you do," Willkie responded coldly. After again stating his staunch opposition to censorship, Flynn regaled the committee with the history of censorship in Hollywood by calling attention to the accusations of immoral filmmaking that was coming from the pulpits in the 1930s. The problem still, as Flynn understood, was that even censorship did not fix everything.

Flynn began reading from a *New York Times* article, dated February 16, 1936, that included an interview with author Sinclair Lewis regarding Hollywood's handling of the film adaptation of the author's *It Can't Happen Here*. Lewis told the story of MGM buying the film rights, securing a script by Sidney Howard and a cast starring Lionel Barrymore, before Will Hays banned any adaptation of the novel. Lewis billed his work as "American propaganda." Howard accused Hollywood of backing out of the film based on a fear of offending Mussolini and Hitler. Of course, MGM's Louis B. Mayer and the MPPDA president Hays both rejected the accusation. Flynn's larger point was that since there was already censorship in place, it should have been possible to pressure for or against other types of films—such as those that may feature an isolationist or antiwar stance.

Mention of several antiwar films followed, such as *All Quiet on the Western Front* and *What Price Glory?* (1926), which made war look unpatriotic in a way not found in current Hollywood films. The journalist may not have been aware of the resurgence of *All Quiet on the Western Front* going on at the time. Flynn surmised his frustration was that the "censorship authority can be used to promote propaganda for any subject or any point of view, for anything under the sun." The war films were too simplistic for Flynn. New pictures should consider similar antiwar positions of the post-World War I pictures.

Hatred of Hitler, according to Flynn, was not sufficient justification for current film trends. Hollywood should hate authoritarianism more than any single representative figure. Painting Hollywood with the brush of fascism, Flynn continued, "I want them to cut out whatever trace of it there is in their business as described by the Assistant Attorney General of the United States." Again, the problem came back to that of control. Showing the same jealousy presented from Nye and Clark the past two days, Flynn noted that it was not fair for one industry to have the loudest voice on any topic. According to Flynn, speaking to a room of thousands of people was useless when movies could reach so many millions. "I am complaining about their right to monopolize the dissemination of truth," lamented Flynn, who felt the film industry was doing with war propaganda what newspapers had done in the past to incite a crime wave by taking the minor crimes reported at the back of the paper and pile them on the front page. Flynn believed that Hollywood was similarly taking minor issues and blowing them out of proportion to drive public opinion.

The committee broke for lunch and Flynn resumed his statement at 2:00 p.m. Continuing to compare Hollywood's propaganda to that of Hitler, Flynn labeled the dictator of Germany as "the model for war propaganda in this country." Providing an overview of Hitler's approach to mass disinformation, Flynn continued to describe Germany's ability to win over people by reducing ideas to simple catch phrases and repeating them over and over. For Flynn, the repetition from Hollywood was "we are next on Hitler's list," "we cannot do business in a world dominated by Hitler," "you cannot make peace with dictators," and "you can aid the allies, but you will not have to go to war." Flynn saw such messages as spewing hatred for Germany in a way analogous to how the Nazis had spread hatred of their own enemies.

Flynn claimed the purpose of Hollywood's war-themed films was vengeance by way of mob mentality. "Hollywood is rather proud lately of its propaganda power," Flynn thought. In 1939, Jack Warner had told the *New York Times* that "the visual power of the screen is tremendous. We propose to use it to acquaint Americans with their heritage," which was the "defense of democracy." Flynn used this quote to argue Hollywood's pride in propaganda, once again restating Warner's line that "the visual power of the screen is tremendous." Flynn's problem was not that Warner was using movies to sell Americanism. The problem was semantic, because the definition of Americanism may differ depending on one's "particular philosophy and fancy." Flynn followed with a line from Warner's interviewer, Douglas Chamberlain, who realized the studio's power of influence: "If Warner succeed in determining just what Americanism is, it is possible that the controversy will end."

After explaining that Warner Bros.' star Edward G. Robinson was also a staunch interventionist, Flynn argued that Hollywood unequivocally took advantage of its propagandistic power. Quoting Paul Harrison of the *World-Telegram*, Flynn pointed to another detractor who felt, "Most of us think there is danger in Warner's policy and that it will certainly be embarrassing to our government. There is a big difference between defensive patriotism and that sort of aggressive criticism." Flynn undoubtedly agreed with Harrison's criticism of "jingoism" in the film industry.

Flynn briefly mentioned Columbia's Jack Cohn, who optioned but ultimately did not produce a film titled *The Mad Dog of Europe*, which was about the rise of Hitler. Cohn had told the *Motion Picture Herald* that "where one person may go to the theater hoping for the strong meat of controversy, hundreds go for lighter but no less important fare." Surprisingly, Flynn did not elaborate on the history of *The Mad Dog of Europe*. The film production was pressured for fear of losing the German market in 1933–34. Joseph Breen also sent a memo to *The Mad Dog of Europe* screenwriter that said, "The purpose of the screen is to entertain and not to propagandize," and that a film like this "might result in a kind of two-edged sword, with the screen being used for propaganda purposes not so worthy."[6] Flynn also recalled the head of RKO, George Schaefer, telling politically active producer Walter Wanger to "hire a hall" or finance controversial films on his own, before moving on to specify a list of films that should be examined.

The first film in question was *Underground*, a powerful Warner Bros. picture about a mobile, subversive radio station in Nazi Germany that informs the Resistance. Flynn quoted a favorable review in the *Motion Picture Herald* that was problematic because the critic also came from Germany. Flynn's point was that even the industry film critics may have been biased, so the only option was to watch and investigate each film. Flynn provided his list, organized by studio:

Warner Bros.

Confessions of a Nazi Spy

Dispatch from Reuters

Dive Bomber

Murder in the Air

Underground

RKO

Convoy

Nurse Edith Cavell

The Mortal Storm

Sky Murder

MGM

Escape

Flight Command

Columbia

Escape to Glory

Mad Men of Europe

Missing Ten Days

Phantom Submarine

They Dare Not Love

This Is England

Voice in the Night

Foreign Correspondent

Twentieth Century Fox

War in the Desert

Men of Lightship 61

The Man I Married

Man Hunt

Four Sons

Paramount

One Night in Lisbon

Mystery Sea Raider

I Wanted Wings

Flynn's list of British films

After Mein Kampf

Anzacs in Action (distributed
    by Twentieth Century Fox)

*Birthplace of America-Our British
    Forebears*

Thumbs Up

U-Boat 29

Pastor Hall

North Sea Patrol

Nigh Train (released as
    Night Train to Munich)

The Lion Has Wings

Flynn also called attention to the newsreels of RKO, MGM, and Columbia.[7] Making sure not to sound off like Nye and Champ Clark, Flynn told the chamber, "Not all of these pictures are poisonous. Some of them are very fine pictures." The final opinion, however, did line up with the other isolationist senators: "The object of these pictures, of course [is] the succession of them—[they] keep pounding at you like the man haranguing the mob in the streets, to get your hatreds in control of your reason and turn you loose on war." Flynn encouraged the committee not to only watch the films but also look into the source material and reports from the Hays Office. Smartly, Flynn sought knowledge

You have heard many refugee stories, but this you will remember as long as you live.

It is about "the Spencer Tracy of France": Jean Gabin

ILLUSTRATION BY SI MESEROW

by
WILBUR MORSE, JR.

"IF YOU refuse, it may mean a concentration camp!"

The thin, nervous little emissary of the Paris Nazi propagandists looked up at tall, bushy-haired Jean Gabin to see what effect this threat would have on the actor's obstinacy.

For an hour, the Paris agent had been vainly arguing with Gabin, in his Riviera retreat, attempting to persuade France's most popular motion-picture idol to take part in a series of French language films which the Germans proposed to produce in a campaign to calm the fears and allay the hatred of the defeated country.

"You seem to forget, Monsieur Gabin, that it is not a German habit to tolerate unfriendly lack of co-operation."

"And you, monsieur," replied the screen star, rising angrily, "you seem to forget that I am still a Frenchman! I tell you again, and for the last time, I will not make these propaganda pictures . . . no matter what the punishment may be for my refusal!"

And as the messenger from the Nazi headquarters in Paris discreetly departed, Jean Gabin, hero of a hundred screen escapes, began to plot his second real-life flight from his German enemies within a year.

His first escape from the Nazi conquerors had been in May, last spring, when Gabin, a sailor on leave from duty with a French minesweeper at Cherbourg, had been caught up in the blitzkrieg on Paris, bombed out of his home in near-by Dreux and evaded capture by the invading German Army by only fifteen minutes.

Then he had fled to Toulon, in the South and, after the Armistice and his automatic demobilization, had remained in Unoccupied France, safe so long as he restrained himself from

PHOTOPLAY *combined with* MOVIE MIRROR

Escape advertisement, July 1941

of the filmmaking process as a way to strengthen his own arguments. Such an approach was lost on both Nye and Champ Clark, who had shown great ignorance of the film industry.

Films like *Man Hunt* and *Underground*, for Flynn, were "designed to arouse the emotions and passions of the people." However, Flynn felt a film like *That*

ESCAPE FROM THE NAZIS

any outright act of antagonism against the hated Hitlerism.

Now the Germans had sought him out in his quiet retreat at Cap Ferrat, near Nice, and were putting on the first pressure that could end only in a concentration camp or his surrender to their demands that he aid their insidious propaganda campaign. Without funds, without a passport to leave the country, Gabin knew that his rescue this time must come from the outside.

Accordingly, he cabled André Devan, his friend of many years and formerly a prominent French film producer, who a few months before had been signed by Twentieth Century-Fox as a producer in Hollywood. Could Devan arrange from America for the proper visas and transportation to get him to Hollywood, Gabin queried.

While he waited for a reply, Jean ironically mused on the number of times Hollywood had cabled him before the war, each tissue-thin billet a more generous offer than the last, urging him to leave his beloved Paris to make pictures in America. Now the plea was reversed. Hollywood, which he had once rejected, was his only hope of succor.

Back from Devan came a cable reporting that not only would he arrange for Gabin's evacuation from France, but that Darryl Zanuck wanted the French star to come to act in his movies. This time the actor eagerly accepted.

So it was that when the liner *Exeter* nosed up through New York harbor one blustery morning in March, a tall, muscular man in a black turtle-necked sweater, a dark suit and an old fur coat, stood on deck eagerly watching the distant dock where he

JULY, 1941

knew Devan awaited him. His once blond wavy hair had turned grey. There was in his eyes the look of a man who has seen death and destruction and despair. But on his lips was the broad smile that has ingratiated him and his simple sincerity to so many French film-goers in the years gone by.

That smile was a smile of triumph For the second time he had escaped seizure by the Germans!

JEAN GABIN told me about those escapes over a leisurely luncheon at the famous Colony Restaurant a few days after he arrived in New York. Around the room, the smartly dressed, faultlessly groomed women who make up the top layer of Manhattan's cafe (Continued on page 58)

"Pepe Le Moko" the French version of "Algiers": Jean Gabin in his great success, playing the role refused by Charles Boyer

Hamilton Woman, which was discussed earlier in the week, was not dangerous, as the anti-Nazi sentiment was a small piece of a much larger story. Regarding *Confessions of a Nazi Spy*, Flynn cited the *New York Times* review: "We don't believe Nazi propaganda ministers let their mouths twitch evilly whenever they mention our constitution. I thought that school of villainy had gone out with the *Beast of Berlin* back in 1924." Flynn also brought up analysis from the *National Board of Review*, which stated, "It's propaganda—propaganda in the sense of exposing something in such a way that people's feelings, or judgement, or both, are likely to be influence on the question involved."

Flynn preferred if all war-themed films, those he called propaganda films, at least labeled themselves as such. Pointing to a Russian documentary film, titled *The Mannerheim Line* (1940), Flynn described how the film opens by stating, "This is propaganda." Only Flynn did not specify that *The Mannerheim Line* was a documentary and not a feature film. Drawing the comparison to Hollywood, Flynn brought out the press packets for *Four Sons, Night Train to Munich, The Man I Married,* and *Man Hunt.* None of them made mention of propaganda, which Flynn argued would do the audience a service by not concealing the true purpose of the films. In addition, there was a British film titled *Mad Men of Europe* (1940) that provided directions for theater managers on how to use the film to engage audiences in the war effort. Flynn was not overly pleased with this display either, even though it presented itself directly as a propaganda film by donating, lobbying, volunteering locally, and even signing up for service. "After all, some of you gentlemen will be running for office soon and here is a liberal education in propaganda," Flynn quipped, drawing laughter from the audience.

Irving Hoffman, in the *Hollywood Reporter*, poked fun at Flynn for bringing the "investigation into the field of absurdity when he insisted that Congress should trace the development of every motion picture script from the germ of its inception through the various drafts written by the scenarists. He even wants to trace through changes made in film editing."[8] Hoffman showed frustration for the "so-called experts" on the subcommittee who showed a complete misunderstanding of how moviemaking works. "They cannot understand the creation of a movie-story based upon teamwork but persist in the outsider's notion that each person's job is a separate and well-defined function."[9] Hoffman also reprinted an open letter in the *Daily News* that Ed Sullivan, the future television personality who was then a columnist and radio host, sent to Senator Nye:

> Your investigation of the movies, to determine whether or not they are being used as a medium of war propaganda, reminds me of the story of the near-sighted man who hired a rig drawn by two horses and went out into the country for some rabbit-shooting. There was a rustle in the underbrush and he pulled the trigger and shot both of his horses dead. That is the position, I think, you are in, Senator Nye. Certainly, there has been war propaganda and you should have suppressed it. It was set forth in a best-selling book, and the name of the book was *Mein Kampf,* and it was written by Adolf Hitler. Had you suppressed that book, the cause of war propaganda would have been dealt a body-blow.[10]

It is curious that with all of the propaganda talk coming from the subcommittee, there was no discussion of the pro-Nazi literature floating around the country. Certainly, a tome like *Mein Kampf* is an easy target, but the mainstream anti-Semitism coming from hate groups and major figures alike was not examined. Lindbergh got a pass; America First was not questioned; hateful leaders like William Dudley Pelley (Silver Legion) and Fritz Kuhn (German-American Bund) were not perceived as threats because they were isolationists; nor was there mention of Father Coughlin, who had been booted off the airwaves in 1939 for his anti-Jewish rhetoric. By 1940 the US government had wised up, passing the Alien Registration Act in 1940 as a way to force immigrants to declare membership in organizations like the German-American Bund.[10] In 1941, the trend of turning a blind eye to domestic anti-Semitic movements was over. Sullivan caught Hollywood critics in the Senate cherry-picking their outrage.

Before the day's events were over, McFarland quarreled with Flynn a few more times. McFarland encouraged Flynn to familiarize himself with the films in question and Flynn encouraged the familiarization with the production process. Flynn told McFarland, "The process might be enlightening to you. I understood you a moment ago to say that you did not claim to be an expert propagandist. You might like to see a propagandist at work." "I think I have seen one today," McFarland quickly responded, and the room exploded into applause. Flynn continued to explain how he was not opposed to propaganda as long as all sides were represented. "What you are really objecting to then," mused McFarland, "is that you have not gotten as much propaganda in the pictures on your side as you would like to have?" The two went on jabbing at each other, evoking continued applause along the way.

McFarland also called attention to Flynn's claims against Warner Bros. and noted that if the stockholders had a problem with the films being produced, they could have spoken out. Flynn had heard no such objection, but still found it problematic that a publicly traded company would make propaganda films—an argument direct from Phelps's anti-Hollywood pamphlet. Flynn provided a concluding remark that denounced the process of filmmaking that had allowed propaganda to reach such a mass audience. McFarland gave a brief response, concluding that "the American people can understand and know propaganda when put upon the screen just as well as you can." The Arizona senator's comments gained applause once again. After three days of examination, the committee broke at 3:50 p.m. and would gather again Monday, September 15.

Flynn much was more researched and nuanced in his argument than Nye and Champ Clark, but it would not be enough to stifle criticism. The Hollywood trade press, as expected, piled on the investigation once again. "Flynn Drools Same Drivel," read a *Variety* headline.[11] The author wrote that Flynn "was punchier than his predecessors on the witness stand, but no more original" and described his arguments as "antiquated squawks."[12] Another pieced titled "Flynn's Puppet Show" called the journalist a "nasty man who wields the long snake whip, to the crack of which the Clark-Wheeler-Nye group responds so eagerly."[13] Flynn was described as someone unable to like or respect anyone who may disagree. The entire investigation was written off as "malarkey."[14] The essay concluded by calling attention to President Roosevelt's words, which had been increasingly directed at the horrors of Hitler. For *Variety*, the Senate should have been investigating the president if they were so concerned with where interventionist support was coming from.

"Senate Hearing Still Big Yawn," ran a headline in the *Hollywood Reporter*.[15] The author, Jack Moffitt, recounted that the investigation had "moved from a state of jubilation to a state of apprehension."[17] Moffitt's frustration was that "the Congress of the United States is composed of a large body of self-effacing men all seeking to be president."[18] Comparing the senators to the famous aviator, Moffitt observed, "It reminds me of Lindbergh after his great Atlantic flight. He rode through the streets of every American city, seated on top of an automobile—because he was so modest."[19] Moffitt complained that the senators were no different from the politicians during the First World War who flip-flopped on their views to connect with the prevailing political winds of the day.

Drew Pearson, also in the *Hollywood Reporter*, focused his column on the prospect of Willkie using the newfound origins of the investigation to his advantage. The new evidence was proof of radio host G. Allison Phelps palling around with isolationist senators, a find that if used by Willkie would "be as sensational as anything uncorked by the Dies committee."[20] Pearson described Phelps as "planting the seeds of hate" as the author of a "muck-racking booklet against the movie industry," *An American's History of Hollywood—The Tower of Babel*.[21] The slant of the pamphlet was clear, as Phelps's title presumed a real American had yet to cover the history of the motion-picture industry. After Phelps worked on the campaign of Senator Bob Reynolds of North Carolina, it was not long before Nye and company moved forward with their resolution to investigate Hollywood. Pearson included a side bar with his column, sardonically referring to the isolationist senators as "busy men" because they "refused to interrupt testimony and see the films involved."[22]

Press coverage outside of Hollywood was largely critical of the investigation as well. *PM*'s Washington Bureau noted McFarland as the "lone supporter of the [Roosevelt] Administration" and described Flynn's words as "in large part a repetition of the previous statements."[23] The *Daily News* showed support by carrying Willkie's statement urging the screening of the films in question. Willkie wanted to prove that the movies had "shown only a pale portrayal of the terror and cruelties of Nazi Germany."[24] Taking direct aim at Flynn, Willkie said, "John Flynn's testimony is merely a redraft of Senator Clark's yesterday—or perhaps John Flynn wrote them both. . . . Let's see the pictures and discontinue this bunk."[25]

Another op-ed in the *Daily News* by Manchester Boddy hammered the Senate's history of abusing power. Boddy argued that similar investigations have "been used as a means toward establishing political machines, crushing political enemies, and filling campaign coffers with cash."[26] The accusations from the isolationist senators were "about 99 percent threat" and had "all the earmarks of a super colossal flop."[27] Boddy also responded to reports that Charlie Chaplin would be subpoenaed to testify: "The people will hear anything and everything that Charlie Chaplin has to say—and it will bitterly resent any 'gag' measure employed to silence him."[28] While the discussion of Chaplin would continue, the actor would never testify. Subpoenas were also issued to the *Hollywood Reporter* publisher Billy Wilkerson and *Confessions of a Nazi Spy* director Antanole Litvak, but neither would end up testifying.

John O'Donnell of the *Times Herald* showed support for the committee, reiterating the monopolistic charges from the isolationist senators. "Six all-powerful magnates, adopting the propaganda techniques of Hitler, are using their monopoly dictatorship to arouse the nation's movie audiences to a 'half-maniacal hatred' and to dictate the foreign policy of the United States," wrote O'Donnell. No mention was given to McFarland's tough line of questioning, as the day was described as a bloodbath for the interventionists while the crowd "howled their delight as the repartee crackled."[29]

Dorothy Thompson, the influential journalist and wife of Sinclair Lewis, had equated the investigation to the infamous Dreyfus affair—a blunder of justice in France that saw a wrongfully accused army captain imprisoned in 1894 before being exonerated in 1906. Alfred Dreyfus, a Jewish staff member of a French general, was suspected to be a German spy, indicted, and sentenced to a life-long banishment to Devil's Island in a closed-door trial. The problem was that the primary evidence against Dreyfus was a handwritten letter, which was never conclusively attributed to him. Two years after the trial, pressure began to mount that Dreyfus was innocent. In 1899, Dreyfus was pardoned and finally exonerated in 1906. The entire affair continued to be relevant because the case represented blatant anti-Semitism, a brand of hatred that grew drastically in the next four decades.[30]

Criticizing the committee's "doubtful legality," Thomson argued that "the America First Committee, working through members of the United States Senate, has set out to frame the entire motion picture industry of this country."[31] The syndicated column directed a death blow to the committee, accusing the

isolationists of trying to "change American [foreign] policy into one of collaboration with Hitler on the model of Vichy."[32] Thompson felt that Senator Nye
and his allies wrongly saw attacking Hitler as a form of warmongering. Pushing
such a view to the point of a Senate investigation, according to Thompson,
was "the greatest Nazi propaganda stunt ever pulled off in the United States."[33]
Thompson concluded her column by arguing that the isolationist senators were
simply colluding with the Nazis in their efforts to minimize the power of film.

The *Yakima Daily Republic* billed the investigation as a bait and switch
"for the purpose of confusing the issue and of branding a great industry with
dishonor in order to promote their own political views and reputations."[34] The
Grandview Herald saw the inquisition as a "disgrace to America" and feared that
an isolationist victory could lead to further investigations of other business
and individuals, ultimately leading the country to "be as thoroughly committed
to the fascist way of life as Germany is or can be."[35] General Hugh S. Johnson
argued in the *Philadelphia Inquirer* that movies had not changed the public's
mind away from isolation, claiming that 70–80 percent of Americans were
"opposed to unnecessary bloody involvement in this war."[36] Gould Lincoln
in the *Evening Star* called the investigation "anti-war isolationist propaganda"
that would likely become a "boomerang."[37]

Arthur Robb, writing in *Editor & Publisher*, took on the question of propaganda versus entertainment in a column titled "The Fourth Estate." Robb
argued that "if there has been a falling-off of attendance at movie theaters, . . .
the reason can be found, in part anyway, with a continuous diet of drums and
bugles, tanks and panes, parachutes and bombs."[38] In addition, Robb argued that
the movies in question were "not propaganda by any fair definition."[39] Though
not sympathetic to Hollywood's war films, Robb was clear in noting the Senate
investigation was akin to a kangaroo court.

CHAPTER SEVEN

Fidler Fiddles

Day Four: Monday, September 15, 1941

At 10:30 a.m., Senators Worth Clark (chairman), McFarland, and Tobey resumed the session by looking at a series of letters written to Worth Clark. One letter was from the Intermountain Theaters Association, whose September 11 meeting solidified their support of the Senate investigation and "its strenuous objection to the excessive war material now being injected into feature pictures and news releases." Another letter came from Fulton Cook, a theater owner in Idaho who was angered at MGM for allegedly forcing a propaganda film into his theater. Cook supplied the letter from Loew's, Inc., while MGM's Maurice Saffle's response was read to the committee:

> I note your letter of May 10 and I notice that among other eliminations you ask that we take out *Land of Liberty*. I wonder if you realize just what this subject is, and why we ask that you play it?
>
> Metro-Goldwyn-Mayer is distributing the picture, at its expense, and putting it in place of one of our own features, on which we might show a profit. We are doing this at the request of the United States Government, who feel that every man, woman, and child in America should see this subject during these times of national defense. In fact, they are so interested in the playing of the subject that we have been asked to wire immediately the names of the exhibitors who eliminate it. All rentals on the picture are turned over to the government.
>
> In view of the above, I am going to ask that you reconsider and try to find a date for this subject.

Cook saw Saffle's letter as a clear threat, specifying the detail about reporting anyone to the government who refuses to play *Land of Liberty*. The film was a feature/documentary compilation about pre-Revolution United States. *Land of Liberty* was edited by Cecil B. DeMille, but the production was undertaken by the MPPDA for the purposes of screening at the 1939 World's Fair and the 1940 Golden Gate International Exposition. Cook wrote back, stating that "the running of my theater should be left to me" and that "propaganda pictures are distasteful." The trade press reviewed the film positively across the spectrum of industry periodicals.[1]

Senator Worth Clark provided his own response to the support by complaining that the majority of press coverage of the subcommittee has been negative. "Our motives have been attacked," Clark announced, "our legality questioned, the facts have been misstated; and, in general, a smear campaign is on." Noticeably intimidated by the bloodbath in the media, Worth Clark declared that the negative coverage "smacks of conspiracy. . . . We are going to find out about it." On that tense note, journalist and radio personality Jimmie Fidler was sworn in before giving his statement. In protest of the senators allowing a gossip journalist as a credible witness, Willkie refused to appear in the courtroom. "I haven't any time to waste listening to one who makes his living purveying gossip, even if the committee has."[2]

Testimony of James M. Fidler

Appearing in a dapper suit that matched his blue eyes, Fidler provided an overview of his life in Hollywood for the past twenty-two years. He began as an actor, transitioned to a press agent, and eventually became a columnist and radio personality, which he had worked as for the past seven years. Fidler's column, "Jimmie Fidler in Hollywood," was syndicated across approximately 140 papers. His radio show aired at 6:15 p.m. on Friday nights. Fidler commanded a team of two dozen reporters that helped gather news and review films. Fidler and his team were regularly invited onto studio lots for preview screenings and celebrity interviews. Much of Fidler's recent coverage had been critical of Hollywood's films and its crusade against fascism, something that did not surprise anyone familiar with Fidler's attitude towards the film colony. Fidler argued that he had taken up arms against film propaganda "because I am sure the public does not want it."

Clark asked if Fidler had any problems with Hollywood based on his anti-propaganda stance. "Yes," Fidler responded, "the motion picture industry in devious ways has tried to censor my column and my radio scripts." Fidler was in a unique spot, as his work was not sponsored from the film industry. Studios often had a hand in approving much of a publication's content, such as fan magazines that were largely funded by advertising from the studios. "I cannot be touched," said Fidler; "I get nothing from the studios." Fidler described the difference between the fan magazines, which were subsidized by the studios, and the columnists like him, who had much more freedom to write what they wanted without fear of repercussions from the industry.

Fidler, a self-proclaimed "gossiper," had been on the radio for the last seven years, and studios, he claimed, were pushing back on his negative reviews for the last four or five. "In most cases," Fidler explained, "they [the studio press departments] said that I should regard myself as a member of the industry; that it was unfair for me to criticize pictures." The reasoning was that films were expensive to make, and Fidler should not be so quick to denounce them on the air. Although Fidler never said a film was a "good" or "bad" picture, he used bells (like some critics use stars), and a "low bell" review irked the studios.

One example of studio intervention in Fidler's reviews came with the 1937 film *Conquest*, starring Greta Garbo and Charles Boyer. Fidler gave the film "two bells," which upset MGM. Studio boss Louis B. Mayer called Don Gilman, the vice president of the National Broadcasting Co., to complain. Though he did not know what was discussed, Fidler said that Gilman wrote a letter to affiliates instructing that "Fidler's reviews be held off the air until 30 days after a picture was released." Shortly thereafter, "The studios and, evidently, the broadcasting companies got together and decided that my reviews on the air had been too frank." Fidler's orders were as follows: the A-list films were required to receive a minimum of "three bells," and any film that would not get a positive review should not be reviewed at all.

Similar instructions were given to Fidler from the Columbia Broadcasting Co., where he began working earlier in 1941. Before going on air for the first time, Fidler was given a series of restrictions by the company's vice president:

> You must conform to the policy of the network. You cannot review pictures, three bells for the big ones, two for the small ones, and so on. We will not permit you to say anything detrimental or harmful to the motion-picture industry.

One of the key reasons for such a policy was that the network sponsors used film stars to sell products. It would be problematic if an advertiser was using a star to sell a product on the air followed by Fidler dissing that star's film. Fidler also found problems reporting news that was printed in some film magazines, in addition to a series of rejected open letters he wanted to read on the air. Columbia quickly responded to Fidler's testimony with a letter to Senator Worth Clark. The studio, according to Columbia, was plagued with legal issues "so long as Jimmie Fidler was on the air because of Fidler's desire to destroy values and reputations in order to build up a big audience to which his sponsor could advertise [to]."[3] The letter made clear that Columbia did not want to make money off of Fidler's style of reporting and preferred to see more balanced coverage.

Fidler had recently moved to Mutual Broadcasting Co., where he had yet to have any serious issues. While his radio show was running freely, his columns were still cause for controversy with the film industry. "I have always tried to speak and write from a strictly unbiased point of view," Fidler said. "Nevertheless my column has been the subject of considerable attempt at censorship by the motion-picture industry." His main example was a column criticizing MGM for increasing the price of *Marie Antoinette* (1938), starring Norma Shearer, Tyrone Power, and John Barrymore. The result was Howard Dietz, vice president of advertising at MGM, writing letters to newspapers that carried Fidler's column and threatening to pull advertising if Fidler were not silenced. Will Hays told Dietz that the industry fought censorship for years and was not going to start imposing it on any one person.

The discussion finally caught back up to motion-picture propaganda, with Fidler denouncing *Confessions of a Nazi Spy*. "In my review," Fidler explained, "I said it was a very finely made picture, a very exciting picture, but that I thought it bred hatred." Fidler received letters from the public protesting the film, and "as others of those pictures came along I received more and more mail from the public." Fidler noted that some mail was coming from theater owners, to which Senator Worth Clark replied, "Oh yes, they are coming in droves." Fidler added that he was approached regularly by people telling him, "Keep fighting [these propaganda films], because these very films are destroying us."

Fidler expanded his analysis by explaining that his criticism was not just against propaganda, but any film that "breeds hatred or makes the American people look at each other in suspicion." Fidler explained that films like John Ford's Depression-era yarns *Grapes of Wrath* (1940) and *Tobacco Road* (1941) should not be made. Fidler went further, expressing his concern over gangster films after receiving letters from parents terrified that crime pictures were negatively influencing their children. "My opinion is largely shaped by the letters from the public," explained Fidler, "and by the opinions of people who have told me things in traveling over the country." Fidler qualified his comments by rolling out his war record and claiming he was not pro- or anti- anything, simply reporting what others had said to him.

It was clear that Fidler was rattled by the negative press of the hearings and wanted to state for the record that he was not anti-Semitic. While Fidler adamantly defended his opinions about current war-themed films, he was smart enough to see what direction the wind was blowing. Every day saw more coverage of the investigation and a prolonged correlation between anti-Semitism and the isolationist movement. Fidler's attitude towards isolationism was, perhaps, what Nye thought he was portraying.

Fidler's stance on motion-picture propaganda was that Hollywood should stick to pure entertainment. "When the industry makes a motion picture that is rather obviously propaganda and they place that motion picture in a theater and charge the public to see it," he reasoned, "then I think they are going beyond their due rights." Showing propaganda instead of entertainment, according to Fidler, was a form of cheating the public. Senator Worth Clark proceeded to read one of Fidler's columns, from August 4, 1941. In the essay, Fidler claimed that "Mr. Movie Bigs are after my scalp" but celebrated Hays for calling to end propaganda films. Fidler still stood by his column, but at the time assumed the propaganda films would not continue like they did. It was also noted that the *Los Angeles Times'* Edwin Schallert had been critical of the propaganda films and had not seen any pushback like Fidler's. Senator Worth Clark then brought up *Harrison's Reports*, a regular review rag, which Fidler agreed was a balanced publication. However, *Harrison's Reports* did not agree with the subcommittee and would eventually refer to the Senate inquiry as a "witch-hunting expedition."[4]

As the afternoon session opened after a two-hour recess, Senator Clark of Idaho brought out one of Schallert's *Los Angeles Times* columns titled "War Propaganda Keeps Patrons from Theaters," dated August 13, 1941. Schallert claimed the newspaper was being flooded with letters from readers who were upset about propaganda in feature films. One letter stated that their "entire household had given up movies for ice skating and chess" as a means to "seek other amusements less prejudiced." Clark did not read the entire article but did insist it be made part of the official record.

During the lunch recess, the Columbia Broadcasting System put together a response to Fidler's testimony in which he had called them out for censoring his programs. Fidler was allowed to pick the statement apart line by line to provide his rebuttal in front of the committee. Columbia's statement claimed the network was "beset by legal difficulties and dangers so long as Jimmie Fidler was on the air." Of course, Fidler contested the claim because the lawyers (Fidler's and Columbia's) vetted each transcript prior to air and any necessary changes would be made before broadcast. Columbia claimed Fidler's goal was to "destroy values and reputations" by broadcasting scandal to boost his audience and maximize advertising dollars. Naturally, Fidler disagreed with the accusation because he covered the same material as every other network.

Senator Tobey began to ask about studios offering money for positive film coverage. Fidler recalled offers from Twentieth Century Fox, who did not

indicate a price, and United Artists, who offered $2,500. Fidler did not know
of any other writers who have taken money from studios. In addition, Fidler
had never been approached about a bribe from MGM or Warner Bros. The two
studios did, however, reduce their advertising in the *Los Angeles Times* when
Schallert was critical of their war films. That was the extent of what Fidler saw
as the studios retaliating because of what was written in a newspaper.

Senator Worth Clark noted Fidler's December 21, 1940, review of *The Great
Dictator*, where the critic anticipated Chaplin's film would flop because early
box-office numbers were low. Fidler argued that the film was a disappoint-
ment because "it flourishes [in] propaganda" and was "too obviously made for
the prime purposes of slinging insults at two foreign rulers." Happy to see the
film underperform, Fidler did not think *The Great Dictator* should have ever
been made. "I still hang onto the seemingly old-fashioned idea that the screen
is a place for forgetfulness and entertainment—not ill-disguised propaganda."

Following discussion of the review, Senator Worth Clark asked Fidler about a
list of films covered in *Harrison's Report* to see if he found them propagandistic.
Fidler's picks were *Man Hunt, The Man I Married, The Voice in the Night* (1941),
Escape, One Night in Lisbon (1941), *Confessions of a Nazi Spy, The Great Dictator,
Foreign Correspondent, So Ends Our Night* (1941), and *Four Sons*. Surprisingly,
Fidler did not find *Underground*, Warner Bros.' anti-Nazi film about a resistance
radio station in Germany, to contain propaganda. Fidler did not see *They Dare
Not Love* (1941), *International Squadron, Mad Men of Europe, Pastor Hall, The
Devil Commands* (1941), *Night Train to Munich, Blackout* (1940), *Mystery Sea
Raider* (1940), or *The Phantom Submarine* (1940). The *Harrison's Report* of the
aforementioned films was then included for the record.

Senator McFarland questioned Fidler on his view of censor intervention
into the industry. Fidler acknowledged his passion for free speech on the radio
and in newspapers, but not in films, because readers and listeners expected
opinions from other mediums but not from movies. McFarland pressed Fidler
about the underperforming propaganda films and asked if anything needed
to be done since much of the public was not going to these films anyway. Low
box office numbers were not enough for Fidler. He wanted the government
to stamp propaganda films as such so audiences know which ones to avoid.
The recurring issue was that movie studios were publicly traded and working
with other people's money—studios had a responsibility to the public and the
shareholders. Part of Fidler's reasoning for this position was that he spoke as
a shareholder himself in Warner Bros. and Monogram Co.

Fidler missed the fact he was providing his own opinions in print and on
the air for publicly traded companies as well. Those shareholders could just as
easily complain about Fidler's commentary as he could about a film produced

JIMMIE FIDLER, left, and GEORGE FISHER, right, newspaper and radio "film gossips," who put on a show for the Senate subcommittee last week.

Fidler and Fisher

at Warner Bros., where he was a shareholder. McFarland let Fidler off the hook with a vivacious comment—"You are still fiddling, publishing your column, and are still on the air. And that is the American way, . . . and that is what we are proud of, because you, Jimmie Fidler, are still fiddling."

The journalist concluded with an open letter that was read over the airwaves the previous week. Fidler's letter reiterated his stance against all propaganda and reminded listeners that it was not just war films, but Depression films and gangster films that were detrimental to society. "I say let Hollywood make pictures that entertain," read Fidler, "pictures that are free of anti-this or anti-that, pictures that sell America." Hollywood moguls were used to hearing such arguments. Gangster films and other edgy pre-Code fare had their share of protestors. The revised Production Code that had been enforced since 1934 was meant to keep the screen clean, but there were always those who felt the Code did not do enough.

Fidler offered additional arguments in a September 21 column: "I don't believe our production heads fully realize their responsibility, even while boasting about the power of the medium they control. It's time now to wake up and to consider something besides profit in plotting a picture."[5] While the moguls often used profit logic as their only motivator, certain producers like Darryl F. Zanuck (who would soon be subpoenaed for this investigation) often sought stories for both profits and cultural resonance. In the coming days, Fidler found himself face to face with Errol Flynn, who reportedly took a swing at the gossip journalist.[6] William J. McNally of the *Minneapolis Tribune* was curious what expertise Fidler had to testify with in the first place. McNally saw Fidler as "a clown witness at a clown proceeding," which he predicted would become a "vast to-do about nothing."[7]

Testimony of George Fisher

The next testimony was from George Fisher, a writer and radio host who had been covering Hollywood gossip for about ten years. Fisher was previously a press agent for Warner Bros. and then began working for their radio station, KFWB. In addition, Fisher had sat in for widely influential columnist Walter Winchell. Fisher's program, titled "Hollywood Whispers," was carried on eighty stations around the country. Fisher had frequent access to film sets during production and was regularly invited to advance screenings of new features. Fisher did not have a prepared statement but explained that he did not experience any of the studio pushback that Fidler described. Senator Clark of Idaho asked for reactions to Fidler's previous comments, including a response to the list of films formerly discussed. Fisher agreed that most of the films noted were propaganda but was not sure about *Man Hunt*, as, "I personally enjoyed [the film] very much because it was so highly imaginative."

Attention was brought onto Fisher's broadcast from July 15, 1939, which discussed the rising criticism of propaganda films. Fisher had defended films against the mounting criticism from figures like Fidler, Winchell, and prominent Hollywood columnist Louella Parsons. Responding to the critical attacks on *Confessions of a Nazi Spy*, *Blockade*, and *Underground*, among others, Fisher fired back, "My colleagues themselves are guilty of falling for the sickening propaganda being put out by emissaries of foreign governments who are most anxious to prevent exposure of their own medieval methods of government." Fisher commended Warner Bros., "who have achieved great acclaim for their timely, topical, off the beaten boy-meets-girl path of moving pictures, have for a long time had the courage to picturize and dramatize newspaper headlines and life's dramas that have attracted the eyes of the world." Fisher noted several of the studio's impressive films such as the gangster films *Little Caesar* (1931) and *The Public Enemy* (1931), labor drama *Black Fury* (1935), the FBI showcase *G-Men* (1935), and antifascist yarns *Black Legion* (1937) and *The Life of Emile Zola* (1937). Enjoying the topical nature of such films, Fisher concluded, "Truth is on the march in the movies and nothing can stop it, despite the propaganda cries of squealing foreign propagandists."

Fisher maintained that films like *Escape* and *The Mortal Storm* were bet-
ter, perhaps in the sense that they were forgivable, examples of propaganda.
As a self-described fan of Chaplin, Fisher was also disappointed in *The Great
Dictator*. Senator McFarland pointed to the famous final speech and argued
Chaplin's film should be considered as a plea for peace and not intervention.
Fisher agreed, but before he could continue Senator McFarland took over with
his own brief statement.

McFarland showed irritation because no concrete evidence about motion
picture propaganda had yet been presented. It was essential to McFarland that
the films in question be viewed; otherwise the discussions would continue to
move off topic. The dancing around censorship from the previous testimonies
also irked the senator. "We had better be careful and not have the burning of the
books which Germany had in 1933," added McFarland, "for that is a beginning
of dictatorship when we burn that which we do not like."[8] The comparison drew
applause from the crowd, reminding the isolationists that their case had not
yet received strong traction in the room of journalists and curious onlookers.

Before the session broke for the evening, Senator Worth Clark brought up
his issue with the recent press coverage. Feeling that the press was ganging up
on the committee, he argued that 75 percent of the press had been critical of
propaganda films. Worth Clark was especially concerned with Drew Pearson's
syndicated column at the *Hollywood Reporter* because the senator felt it had
become libelous. Worth Clark assured his colleagues that W. R. Wilkerson,
publisher of the *Hollywood Reporter*, had been subpoenaed and would testify
before the committee. The investigation broke until the following Monday,
which would allow ample time for the press to weigh in.

Shortly after the day's proceedings, the *Washington Post* carried an editorial titled "Movies Biased? Editor Asks If Inquiry Is" by editor Herbert Agar of
the *Louisville Courier-Journal*. "Do they want the motion picture industry to
pretend that the Nazis are not cruelly assaulting our civilization," asked Agar,
"[and] are not relentlessly destroying freedom and kindliness wherever their
bloody rule extends?"[9] Agar echoed the views of many Hollywood defenders
in his local newspaper: "It is not war-mongering to tell the truth . . . it is not our
fault that the truth is cruel. But it will certainly be our fault if we are too dull
or too cowardly to face the cruel facts."[10] These words were carried across the
country through the Associate Press. Agar knew what the isolationist senators
continued to avoid, that it was impossible to sidestep the evils being perpetuated
by the Nazis. As more of the Nazi atrocities made headlines, anyone pushing
against films attacking fascism could easily be seen as a fascist sympathizer.

As expected, the Hollywood press continued to batter the investigation. *Variety* reported that the committee used "sketchy information on warmongering"

Book burning scene from *The Mortal Storm*

to provide a "wailing wall for Jimmie Fidler."[11] Although Fisher was "touted as a bombshell" witness, he was written off as a "dud" because his testimony was far from damning.[12] *Variety* also noticed Willkie's absence on Monday. Referring to Fidler, Willkie said, "I haven't any time to waste listening to one who makes his living purveying gossip."[13] Willkie did not appreciate the committee taking time to listen to someone "who [made] his living by unsupported and unproven statements about other people" and attacked film and radio for

ZANUCK ATTACKS CENSOR ATTEMPT

Propaganda Given Zanuck Definition

Washington, Sept. 28.—At the Senate committee hearing on Friday Chairman Clark asked Darryl Zanuck for his definition of propaganda, as he has done with every other witness.

"I usually find that when someone produces something you do not like, you call it propaganda," Zanuck replied.

"I think that is probably a pretty fair statement of the situation," Clark admitted.

British Studios Are Humming, Increase Expected: Jackson

All British studios are working at top speed, without exception, and hope to turn out better than last year's 50 per cent of the 1938, or pre-war, number of productions, Louis Jackson, head of Anglo-American Films Corp.

Tells Subcommittee Films Condemned Are Based On Published Stories

WASHINGTON, Sept. 28.—Two 20th Century-Fox films, "Man Hunt" and "The Man I Married," which have been cited as "propaganda films" at the Senate subcommittee hearings, were widely circulated in book form and in popular magazines throughout the country.

Darryl F. Zanuck

Darryl F. Zanuck, vice-president in charge of production for 20th Century - Fox, informed the subcommittee on Friday.

A third picture, "The Great Commandment," which the company was charged by committee (Continued on page 5)

Zanuck goes after senators

attempting to control his "golden voice."[14] Much of *Variety*'s coverage echoed the statements from McFarland, including comparisons to book burning.

Los Angeles district attorney Jay Moidel spoke at the Lawyer's Club Bill of Rights event on the night of September 15: "The current Senate sub-committee investigation of alleged war propaganda in motion pictures is helping to bring about one of Hitler's objectives—a house divided against itself in the United States."[15] Another district attorney, John F. Dockweiler, had more to say and raised questions about the investigation's legality. "Does the sub-committee want the movie industry to be fifty percent pro-Nazi and fifty percent pro-American?" asked Dockweiler. The district attorney continued cynically, "Maybe the sub-committee wants to convert the movie industry into a Nazi-American bund, to the extent of only fifty percent, of course, to keep it fair."[16] Continuing to get heated, Dockweiler wondered if the anti-Hollywood senators truly understood the United States' enemies:

Was it the Warner Brothers or the Luftwaffe that bombed Rotterdam and murdered thousands of peace-loving and defenseless Dutch people? Was it the Metro-
Goldwyn-Mayer Co. or the Nazis who invaded and crushed innocent Belgium?
Was it Darryl Zanuck and the Schenck brothers who attacked and enslaved the
brave Polish people, or was it Hitler and Goering? Was it Jesse Lasky who shot
down the gallant Norwegians fighting for their native land, or was it Hitler?[17]

Dockweiler's words have a similar tone and message to that of Senator McFarland over the previous days of testimony. Like McFarland, Dockweiler was
looking forward to hearing the film industry representatives' defense against
the long list of accusations that had been put on the table in the first sessions
of this subcommittee.

Darryl Zanuck responded while attending the American Legion convention in Milwaukee, proudly pleading guilty to producing anti-Nazi and pro-
defense films. "The motion picture is produced to entertain and to inform,"
argued Zanuck, "but the picture offers more than entertainment—the picture
is a true reflection of the American way of life."[18] Zanuck's characterization
of the industry dates back to his days producing socially conscious and edgy
films for Warner Bros. in the late 1920s and early 1930s. The producer also
brought attention to the fact that studios were working with the government
to make recruitment and defense films at cost. "Can you name me even one
other industry working for our Government without profit?" Zanuck asked.
"We consider it a patriotic duty."[19]

The *Hollywood Reporter* focused on the day's discussion of bribery accusations, which was assumed to be a reference to Russell Birdwell and Harry
Brand. Both men issued statements in their own defense. Birdwell called Fidler
"Hollywood's number one liar" and denied offering him any money, stating,
"Fidler's opinions are not worth 25 cents, much less $2,500."[20] Brand, who was
in Milwaukee with Zanuck, agreed that Twentieth Century Fox paid Fidler to
"make an advertising trailer . . . but his interpretation that the payment was an
attempt to 'buy his soul' is a deliberate attempt to distort facts as he so repeat-
edly does in reporting the Hollywood scene."[21] Brand explained that Fidler
was known around Los Angeles as a kind of snake oil salesmen, who tried to
get people to invest in his interests ranging from a dress shop to screenplays.

Herb Stein of the *Hollywood Reporter* chimed in by calling Fidler "Hollywood's Lord-Haw! Haw!"[22] The nickname, Lord Haw-Haw, was originally given
to William Joyce, a known Nazi radio propagandist, who regularly featured in
the program *Germany Calling* that ran until 1945 when Joyce was captured by
the British. Joyce was the first of many broadcasters to gain the nickname of
Lord Haw-Haw, often cited for their "aw shucks" manner of speaking. Stein took

aim at Fidler for attacking the town that had provided him a good living. "It's a good old town, Jimmie," Stein wrote, "chuck full of good old people, most of whom you've slapped around."[23] Stein researched Fidler's claims, finding that Fidler gave "five bells" to film productions that he accused of bribery without evidence. Stein also mentioned that Fidler was offered $40,000 from Warner Bros. to appear in a film. "Your slapping days are about over," promised Stein, who concluded with "love and kisses from Herb."[24]

Writing in the *Los Angeles Times*, Westbrook Pegler provided a useful overview of the investigation up to this point as well as some historical context. Pegler called the investigation a "dishonest procedure" and attacked the "so-called isolationists who may now be pro-Hitler."[25] One of the reasons Pegler used as part of a growing distrust of Hollywood was the coverage of industry scandals in the 1920s. Pegler argued that "shabby sycophants" wrote about Hollywood's scandals that "broke over the country in a slimy wave after the Fatty Arbuckle, William Desmond Taylor, and Wallie Reid incidents."[26] Arbuckle, a world-famous screen comedian, was accused of rape, avoided conviction, but was found guilty in the court of public opinion. Taylor was murdered and his death remains unsolved. Reid became a notorious drug addict and died in 1923. Pegler is correct in noting that each of these incidents were key moments when the media cashed in to create the image of a Hollywood Babylon. "The real news of the moving pictured trade has been smothered in cheap publicity," argued Pegler, and "served in the guise of gossip."[27]

A strong letter to the editor by Pulitzer Prize-winning author Louis Bromfield was published in the September 16 edition of the *Washington Post*. Bromfield was an immigrant who fled oppression in Europe and found many parallels between what he saw in the old country and what was occurring in the Senate subcommittee. "Both Nazis and Fascists set up committees at a wholesale rate to do away with elements, individuals, and philosophies which stood in their way," Bromfield remembered.[28] Not allowing Willkie to testify was evidence for Bromfield of such an approach. "During these early Nazi trials there was always a 'stooge' placed on the committee to give the illusion of impartiality," the author recalled; "however, it appears that Senator McFarland is unwilling to remain in the role of stooge and has turned into a viper."[29] Bromfield also saw the investigation's rhetoric as "vague Jew-baiting" coming "right out of Dr. Goebbels' handbook."[30] For immigrants like Bromfield, the parallel was all too easy to draw between the investigation and the ideological pressures forced on adversaries in Germany.

Coming off of vacation and into the madness of the Senate investigation, the *Los Angeles Times'* Edwin Schallert carefully weighed in on September 17. Schallert mused that the press coverage could equally hurt or help the film business. Offering historical context, Schallert reminded readers of World War I films that "were born out of the heat and fervor of preparedness and patriotism, which influenced all forms of expression—prose, song, poetry—prevailing arts of the day, along with the cinema."[31] Those films produced between 1916 and 1919 did not, however, according to Schallert, draw nearly as much negative attention. Perhaps these films did not seem subversive because they were based on popular and "already successful printed page stories."[32] One could make the same argument about the films listed in the 1941 investigation.

As expected, the Hearst Press and other critical publications told a very different story. Citing only the isolationists, the *Los Angeles Examiner* and the *Hollywood Citizen-News* both quoted Fidler at great length and built up the claim that propaganda films were inbound from Russia. Attention was specifically given to the list of films Fidler supplied as examples of propaganda and the letters read by Worth Clark before Fidler's statement. Knowing they were in the clear, the *Los Angeles Examiner* also noted Clark's complaint of conspiracy amongst the Hollywood press.[33] *Hollywood Citizen-News* printed Fidler's telegram to Worth Clark. When the senator found out Willkie would not be in attendance, he wrote, "I would like to see what his face looks like without egg on it."[34] Ray Tucker, in an additional column for *Hollywood Citizen-News*, painted the Hollywood moguls as shifty and untrustworthy [an age-old Jewish stereotype] with an overstated claim that there were "many producers under income tax investigation or indictment" and concluded by describing Willkie as a condescending politician.[35]

First Recess, Media Frenzy

On September 17, California Governor Culbert L. Olson mailed a letter of protest to the US Senate subcommittee on motion-picture propaganda. Addressing the letter to senator and subcommittee chairman D. Worth Clark, Olson wrote on behalf of the home state of Hollywood that California "looks with disfavor upon the implications of your committee's investigation, not because this important industry of our state has anything to fear from such investigation, but because the investigation itself is considered an unjustifiable attack upon it."[1] For Olson, Hollywood's anti-Nazi films were a response "to the spirit of American unity in our 'all out' effort to stop the beastly aggressions of the Axis powers."[2] In closing, Olson argued that "the moving picture industry should be praised, not condemned."[3]

Undeterred, Senator Nye spent time working to widen the investigation, "I have submitted and am preparing to submit angles calling for testimony of certain witnesses, some from within the film industry. I am getting many tips from Hollywood."[4] Like Nye's claims of familiarity with Hollywood films, his connection to any actual industry insider was also flimsy at best. Perhaps, for Nye, anyone who had actually viewed the films in question could be considered an insider compared to the isolationist senator.

The *Hollywood Reporter*'s Jack Moffitt attended a White House press conference while in town. Visualizing President Roosevelt based on the satiric cartoons frequently running in the newspapers, Moffitt was pleasantly surprised by what he saw when given an opportunity to see the Commander in Chief. Everything about the president "indicated that he was worn—but not exhausted—by a terrific exertion."[5] Moffitt continued, "I had the feeling that a man—a tired man—was fighting for my children. I thanked God for the stubbornness I saw in that straight chiseled nose and that high intellectual forehead."[6] Moffitt's pleasant experience would continue as the discussion turned briefly to the Senate probe.

"The President laughed at the movie witch hunt," Moffitt reported.[7] Roosevelt had not been following the investigation closely, though he was a subscriber to the *Hollywood Reporter* with its daily coverage of the investigation.[8] Keeping Hollywood commentary to a minimum, the president held up a newspaper showing a drawing of Charlie Chaplin dressed as his tramp holding a subpoena to appear before the subcommittee. A blurb from Chaplin read, "What could I possibly tell those past-masters about comedy?" Moffitt summarized the implications of the exchange: "If the country laughs, as its Chief Executive laughed, the straw man built by this Congressional minority will vanish in a hurricane of laugher back to the Senatorial wizards."[9] Roosevelt's brief response to the Hollywood debacle was certainly a sign of things to come. Brushing off the president's dismissal, Senator D. Worth Clark assumed that because most of the films in question were relatively new, a busy president likely did not yet have time to view them.[10]

Additional coverage in the *Hollywood Reporter* noted that members of the American Federation of Labor Unions (AFL) took a stand against the Senate investigation in protest of this "attempt to spread racial discord as a forerunner to national disunity, and curtailment of freedom of expression."[11] The criticism of the investigation by unions around the country would continue to ramp up. Eventually the subcommittee would end up receiving a formal letter of protest from hundreds of different trade unions across the nation.

Drew Pearson, also in the *Hollywood Reporter*, printed his open letter to Senator D. Worth Clark. Pearson wrote of a phone conversation he had with Worth Clark in which the senator told Pearson he would not be subpoenaed because of his Washington connections. Perhaps Worth Clark feared these connections, whatever they were. Conversely, Worth Clark told Pearson that he would like to subpoena William Wilkerson to make him "suffer the tortures of a senate inquisition."[12] What Worth Clark may not have known, was that Wilkerson was no ally of the studio moguls. In fact, while the *Hollywood Reporter* had writers defending the industry, Wilkerson himself was known to detest the Jewish moguls who he blamed for quashing his own dreams of running a studio.[13] Wilkerson would not be subpoenaed to Washington, but one can imagine the fireworks if he had been provided a platform to unload on the studios.

Pearson argued that the looming threat of a formal Senate inquiry was made up of "tactics which, if they get started in this country, are going to chisel down the freedom of the press, the freedom of the church, and the freedom of the arts and all other freedoms."[14] Pearson reminded Worth Clark of his historical insignificance, noting that his committee was made up of "little pebbles. . . .

The stream flows long after you."[15] In conclusion, Pearson offered himself up to the committee at their convenience. The invitation would not be entertained.

Hollywood Citizen-News called attention to the fact that "the extremes to which Senators Nye and Clark have been forced in their efforts to help Hitler by smearing the motion picture industry were made apparent by their use of Jimmie Fidler."[16] Contrary to the stories Fidler told during his testimony, the editors of the *Hollywood Citizen-News* argued that a divide between studio executives and journalists did not exist. The newspaper encouraged the subcommittee to call a range of Hollywood journalists to Washington to get a more complete picture.

The *Los Angeles Daily News* certainly did not agree with the majority of the Hollywood press, referring to the film industry's war films as "box office poison."[17] Frederick Othman called out most anti-Nazi films as failures, asking, "What's the use of unreeling films in empty theaters?"[18] Othman agreed that Nazis make for good villains, but noted that *Pastor Hall, Confessions of a Nazi Spy, Four Sons*, and *The Mortal Storm* each underperformed. *Man Hunt* was Othman's exception, to which the journalist concluded, "The cash register seems to have made the decision. Propaganda is dull, but Nazis chasing beautiful blondes are exciting."[19]

The *Motion Picture Herald* took the long-form journalist approach with a piece titled "The Inquiry and the Answer." The September 20 article suggested that the real propaganda rests with the senators: "Interestingly, but hardly consistently, this charge of propaganda laid against the motion picture and its Hollywood is made by propagandists for propaganda."[20] Hollywood is always influenced by its surroundings, both socially and culturally, argued the *Motion Picture Herald*. Each season brings on another type of film, so it should be of no surprise that the rising concern about fascism in Europe would get attention in film just as it has in the press and in literature. "The motion picture is itself a great instrument of public relations," according to the *Motion Picture Herald*, "and it has in its service many experts in the art of communication, with demonstrations of performance in that field of public relations."[21]

Throughout the recess, the committee held strong on their claim of legality regarding the investigation. Senator Worth Clark told journalists, "This procedure [of investigating to see if they should investigate] consistently has been followed in the Senate . . . before we can ask the Senate to authorize a formal investigation we have to have something to present."[22] Worth Clark mentioned that the goal was to see if the Senate should dig deeper into the film industry for purposes of stopping propaganda or breaking up a monopoly. If the subcommittee found that more work should be done, "Then we may go directly to the Senate and ask for a formal investigation."[23]

One publication unsurprisingly confident in the Senate investigation was the *Free American*, the newspaper for the pro-Nazi German-American Bund. The *Free American* referred to the anti-Nazi movies as "atrocity films," defined Hollywood as a "pictorial dope industry," and compared Willkie to Judas.[24] Another editorial in the Bund's newspaper, "The Enemies of the State," called attention to the "racially alien" studio moguls who were "using freedom of thought for cover" and had "conducted the lowest hate-mongering propaganda."[25] In addition, the essay stated, "The calamity which has befallen the Jews is just a punishment by God," and goes on to blame the Jews for their own problems.[26]

Interestingly, the essay refers to Hollywood as a place of "mass stupidity," which is exactly how Warner Bros.' *Confessions of a Nazi Spy* described the Nazi mentality in 1939. Towards the end of the article, predictably, the author calls out the Warner Bros.' film as "a hate-dripping, completely false presentation of Germandom."[27] During a speech at an Ohio Democratic rally, McFarland spoke of confronting John T. Flynn about the anti-Semitic alliance between the Bund and America First movements.[28] Flynn pushed back about the accusation of prejudice but did admit that the Bund was encouraging its members to join America First. Seeing the Bund becoming more mainstream, McFarland issued a warning to isolationists who "have become so desperate and intolerant that they would invoke race prejudice as a means of imposing their will on the American people."[29]

On September 20, 1941, *Film Bulletin: The Independent Exhibitors Trade Journal* ran a cover image that said, "The Hate-Mongering Movie Inquisition Must Not Be Halted."[30] A blurb ran along the side that read, "The foul-smelling hole that Senator Gerald P. Nye has dug them into is getting unbearable and they would like to crawl out with some remnants of their self-respect and with a minimum of attention. We urge the leaders of the motion picture industry not to let them off so easily."[31] The next week would see the Hollywood moguls finally face-to-face with the critical senators.

During the recess Senator Nye pushed back against Willkie's comments regarding Lindbergh. Nye argued that the aviator spoke "without being anti-Semitic," and, "If I were one of them [Jews], I should feel as they do toward those who have persecuted my people."[32] Still not understanding that the Nazis threatened the entire free world, Nye's next comment contradicted his attempt at Jewish sympathy: "But I should not try to let my natural hatred blind me to the first and best interest of my own country."[33] It was this type of reasoning that resulted in headlines such as this, from the *Washington Post*: "Fact, If in Film Form, Annoys That Committee."[34]

Influential gossip journalist Walter Winchell weighed in with his discussion with Irving Hoffman of the *Hollywood Reporter*. When asked if he would return to the hearings after the recess, Hoffman declined. "I'm fed up with the dirty work and low punching," Hoffman said. "Too much like Hollywood?" he was asked. "No," Hoffman replied, "too much like Germany."[35] Senator Nye was not doing much to combat such a comparison, as his September 21 talk at the Biltmore Hotel was picketed by hundreds after the senator aligned himself with Lindbergh's views about the Jews. Several signs read, "The Fuehrer thanks you for your many services."[36] Even some isolationists had to distance themselves from Nye's blatant prejudices, such as the Keep America Out of War Congress, who issued a statement rejecting the notion that "the American citizens of Jewish extraction or religion are a separate group, apart from the rest of the American people, or that they react as a separate group, or that they are unanimously for our entrance into the European war."[37]

With the constant accusations of racism associated with the Senate subcommittee, other journalists predicted the hearings were nearing an end. In the *Hollywood Reporter*, Pearson called attention to Senator Wheeler's leaving the courtroom early. Perhaps Wheeler's exit was an "indication that the Senate Inquisition has about run its course."[38] The *San Francisco Chronicle* sardonically mocked the subcommittee by asking that they also investigate the large amount of anti-Nazi literature. Works by William L. Shirer, Alice Duer Miller, Virginia Cowles, and Gottfried Leske were "being bought and read by the American people and are hot anti-Nazi and pro-British documents" that "must be hateful to Wheeler, Nye, the Clarks, Tobey, and Brooks."[39] In other words, it was clear that the subcommittee could divide filmgoers; could they do the same for book readers?

The recess offered time for other publications to catch up and weigh in on the investigation. *Newsweek* provided a straightforward overview of the previous day's proceedings.[40] The *New Republic* used its pages to argue the legality of the investigation and to point out that most of the senators were hand-picked to shift that balance towards the isolationists. Defending Hollywood's production trends, the *New Republic* wrote that "the purpose of the Wheeler attack is to frighten Hollywood into silence."[41] For the writers at the *New Republic*, it was clear that the senators were on the wrong side of history. The same attitude was seen in the *New York Journal-American*, which argued, "Senator Nye and his intellectual klunkers defined their terms before setting out on a lynching bee."[42]

Time magazine weighed in with an extensive overview of the days leading up to the recess. *Time* sided with Hollywood and cited industry reporter Jack Moffitt at length. The writers also gave credibility to Willkie's interjections, noting that he would grab the microphone to defend himself, then "growled and snorted the rest of the time with the agony of a man who has good answers he isn't allowed to make."[43] Making it clear that Willkie was denied a right to respond, the article also noted Nye's denial of anti-Semitism while making statements such as, "If anti-Semitism exists in America, the Jews have themselves to blame."[44] *Time* detailed the senator's arguments before describing many of the films in question. *Escape* was shown as reviewed in the *Saturday Evening Post*, with the novel cover by Ethel Vance and its Book of the Month Club advertisement. *Convoy, The Great Dictator, Manhunt, That Hamilton Woman, Sergeant York*, and *I Married a Nazi* were each featured via screenshot and given positive coverage. The final page of *Time*'s feature showed the courtroom during session and noted the crowd's "boos, titters, laughter, and applause," which "turned the proceedings into Washington's funniest political circus of the year."[45] In conclusion, the caption reminded readers once again that Willkie "was denied the right to cross-examination."[46]

Not all coverage was critical of the senators, however. *Social Justice*, a national weekly publication founded by anti-Semitic radio priest Father Charles Coughlin, used several pages to smear Hollywood. For the writers at *Social Justice*, Hollywood must have bought and paid for all of the journalists defending them during these hearings. The publication had its own Hollywood source, Bill Wells, who claimed the industry was "crawling with communists and fellow travelers" who had blacklisted their enemies.[47] Wells also argued that the Jewish organization B'nai B'rith and the Anti-Defamation League had many representatives infiltrating the ranks of Hollywood. These organizations, in addition to the Anti-Nazi league, should be investigated, according to Wells. Siding with the testimony of Jimmie Fidler, which *Social Justice* quoted at length, the publication closed by arguing that it was the same group of filmmakers and radio personalities pushing war propaganda that were able to get Father Coughlin kicked off of the air.

On September 22, the Screen Actors Guild passed a resolution opposing the Senate investigation. The resolution was sent to Wheeler and Nye, and declared, "Be it resolved, that the Screen Actors Guild does herby condemn the actions of the subcommittee as an immediate threat to free thought, free speech, and to the very fundamentals of liberty upon which our great nation was founded, and demand that this inquiry be stopped."[48]

After the recess was over, the following days would finally see the Hollywood giants granted an opportunity to defend their industry. Nicholas Schenck, Harry Warner, and Darryl Zanuck all took turns defending Hollywood. The fireworks would begin again on Tuesday, September 23, 1941. After a week of jousting in the press, the subcommittee was ready to get back to work.

PART FOUR

HOLLYWOOD'S

DEFENSE

Schenck testifying against Senate Resolution 152

CHAPTER EIGHT

Schenck Stands Strong

Day Five: Tuesday September 23

Before the scheduled testimony of the day, Chairman Clark of Idaho permitted Senator Sheridan Downey of California to say a few words. Downey's appearance was unsurprising after seeing the recent letter of protest from the California governor. Downey spoke his concerns over the "ill-defined term of propaganda as an excuse for censorship or harassing investigation." Certainly, the subcommittee could have based their definition of propaganda on the work of Edward Bernays. In fact, Bernays would have been a perfect expert to engage during a national discussion on propaganda. Instead, rumor had it that the isolationist senators had Flynn working with a team in New York studying the Hollywood films Nye and Clark should have watched themselves.[1] Nothing would come of Flynn's extra research, because Hollywood would valiantly defend itself and embarrass the isolationist senators in the process.

Downey spoke to the subcommittee having watched all of the movies in question. If films such as *Man Hunt, Land of Liberty, I Married a Nazi, Sergeant York, Dive Bomber, Escape,* and *The Mortal Storm* "incited in the spectators any discernible fervor for intervention which they had not brought with them," Downey mused, "then I must be both blind and deaf." Downey's point was that the anti-Nazi sentiment had often been in the audience long before viewing any of the films. Citing a Gallup poll from a few years prior, Downey argued that "the movies reacted to their public, not the public to its movies." The evidence of this claim can be seen in the large number of headline-driven films made each year. The anti-Nazi productions were just another version of ripping from the newspapers, just like Warner Bros. did with gangster films for years.

Interestingly, Downey's defense of Hollywood may lead one to believe he was an interventionist. He was not, though he voted for the Lend-Lease bill and supported any aid to Great Britain "short of war." Downey stood in defense of Hollywood simply on the industry's right to create and distribute any content it desired. In addition, Downey reminded the senators that Hitler created the greatest anti-Nazi propaganda himself, both in his own actions and writing *Mein Kampf.* "I am happy to let our people [Americans] sift the false from true," Downey declared, as a rare isolationist not bothered by Hollywood's anti-Nazi films. Beyond the question of intervention, it is also understandable that a senator from California would want to defend the state's most visible industry.

Senator Worth Clark responded to Downey's statement by arguing that the subcommittee did not want censorship and, in fact, believed that because Hollywood was controlled by a select few people, the screen was in need of liberation. Because the subcommittee did not believe the screen was free, Worth Clark felt that Downey "built up a man of straw and then proceeded to demolish him." Senator McFarland chimed in, "I might say that this general investigation is a straw investigation," drawing laughter. "It may be straw in the wind," Worth Clark fired back followed by a round of applause.

The next witness marked the much-anticipated appearance of the first studio mogul, Nicholas Schenck, president of Loew's, Inc. Schenck was one of the first founders of what became known as the Hollywood studio system, helping put MGM and Loew's, Inc. on the map. Loew's was the second studio listed on the New York Stock Exchange, second only behind Adolph Zukor's Paramount.[2] Schenck was a mogul who navigated the Great Depression with brilliance by cutting salaries, minimizing output, and grooming some of MGM's top celebrities.[3] Scheck also weathered another storm when his studio lost Hollywood's top producer, Irving Thalberg, who died of a heart condition at age thirty-seven. The studio increased its B-picture output and invested in double features, which gave MGM alone the profits of all other studios combined.[4]

After Schenck was sworn in, Senator McFarland read two telegrams to the subcommittee. The first was from Russell Birdwell denying Fidler's claim that Birdwell offered him money for a positive review of a film. Birdwell referred to Fidler as "Hollywood's number one liar." The second telegram, from Harry Brand, also denied Fidler's similar words regarding a bribe. Brand noted that Fidler was paid to appear in a film trailer but was in no way paid for a puff piece. Brand also mentioned a gown scandal in which Fidler had caused actress Alice Faye some embarrassment. McFarland wanted to read these telegrams "to show how far afield we can get in this kind of hearing." Frustrated with the conversation continually moving beyond the films in question, McFarland felt that the subcommittee "should be viewing pictures, if we do anything at all." Senator Worth Clark assured McFarland that the films would be screened.

Testimony of Nicholas Schenck

As Schenck's testimony was about to begin, McFarland told the mogul he could have his counsel beside him as he spoke. "We are perfectly confident that Mr. Schenck can take care of himself," Willkie responded as he waived the right. "Despite the newspaper comments," noted Senator Worth Clark, "you have nothing to fear in the way of unfairness from this committee." Worth Clark continued to assure Scheck that he would get a fair shake and that politicians around town had nothing but praise for the studio mogul.

The opening questions focused on the stock distribution and holdings of Loew's, Inc. Senator Clark of Idaho appeared confused when Schenck did not know the answers to his economic questions. Scheck was not denying knowledge but simply stated that these situations were the focus of their controller and "meant nothing to me, it was purely mechanics." Schenck was not dodging questions here, but he did not make it immediately clear for the subcommittee what his role was at the studio. Worth Clark moved on to get an idea of what Loew's theater chains looked like, which were mostly first-class and first-run outfits. That discussion was halted when Senator Tobey intervened.

Tobey, echoing Worth Clark's concerns, was "troubled" by Schenck's "lack of familiarity with the companies you are a director of." Tobey argued that the "title of director or trustee connotes something of a sort of fiduciary capacity to me, where such officer is representing people who have an interest in the companies." Tobey was confused about why Scheck's memory appeared to be lucid on "matters of far less importance" such as theater owners but could not remember details about stockholders' interests. "I pause in a sense of wonderment at that," said Tobey.

Schenck defended against the senator's concerns. "Until 1927 I was the so-called second in command, but I did all the work," he recalled, as his words drew laughter and applause. Marcus Loew was the founder of Loew's, Inc. and died in 1927. Schenck told the subcommittee that he personally supervised every theater mentioned by spending several months at each of them "that remains with you." Tobey asked if Scheck attended meetings at the companies where he was affiliated, which was answered affirmatively. When Tobey described Schenck as a director of several boards, the mogul added, "And I am a good one, I think," to another round of laughter and applause.

"If you do not know the name of the company and the parties you are act-
ing for, how can you act for them," asked Tobey. "Well, it is not the point for
me to remember," responded Schenck. "In view of your testimony so far let
me just say this to you," said Tobey, "if you are exhibit A in the matter of the
average corporate director in this country, then God save the stockholders."
Tobey's quip initiated yet another stint of laughter and applause from a crowd
increasingly anxious for more verbal sparring.

Schenck was getting aggravated and told the courtroom he had not taken a
vacation day in years. Tobey argued that this testimony must be a vacation for
Schenck, to which he fired back, "I do not think you should put me through this
kind of a work-out when I honestly tell you that I know a lot about these things,
. . . and I do not consider it any lack of responsibility in my siting here and not
being able to remember some corporate names." The applause resumed once
again and continued for some time as Tobey began to respond. Unimpressed
with the audience, as they showed allegiance for Hollywood, Tobey called them
out as "professional claqueurs" before giving up entirely.

McFarland stepped in to clarify that Schenck may not know individual
corporation names because they were only known to the controllers of Loew's
and the employees engaged in the day-to-day operations of the corporations.
Schenck's business was usually regarding the overarching policies of the parent
corporation, Loew's, Inc. "That is correct, and exactly how it operates," confirmed Schenck. "I thank you sir. I think you have brought it out beautifully."
Schenck's gratitude initiated more laughter and applause and made for a clean
break for lunch at 11:55 a.m.

The proceedings resumed at 2:00 p.m., when Schenck had a few more
answers for the subcommittee. Schenck noted that Loew's, Inc. held ninety-
four corporations in the United States and fifty-six across the rest of the world.
Moving on to the production side of the discussion, it was pointed out that
Loew's had produced on average fifty feature films a year in recent years—a
number similar to Paramount, Twentieth Century Fox, and Warner Bros. The
subcommittee noted that RKO and Universal produced a slightly smaller number
of films each year, with United Artists, Republic, and Monogram being closer
to twenty films per year. Senator Clark observed that with these numbers, 70
percent of all feature films were made by eight film companies (not including
Monogram). Of course, Clark set this up to showcase a problem, but Schenck
was unintimidated and noted that those eight companies were investing the
most money, so naturally they were producing the majority of films.

Explaining how each individual film company had varying control over the
films exhibited around the country, Schenck defended their business practice
by showing that while each company had a substantial part of the market,

Man Hunt advertisement, June 7, 1941

they continued to compete with each other. Every studio produced films and exhibited them in their own theaters, but they also sold their films to competitor's theaters and bought from competitors for their own theaters. For example, Schenck explained, "We have 129 theaters. That does not mean anything. We play in between eleven and twelve thousand theaters." The 129 number, being a small percentage of the total in the country, was nothing more than a "show window" for advertising "as we think it should be done."

Worth Clark's concern was that the film industry was simply appearing as a competitive market when the studio bosses could conspire to ensure their success. Schenck assured the subcommittee nothing of the sort occured and pointed to the 1940 consent decree that limited block booking to five films. It was previously common practice to make theater bid blindly for larger packages of films. The 1940 consent decree rid the industry of blind bidding for a much more balanced trade-show approach, where exhibitors could see films before ordering them. Still pushing, Worth Clark asked, "If you did get together [Loew's, Paramount, Warner Bros.], could a picture produced by any one of these three outside corporations [Columbia, Universal, Twentieth Century Fox] succeed without being played in your outlets?" Schenck alleged everyone was aware of the laws against such a practice and went as far to say that nothing of the sort even happened in the early days, before the newly formed companies knew of such laws. In addition, Schenck told a story about how one company refusing films from a competitor did not help sales. A few years prior, Harry Warner had an argument with Schenck where the two could not compromise on an exhibition deal. Schenck walked, sold his films elsewhere, and continued to serve those customers (theaters). Warner was in the room for Schenck's story and added no objection.

Another popular line of attack for the isolationist senators was the charge of nepotism, because of the family hiring in Hollywood that extended as far as the Roosevelts once FDR came to power.[5] While Worth Clark spoke of nepotism, he danced around using the word. Arthur Loew was vice president of Loew's, Inc, and his father-in-law, Adolph Zukor, was the founder of Paramount. Schenck assured Worth Clark that he had been a strong competitor of Arthur Loew for many years, and his marriage to Zukor's daughter, Mildred, had not affected business. In addition, Schenck pointed out that Arthur's focus as vice president was on foreign exhibition and had nothing to do with production. Schenck prevailed through the barrage of questioning, all while smiling through a lit cigarette.[6]

Loew's had first purchased Metro, then Goldwyn, followed by Louis B. Mayer Pictures to create MGM as it was then known. Schenck helped advise each purchase and its merger into the Loew's company by letting go of several studio bosses and keeping the likes of Louis B. Mayer and Irving Thalberg. As part of the industry shake up, David O. Selznick worked as a producer at MGM for a time. Adding to the family industry argument, it was pointed out that Selznick married Louis B. Mayer's daughter but eventually moved to other companies (including his own, Selznick International Pictures). Countering the implication that such a move would hamper business, Schenck hired director Mervyn LeRoy, a contract director at Warner Bros., and married Harry Warner's daughter. LeRoy was now working for MGM, to Schenck's delight, "And we were fortunate enough to take him away from Warner, just as we always try to do with one another when we have the opportunity." Inciting laughter back into the room, Schenck concluded, "He does splendid work. He, by the way, directed *Escape*."

Echoing many of the arguments found in Phelps's *An American's History of Hollywood: The Tower of Babel*, Worth Clark continued to hammer his point that Hollywood could possibly collude "when they get together." "We are never together," Schenck said. "You might be," Clark responded. "You cannot take the thing 'we might be,'" the mogul fired back.

Lobbing out another hypothetical, Worth Clark asked, "Let us suppose that I am an independent producer and I have a million dollars and suppose I have the brains and imagination and creative ability, where would I get any moving picture stars?" "I will tell you where you would likely wind up," said Schenck, "you would wind up with MGM," prompting more laughter and applause. However, Clark asked if he wanted to produce a film independently, could he still get MGM stars? Of course, the answer here is no because the major studio's stars were all under contract. There were free-lance stars, as Schenck made clear, but also admitted that the major studios have the majority of film stars under contract "because that is what we are in business for." Schenck explained further,

We are building new ones [stars] all the time. I can call out numerous people on our lot every day that are coming along. That is our business. After all, Bill Powell cannot live forever. He is tremendous today. And so it is with Gary Cooper, and Clark Gable. They cannot live forever. We must build new people, and we spend an awful lot of money to do it. I have a stock company of 150 people. We do not use them. We train them. We will do everything we can to get benefits out of them some day. That is an investment. How could an outsider come in and say: "I want this one or that one." That would not be fair.

Schenck also explained the process of loaning out stars, which did happen between the studios, especially if the project would help the star's image. MGM did this with Clark Cable by loaning him to Columbia for *It Happened One*

Night (1934), a film Schenck thinks was one of the best of that year and boosted the careers of both Cable and his costar Claudette Colbert. It may be easier, however, for a studio to pick off a director. Schenck told the room that Warner Bros. was able to land Frank Capra because Capra was given use of Warner's contract stars and the studio offered to distribute the film as added incentive. Such insider stories proved that the studios, while competitive, would also make moves that helped the entire industry when necessary.

As Schenck explained the process of grooming stars and finding directorial talent, Senator Tobey chimed in with a counternarrative where an outsider, James Roosevelt, became involved with a major studio. Tobey's story of this "rank outsider" who "became a great moving-picture producer," drew a great amount of laughter from the audience. The reaction was two-fold. First, Roosevelt is the eldest son of President Roosevelt, who was widely supported in Hollywood, so calling him an outsider was a gross underestimation of his status. Second, Roosevelt had been working with Schenck in 1940 when he was convicted of tax evasion.[7] The crowd laughed as the unflattering statement was spoken into the record. Scheck's only response was a simple, "Oh well."

The subcommittee continued to seek clarification on how studios acquired film rights, the contents of their studio libraries, to which Scheck noted that the studio production heads could better answer regarding these details. Schenck suggested talking with someone like Louis B. Mayer or Darryl Zanuck, who was subpoenaed to testify in the coming days. Other questions came up about Will Hays, head of the MPPDA, and Schenck explained Hays's role as a censor whose only job was to help decide what should and should not be seen on film by the public.

Senator Worth Clark continued to search for ways to get Scheck to slip up and admit that the major studios kept outsiders out of competition. Scheck argued that it was not the studios that held up independent film investments, it was the banks who were wary or funding motion-pictures, which is why studios tried to invest their profits into new films (instead of taking out risky loans). Never playing into Worth Clark's traps, Schenck noted that while the film business had been profitable, it was also risky, which was the reason most films were made by the established studios. In fact, Schenck felt the film market was at capacity and that many theaters could get by without double-bills.

After more pushback from Worth Clark, Schenck explained that all studios buy from one another. "We buy the best we can," Schenck rationalized. Worth Clark, still skeptical, assumed that the smaller studio's films were purchased for less money to keep them small. Scheck pointed out that prices all come from supply and demand and that each new film purchase was a new discussion. Keeping the details vague, both out of fidelity to the industry as well as ignorance of specific details he could not ascertain, Schenck survived the day. The hearings broke for the evening at 4:10 p.m. and would reconvene to finish Schenck's testimony the following morning.

Press Coverage of Day Five

The *Film Daily's* Oscar Hume wrote positively of Governor Downey's words. Hume observed that Downey "took up the cudgel for the industry and ripped apart, one by one, the straw men which the isolationist witnesses have built up against the nation's movie-makers."[8] The coverage provided a lengthy overview of Downey's words, as well as a rumor from the previous evening's rehearsal for Eddie Cantor's "It's Time to Smile" radio show. In preparation for the September 24 show, Joe DiMaggio was noted as being "ignorant about motion pictures," to which Carole Landis quipped, "Then what is he doing with the New York Yankees? He ought to be with the Washington Senators."[9]

The *Film Daily* found another ripple effect from the hearings regarding Warner Bros.' *Underground*. Since the picture was noted a few times during the investigation, public interest increased significantly. The studio saw *Underground's* profits increase from 132 percent before the investigation to 162 percent after the investigation began.[10] While some of the war films were reportedly underperforming at the box office, such an increase in the popularity of anti-Nazi films seen by *Underground* would undoubtedly make most isolationists' blood boil.

In addition, the *Film Daily* reported the results of a large poll that asked the nation's film critics about the war propaganda investigation. The poll went out to 210 critics and received 113 respondents, mostly voting in defense of the film industry. The questions were preceded by a telegram that read:

> *The Film Daily* invites you as an outstanding American film critic to express your opinion on issues involved in the following:
>
> Senator Gerald Nye has charged that motion pictures are designed to create a war hysteria in this country and that the movies have ceased to be instruments of entertainment and have become the most gigantic engines of propaganda in existence to rouse a war fever in America and plunge this nation into destruction.
>
> In support of these charges the following pictures have been named by Senators Gerald Nye, Bennett Clark, and D. Worth Clark:

Mystery Sea Raider, Phantom Sea Raider, They Dare Not Love, Murder in the Air, The Man I Married, One Night in Lisbon, The Devil Commands, So Ends Our Night, Four Sons, Dispatch from Reuters, Sergeant York, Dive Bomber, Nurse Edith Cavell, Flight Command, International Squadron, Manhunt, Escape, Mortal Storm, Confessions of a Nazi Spy, Foreign Correspondent, Underground, The Great Dictator, War in the Desert.

Will you please wire immediately press rate collect, answering yes or no to the following questions in order given:[11]

The questions and answers were returned as follows:

1. In your opinion, are the listed pictures collectively designed to influence the public mind in the direction of participation in the European War? **Yes-7 No-103**

2. Do you believe pictures such as *Confessions of a Nazi Spy, Sergeant York, Escape, Underground, The Man I Married, Man Hunt,* and *The Great Dictator* have the effect of creating a greater appreciation of our Democracy and American Liberties? **Yes-103 No-9**

3. Do you believe it is improper for American-made motion pictures to portray conditions in Germany under the Nazi regime? **Yes-4 No-109**

4. Do you believe Congress should take any action which would make impossible the production of pictures such as those listed? **Yes-0 No-113**[12]

While all questions were largely answered in favor of the film industry, the only unanimous answer was that all critics who responded to the poll did not believe the US government should interfere with film productions. Several critics polled elaborated on their votes and were quoted in the *Film Daily* alongside the questions. Henry J. Murdock of the *Philadelphia Evening Public Ledger* saw the investigation as "foolish" and predicted a tax increase after the Senate wasted money on this subcommittee. Charles F. Mulcahy of the Youngstown, Ohio, *Vindicator* wrote, "Congress ought to keep hands off [the] movies unless it is ready to subsidize the industry." Thomas Ewing Dabney of the *New Orleans States* observed, "I have found no one who has been made jingoistic by these films." Boyd Martin of the *Louisville Courier-Journal* feared that the subcommittee investigation could result in increased internal film censorship.[13]

The industry coverage of Tuesday's hearing, as expected, was largely supportive of Schenck's testimony, even with the mogul's clear ignorance regarding the studio's day-to-day practices. Jack Moffitt wrote under a headline in the *Hollywood Reporter* that read Schenck "Teaches Inquisitors Some Common Facts About Pix; Wins Over His Audience." Moffitt saw that "chairman Clark tried to jockey him [Schenck] into some damaging admissions, but it was

4   MOTION PICTURE DAILY   Friday, September 26, 1941

Industry Leaders at Senate's Film Hearings

Photos copyright Harris & Ewing

Leading executives of the industry as they appeared this week at the hearings of the Senate subcommittee investigating the film industry in Washington. The picture at the left shows Nicholas M. Schenck, president of Loew's, Inc., conferring with Wendell Willkie, counsel for the industry in the investigation. In the photo at the right is seen Harry M. Warner, president of Warner Brothers, who testified yesterday. Seated directly behind Warner is Herbert Freston, of the Warner legal staff.

Nicholas Schenck and Harry Warner in Washington, DC

like trying to jockey Rex, King of the Wild Horses."[14] Schenck certainly had the upper hand by the day's end, which Moffitt also observed: "By afternoon, he [Schenck] actually was helping the boys with their questions."[15] Amused by the range of topics, Moffitt poked at the committee for spending large amounts of time discussing the marital relations of executives and how that might affect business. The conclusion was, of course, that it did not, and in some circumstances actually made competition stronger. For Moffitt, "Senator Clark looked like a boy who gets stuck at a birthday party while trying to pin the tail on the donkey."[16]

Moffitt also noted that Senator Tobey's son, Charles Jr., was regularly seen approaching his father with pieces of paper. Senator Tobey "was being coached by his little boy," who Moffitt described as "a beetle-face youth with a bookish aspect."[17] When Scheck showed brief weakness in not knowing the names of some of Loew's smaller companies, "Junior raced forward like Pluto bringing Donald Duck the Morning Gazette."[18]

Variety reported that watching the senators put Schenck under the hot light was "sort of a tooth-pulling process."[19] Amused with the humorous quips from Schenck, *Variety* listed several of their favorites, including, "If you are interested in contract terms make a deal with Warners. If you are interested in results, make a deal with me."[20] Admitting that the mogul was weak on some questions, *Variety* felt Schenck held strong during the most important discussions of the day, including his knowledge of how Loew's theater chain compared to others.

Additional coverage in the *Hollywood Reporter* shed light on the national labor unions that were increasingly speaking out on the investigation. Thomas J. Lyons, president of the New York State Federation of Labor, gave a statement to the Stop Film Censorship Committee and its approximately one thousand members working in Los Angeles. Lyons's statement confronted the "doubtful legitimacy" of the subcommittee and argued the senators had "given aid and comfort to anti-democratic elements by seeking to stir up religious and racial hatreds with the hope of confusing and dividing our people."[21]

The senators still had their supporters. Margaret Frakes wrote in the *Christian Century* that it was "difficult to enjoy a program in any motion picture theater these days" because most films are an "out-and-out glorification of the armed services" or "a bitterly anti-Nazi melodrama."[22] Clearly unimpressed with Hollywood's recent output, Frakes did not approve of the industry's coverage, with lines such as, "If *Variety* is to be believed."[23] Frakes also pointed to the immigrant status of many in Hollywood, whose background from currently war-torn countries made them an easy sell on armed conflict. Admitting that some of the anti-Nazi films were "rather honest and restrained at first," Frakes felt that they "have become more and more bitter in their denunciations, with the Nazis painted as such monsters they become almost caricatures."[24]

The following morning, Nicholas Schenck would resume his testimony. The subcommittee would also hear from Howard Dietz. On the night of September 23, a party was held at Drew Pearson's residence in Georgetown in support of Schenck's testimony.[25] The star-studded event included Greta Garbo, Spencer Tracy, Errol Flynn, Howard Dietz, Darryl Zanuck, Wendell Willkie, and Harry Warner, who dodged reporters all night. The *Hollywood Reporter* publisher William Wilkerson also made an appearance. It is possible Wilkerson was expecting to testify, but he would never be called. It was not a Hollywood-only event, as Senators Robert Reynolds and Ernest McFarland, as well as FBI director J. Edgar Hoover, were seen working the room. While the investigation was not yet over, there was undoubtedly cause for celebration as the isolationist senators continued to dig themselves into a deeper hole every day. Hollywood's anti-Nazi films would not be going anywhere.

CHAPTER NINE

Dietz Delivers

Day Six: Wednesday September 24

Senators Worth Clark, McFarland, Tobey, and Brooks resumed the hearings at 10:30 a.m. Once again, McFarland received an additional telegram that he read for the record. This one was from Jimmie Fidler, responding to the previous day's telegrams that took aim at Fidler's testimony. Fidler opened by arguing he "made no issue of the Alice Faye gown matter," as the audience laughed. Fidler hoped to set the record straight since the previous letter opened the issue. He denied the accusations by writing, "As for Brand's unfair charge that it [the dress] fell apart at the first wearing and caused Miss Faye humiliation, that is not true." The room broke into amused laughter once again, as the letter had further proven McFarland's previous points about the subcommittee getting distracted on irrelevant details. "I will say that I have gotten as deeply into this gown matter as I can," McFarland joked. Fidler was unhappy that Brand's letter made front-page news, and understandably hoped to cool the issue so it would not unnecessarily affect the dress shop. As McFarland finished the letter, the gallery was full of conversation, and Senator Worth Clark had to call the room to order. The point was made as the room fell into distracted discussion similar to how the investigation continued to veer in directions other than the focus of propaganda or monopoly. As the room gathered its composure, Nicholas Schenck continued his testimony.

Nicholas Schenck, Continued:

After seeking additional clarification on who owned the theaters and at what percent stake, Schenck simplified it by explaining that while studios had some stake in a certain number of theaters, each one had to be sold to separately. Just because a theater says "Paramount" did not automatically mean the studio had a golden ticket at that venue. Somewhat satisfied with the clarification, Worth Clark quickly moved the discussion towards the truly pressing matter, motion-picture propaganda. Schenck promptly established his stance: "In no way can I agree with you that the so-called pictures you refer to . . . for instance our three pictures, *The Mortal Storm, Escape*, and *Flight Command*, are any propaganda war pictures." Going further, and because Clark was still unclear about the relationship between studios and theater, Schenck explained that many theaters could preview films and cancel them early if necessary. Therefore, if a theater manager did not like (or approve of) a film, they could cancel it and order something else.

Schenck used an example of MGM's *Marie Antoinette* (1938), which had nearly nine hundred cancellations. "I suppose they did not think certain people would like it. It is purely a matter of judgement," Schenck explained. Clark assumed, however, that if it was a propaganda picture like *The Mortal Storm*, the theaters would have to play it. "Certainly not," Schenck declared. Tobey leaned into the microphone and asked, "Now when *Marie Antoinette* was made—I mean when the picture about her was made." The audience howled in laughter and Tobey, amused with his unintentional quip, said, "That's quite a bon mot, I commend it to Mr. Moffitt."[1] The pleasant laughter was a brief aberration, as the audience would spend the rest of the day hissing at Tobey's questions.[2]

Continuing his "rapid-fire questions," Worth Clark tried another angle, hoping to get Schenck to admit that *Land of Liberty*, which was funded from across the industry with all profits to charity, was a propaganda picture.[3] "It is a patriotic picture," responded Schenck. "I think every citizen and every child should see it." Clark questioned the charity angle, arguing that the money could go "for bundles to Great Britain." Schenck noted one occasion, after an entire city was bombed out, that they sent fifty thousand dollars for aid purposes. Interposing, McFarland added, "I would like to state here that I think that is a very worthy purpose, and I want to commend you for your actions." As the room broke into applause, Worth Clark backpedaled, hoping to prove that exhibitors were forced to show films where the profits aided the war effort. Again, hoping to get traction on the argument that studios forced their patriotic films on theaters, Worth Clark asked if theaters would receive threats if they did not take certain films. Schenck said no, and Worth Clark moved on, but the mogul continued to control the session.

After more discussion of *Land of Liberty*, Schenck encouraged Clark to see the film himself. "I happened to see this picture," said McFarland, "and I think it is a wonderful picture. It is my thought that if this committee would see these pictures we might all agree that they were good, and we could quit and go home." Responding to McFarland and trying to counter yet another round of applause, Clark stated bluntly, "We are very glad to have you with us at any time, but whenever you think we are wasting time, you do not need to be here." Worth Clark's rebuttal received additional applause, while McFarland replied, "If it was not my duty to be here, I would not be here."

Hoping to close Schenck's session, Worth Clark asked the mogul his definition of freedom of speech. "The right to express yourself," answered Schenck. Hoping to corner Schenck into supporting legislative control of the media, Worth Clark asked him about newspapers and radio. Schenck articulated their right to free expression and his disagreement with any legislation that would hinder those mediums or the writers and commentators using them. When asked about the *Los Angeles Times* being pressured to rid itself of Fidler's column, Schenck noted that he would not "tolerate any of our men ever threatening any individual or newspaper because we were not given what we thought we should be in the line of criticism." Schenck assured the senators that if any of his employees got into it with the newspapers, that employee would quickly be fired.

Clark gave the floor to Senator Tobey, who echoed Phelp's allegations about studios yanking advertising. Tobey pushed Schenck on his opinion regarding the situations with the *Los Angeles Times*, where studio heads allegedly pressured the newspaper to rid itself of Fidler's column or they would pull all film advertising.[4] Schenck responded to the series of questions by referring them to Howard Dietz, head of MGM publicity. The senators did not like this answer. "I am not questioning him now," fired back Tobey, "I am questioning you, sir." The senators wanted words from Schenck, the president of Loew's, but the mogul continued to defer to Dietz. The isolationist senators had not gotten the damning quotes they wanted, and the session broke at 11:55 a.m.

Testimony of Howard Dietz

The subcommittee reconvened at 2:10 p.m., with a telegram sent to Senator Worth Clark from Louis De Rochemont, producer of the *March of Time* newsreel series. De Rochemont advised Worth Clark that members of the Royal Norwegian Air Force were flying to Washington to screen for the subcommittee the latest newsreel, titled "Norway in Revolt." Senator Brooks dismissed the screening invitation, stating that Norway "probably needs them [the fighter pilots] there much more than it does here." McFarland made it clear he would be happy to watch the film and meet with the pilots, which prompted the first round of applause in the afternoon session.

Howard Dietz was sworn in next. As director of advertising and publicity for MGM, Dietz had a deep industrial knowledge after working with the company since 1924. Dietz informed the subcommittee that his team organized film promotions and worked with local representatives and the staff at the studio in California.

Tobey threw the same questions at Dietz about defining freedom of the press. "Freedom of speech within those definitions as relates to the press itself," Dietz answered. Defining censorship of the press, Dietz argued it would take "a legal measure to restrain the press." Tobey pressed Dietz on the possibility of legislation against censorship of the press, but Dietz noted that the Constitution already protected the freedoms of the press—no new laws should be necessary.

Tobey then sought Dietz's thoughts on the rumor that Hollywood moguls threatened to pull advertising from the *Los Angeles Times* as a result of their publishing Fidler's column. Dietz labeled Fidler's sworn testimony as pure gossip and nothing more. When probed for evidence, Dietz asked if Tobey could first have any proof that Fidler's report was true. Of course, it is difficult to prove that something did not happen. By this point, however, the subcommittee was driven by the legal aphorism that absence of evidence is not the evidence of absence. "I would not accuse Mr. Fidler of perjury, but I would say that Mr. Fidler is a congenital liar," Dietz proclaimed, "and it would be going against his conscience to tell the truth." Provoking a great deal of laughter and riotous applause, Dietz simply argued that he could not debate the facts of a situation that was not grounded in truth.

The only facts that Dietz could discuss were from Fidler's accusation that Dietz penned letters to over a hundred newspapers asking them to pull Fidler's column. Dietz claimed he did not write a single letter to any newspaper. Going further, Dietz refuted Fidler's claims that MGM often worked to censor the press. "I would like to add that many of us are opposed to this investigation because it is an attempt to restrict the freedom of the screen," Dietz concluded, drawing additional applause from the room.

Tobey continued to throw Fidler's testimony at Dietz, pressing him about a specific situation involving a letter to a Mr. Stahlman, publisher of the *Nashville Banner*. Dietz admitted to communicating with Stahlman in regards to marketing in that region; however, there were no letters of censure sent to the *Nashville Banner*. Tobey reminded Dietz of Fidler's story that Will Hays had to "call off the dogs" in regards to MGM's activities surrounding the release of *Marie Antoinette*. Dietz told the subcommittee that he called Mr. Stahlman after hearing Fidler's testimony. The only threat on the newspaper came from a local theater manager who complained to the *Nashville Banner* after Fidler had personally attacked actress Norma Shearer in one of his columns. That theater manager, a man named Crull, was not speaking for MGM and had no real authority in the manner—he was just speaking from personal emotion. Dietz compared local theaters to retail stores: each serves a different community, and the manager responds to that community in the way they see fit.

When asked about the newspapers that carry Fidler's column, Dietz posited that publishers do not always agree with their op-ed columnists. Some newspaper publishers "may think there is very little harm in his column and that there is some circulation value to it," offered Dietz, who understood that "it may be good business to carry it."

As Tobey continued to push Dietz on the *Nashville Banner* issue, McFarland stepped in to clarify that this alleged threat to pull advertising occurred before the current concern over war propaganda films. "This whole thing has nothing to do with this investigation," snarled McFarland. Tobey strongly disagreed and reminded the Arizona senator that while the room regularly applauded comments questioning the subcommittee's intentions, it was their job not only to investigate alleged war propaganda but also the charges of monopoly in the film industry. Tobey maintained that the current goal was to fact check the previous sworn testimonies, which would be accepted until proven false. However, McFarland argued that the subcommittee should have to prove their accusations before asking anyone to disprove them.

Again trying to convince the senators that Fidler could not be trusted, Dietz enlightened the subcommittee on the journalist's usual modus operandi. Fidler was known in Hollywood for reviewing films before they were released, sometimes before they were even completed, often without having seen the film, and presented himself as an insider providing facts. Dietz argued that the vast majority of critics were fair and honest, and as long as that remained the case, the studios did not push back if any individual critic received a film poorly. The problem for many was that Fidler went above and beyond to be nasty, dishonest, and careless with his reporting.

The subcommittee worked to clarify the chain of command in terms of studio advertising. While Tobey and Worth Clark tried to pin a local decision of a theater manager on MGM management, Dietz showed the senators that no theater operator had authority to make advertising decisions. They could inquire to see if MGM was interested in publicity in their area, but all marketing decisions come from the studio advertising team lead by Dietz. Local theaters did not even get consulted about advertising in their area. By this point, Worth Clark began to wonder if Fidler had mistaken Crull for Dietz.

Dietz explained that studios did not have lasting contracts with newspapers. Deals were only set for a short period, the length of any single advertisement run. In the case of the *Los Angeles Times*, which Tobey kept bringing back into the discussion, Dietz noted that studio management like Louis B. Mayer and Harry Warner regularly met with the Chandlers (publishers of the *Los Angeles Times*) and always worked to keep a good relationship between the movie business and newspaper business. Such conversations did not focus on any writer's column and instead focused on the larger picture. Studio bosses and publishers were less concerned with any given journalist and more concerned with circulation numbers and advertising dollars.

Schenck Resumed

Dietz left the stand, and the senators resumed questions for Schenck, who added that he visited the MGM studio a few times a year for a total of about five to six weeks spent at the studio. Schenck's visits to the studio were usually to resolve issues that had arisen, such as contract disputes and other financials like future investments (novel or story rights for films). His business never dealt with active productions.

Moving the inquiry back to alleged war propaganda filmmaking, Worth Clark sought Schenck's thoughts on the definition of a propaganda picture as "one which contains in it certain incidents which might incite hate or incite a desire of those who saw it, or some of those who saw it, to go to war." "Let us put on the record," asserted Schenck, "that I disagree every time with the term 'propaganda picture.'" This was the most direct answer Schenck gave, but the senators were regularly unsatisfied with the mogul's replies. Worth Clark and Tobey felt that Schenck was not indignant enough over the allegations made by Fidler. *Variety* described Worth Clark as "irate" and Tobey's responses as regularly "raising a rumpus," especially when Schenck said he was previously unaware of any situation involving the *Nashville Banner*.[5]

In the *Hollywood Reporter*, Jack Moffitt wrote that Schenck "let the Senator have facts—right in the kisser."[6] Moffit argued that "America wants to bond with the Bund," referring to the isolationist and Nazi-influenced organization.[7] "For almost three weeks, Senator [Worth] Clark has been on safari in the head-line-hunting country," Moffitt mused. "He has avoided every waterhole where a fact might be lurking. The spoor of any qualified expert causes him to start up country."[8]

Worth Clark began to ask about MGM films, even though Schecnk was rarely asked to consult on a production. In regards to *The Mortal Storm*, Schenck said he provided no input on the film. When asked about its subject, Schecnk replied, "I think it is a great picture," drawing applause from the room, who also appeared to approve of the film. When probed if the film incited hatred,

Schenck denied the claim. "I will say this," Schenck added, "that it gives a little additional information so that people know what is going on on the other side—Hitler and his army and Hitlerism, all through. But it only touches on some of the things that are happening as we know it from newspapers and from people coming back." Again, drawing applause from the audience and frustration from Worth Clark, Schenck showed his unequivocal support of socially conscious war films.

Worth Clark asked Schenck about his opinion regarding critic and gossip columnist Louella Parsons. Schenck declined to comment but Worth Clark baited him with Parsons's review of *The Mortal Storm*. Parsons wrote, "There is unspeakable brutality and heartaches so real that it must affect everyone who sees the picture." Scheck stood strong by declining to comment on the critic and advised Clark to see the film for himself. Scheck described the film as a small percentage of what was known to be happening in Germany. "We know hundreds of thousands of people are being destroyed," Schenck added. "That applies to Jews and Catholics and everybody that does not believe in the Nazi regime; and they are destroyed in every possible way." It was not a propaganda film, Schenck argued, as it was a story about a few people based on a best-selling book.

Schenck then provided Worth Clark with an overview of how the story-finding process worked at MGM. The studio had readers—people who find and review potential stories—all over the world. "Everything that is published or unpublished is read," Schenck explained. The stories that show promise are then kicked up the corporate ladder. Once it gained traction at the studio, the 26 producers, 150 writers, and 20 plus directors went to work.

Trying to trip the mogul, Worth Clark asked if Schenck was making films about atrocities in other countries, why not make films about Russia? Smiling "as the wolf smiled when mugging Red Riding Hood's grandma," Clark thought he had Schenck pegged.[9] However, MGM did make an anticommunist film in the form of the popular comedy titled *Ninotchka* (1939) with Greta Garbo. Schenck described the studio's jabs at communism while Worth Clark "fidgeted and waved a long yellow pencil," wrote the *Hollywood Reporter*. "He seemed to be stenciling invisible oaths on the ozone."[10]

Towards the end of the day, the discussion turned to the Production Code, which was first instituted by the MPPDA in 1922, adhered to haphazardly in the following decade, and revised a few times before being strongly enforced in 1934. Senator Tobey quoted a line in hopes of tripping Schenck with the film industry's own rules. One line of the code, read by Tobey, was, "The history, institutions, prominent people, and citizenry of other nations shall be represented fairly." When pressed if a film like *The Mortal Storm* is fair to

Germany, Schenck answered in the affirmative. In addition, he added, "I don't think you want unity with Hitler." This line prompted the *Hollywood Reporter* to ask, "In other words, what racial group except the Bund could be offended by an anti-Nazi picture?"[11] As previously noted, that film did not go nearly as far as it could have in depicting the truth about Germany. For Schenck, a film like *The Mortal Storm* was instructive and gave viewers information, which was part of the purpose of motion pictures as outlined by MPPDA president Will Hays.[12] What they did with it when they left the theater was up to them.

Writer Lillian Hellman called the film investigation "a disgrace."[13] Hellman defended Hollywood, saying the anti-Nazi stance was not new and the studios should have been pushing such films much earlier. The next day would find an even stronger defense of Tinseltown when the shrewd Harry Warner went up against the subcommittee.

PART FIVE
HOLLYWOOD'S
VICTORY

CHAPTER TEN

Warner's War

Day Seven: Thursday September 25, 1941

As the seventh day came to order, Senator Worth Clark was notified of a film screening of *Land of Liberty* to be held for Congress at the National Archives building the next day. Worth Clark was anxious to see the film: "I have no doubt that it is a splendid picture." The gallery was overwhelmingly packed with Hollywood supporters, nearly two hundred and fifty, but much of the traditional press was lacking. The few non-Hollywood press representatives would soon find themselves taken with Harry Warner's words. The tide was strongly in support of Hollywood, as the *Film Daily* presented excerpts from well over thirty papers from around the nation that displayed emphatic support of the studios and disdain for the Senate investigation.[1] Awaiting Warner's testimony were Senators Worth Clark, McFarland, Tobey, and Brooks. Without further discussion, Harry Warner, president of Warner Bros., was sworn in.

Testimony of Harry Warner

The stoic and mild-mannered president of Warner Bros. opened by assuring the subcommittee he had taken their allegations seriously, had thought them through, and wholeheartedly denied them as "reckless and unfounded." Warner admitted that the isolationist "gossip" about the studios had been "widely disseminated" and took issue that his studio and his name had been mentioned in many articles accusing Hollywood of warmongering. The mogul was on the offensive right out the gate.

While the previous sessions opened with the senators firing questions at film industry associates, Warner opened the day with a lengthy, emphatic defense of

= THE 𝕵𝕚𝕷𝕞 =

Intimate in Character
International in Scope
Independent in Thought

The Daily Newspaper
Of Motion Pictures
Twenty-Two Years Old

= DAILY =

80, NO. 61   NEW YORK, THURSDAY, SEPTEMBER 25, 1941   TEN CENTS

PROBERS FIRE JUST BLANKS AT SCHENCK

Hollywood press continues its attack

his own to be delivered before any questions could be asked. Believing Nazism to be "a world revolution whose ultimate objective is to destroy our democracy, wipe out all religion, and enslave our people—just as Germany has destroyed and enslaved Poland, Belgium, Holland, France, and all the other countries," Warner was happy to dedicate himself fully to the cause of defeating the Nazis.

Warner expressed his concerns for all people, not just Jews, as he felt the battle against the Nazis was the last step in "the world struggle for freedom." Always in line with President Roosevelt's policies, Warner supported giving Europe aid to defeat the Nazis but remained unsure as to whether the United States should get directly involved. "The President knows the world situation and our country's problems better than any other man," Warner added. "I would follow his recommendation concerning a declaration of war." Warner's primary concern was that if the Nazis took over Europe, they would become the world's leader.

Moving on to the accusations made about Warner Bros. films, Warner threw the isolationists' words back in their faces. He singled out allegations by Nye, Champ Clark, and Flynn, who argued that Warner Bros.' *Sergeant York* was "made to create war hysteria" and added *Confessions of a Nazi Spy* and *Underground* to an "isolationist blacklist." "These witnesses have not seen these pictures," Warner shot back, "so I cannot imagine how they can judge them." The millions of moviegoers who had paid good money to see and enjoy these films, each of which had made a profit according to Warner, had proven the public's favorability.

Specifically, Warner describes *Sergeant York* as "a factual portrait of the life of one of the great heroes of the last war. If that is propaganda, we plead guilty. *Confessions of a Nazi spy* is a factual portrayal of a Nazi spy ring that actually operated in New York City. If that is propaganda, we plead guilty." Warner assured the subcommittee that their films were "carefully prepared," based on facts, and were "not twisted to serve any ulterior purpose." The studio was so proud of *Sergeant York* that three days prior, Jack Warner took out a five-page ad in the *Hollywood Reporter*. Followed by pages of screenshots, Jack Warner's quote led the advertisement: "It is my great pleasure to express my appreciation to all those who participated in the production of *Sergeant York*, already a screen symbol and tradition." Warner continued, "I wish to acknowledge publicly each individual's vital contribution to its making and to express the hope that it will be to them, as it is to me, a continuing source of pride."[2]

Harry Warner took the accuracy of his studio's films seriously. He added, "The only sin of which Warner Bros. is guilty is that of accurately recording on the screen the world as it is or as it has been." Warner was prepared to bring in numerous witnesses to prove that his studio "has not duped its patrons but has, in fact, kept its obligation to the movie-going public." Warner feared that the isolationists wanted the studio to change their obligation to the public. "This," the mogul charged, "Warner Bros. will never do."

The mogul's next line of offense was to organize the subcommittee's vague arguments into digestible and defensible categories. Warner summarized and then responded to each one. First, the notion that Warner Bros. was making films "for the purpose allegedly of inciting our country into war." Warner reminded the senators that for the past twenty years they had had the same approach to filmmaking, which was to depict the world as it was. Second, the argument that Warner Bros. films about the war were "inaccurate and are twisted for an ulterior purpose"; again, Warner defended his studio's approach to researching films and presenting real stories. These films "show the world as it is," he added. Third, the idea that the studio was making films that nobody wanted to see. "The proof of the pudding is in the eating," said Warner, as these films had all made money. In addition, he predicted *Sergeant York* would be their biggest film in years. Fourth, the accusation that "in some mysterious way, the Government orders us to make this or that type of picture." While Warner Bros. had cooperated with the national defense program by making short films, Warner explained that each film was made "voluntarily and proudly." No orders from the government were ever received.

Before any more assumptions could be made about the studio's story-acquisition practices, Warner educated the subcommittee on his studio's operations so the subcommittee could "no longer be dependent for your information on the half-truth and the misinformed witness." Harry, of course, was president of the company, while his brother Jack was head of production at the studio. The third living Warner brother, Albert, was head of distribution. Warner Bros. had become the powerhouse it was, Harry Warner explained, because of their decision to invest in the talking picture. Their company had begun with a small nickelodeon outfit in Pennsylvania in 1906, expanded its operations, and eventually had enough money to open its own production facility. By the

1920s, the Warners were investing in stories and already making films about the world as it was.

The studio's most important contribution, according to Warner, was their investment in sound technology—a move initiated by the late Sam Warner. Harry Warner knew that exhibiting silent films with large orchestral accompaniments was something only maintainable in large cities. Pushing a technology to accompany all films, in any city, could expand the accessibility of the most dynamic film experiences of the day. The decision to invest in sound technology was based on the same principals used to begin exhibiting in 1906: "We wanted to please, entertain, and inform our fellow townsmen. Today that is the objective of our studios, on a national scale." Though the drive for sound on film was a long battle that featured Thomas Edison, William Fox, Albert E. Smith, and the Warner Bros. studio, the Warners eventually proved the technology profitable with *The Jazz Singer* (1927) and *The Singing Fool* (1928).

Differing from Schenck, who placed all production decisions with those at the studio, Warner declared, "I, as president of the company, wish to assume the full responsibility for the pictures we produce. That is the responsibility that should be mine, and one from which I do not shirk." Certainly, this did not mean that the studio president chose each film project, but rather that Warner's duty had been to keep a strong team who could present material that would be engaging and entertaining to the public. "I have the idea that our accusers believe that I, together with one or two others, sit down in secret conference and plot the kind of pictures which we propose to make," Warner explained. "Nothing could be further from the fact," he added—the studio's success was dependent on the millions of viewers who enjoyed Warner Bros.' films.

Warner's measured statement moved on to specific films that had "tried to portray on the screen current happenings of our times." Warner listed *I Am a Fugitive From a Chain Gang*, about a real fugitive from justice during the Great Depression; *British Agent*, based on the book about communist Russia; *Black Fury*, about the working conditions in the coal-mining industry; *The Story of Louis Pasteur*, about the famous French scientist; *Juarez*, about "the Abraham Lincoln of Mexico;" and *The Life of Emile Zola*, about the man "who aroused the conscious of the world on behalf of Dreyfus—the victim of religious bigotry." Warner explained how his studio had been making "topical pictures" for decades prior to any Nazi threat and provided the subcommittee with a full dossier of how several of their films were made, including *Confessions of a Nazi Spy*, *Sergeant York*, *Underground*, and *International Squadron*.

Wanting to present at least one of these case studies to the subcommittee himself, Warner provided them with a history of *Confessions of a Nazi Spy*. The narrative was taken from the real events that were exposed in June of 1938, where

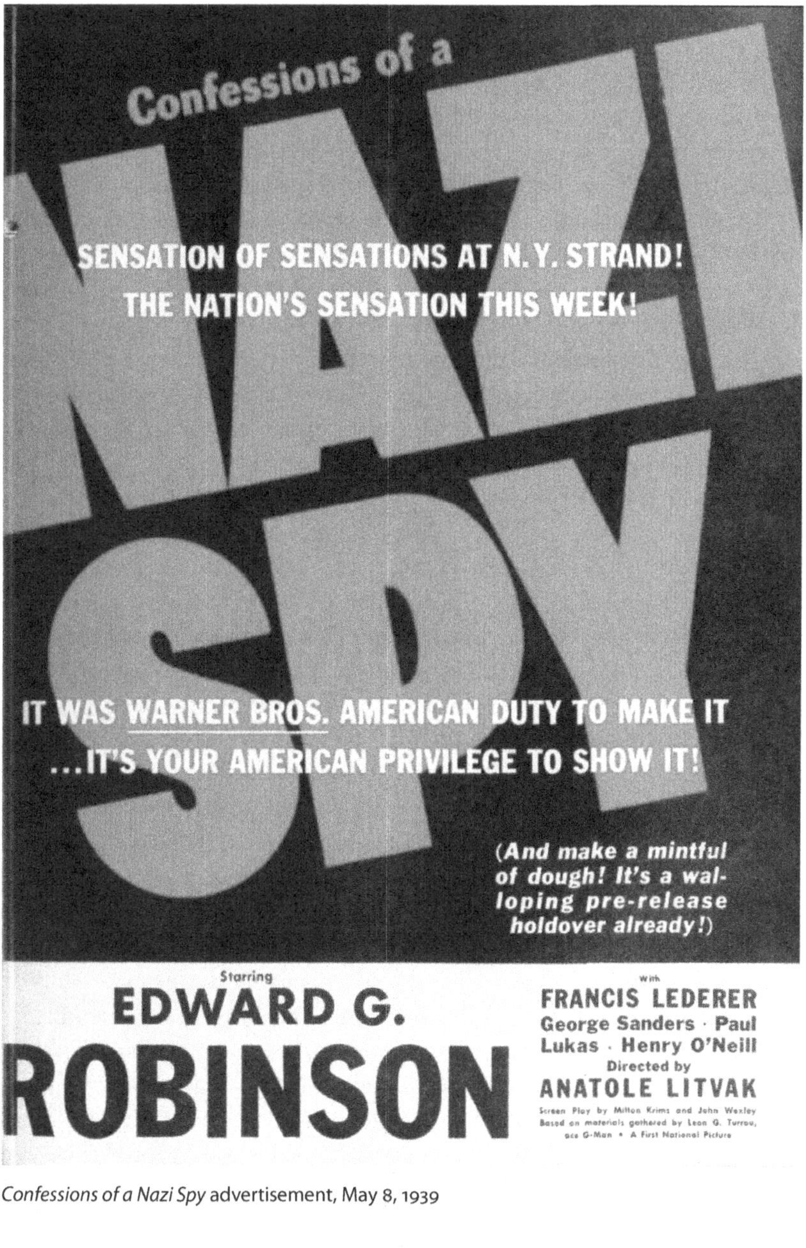

Confessions of a Nazi Spy advertisement, May 8, 1939

a Nazi spy ring was uncovered in New York and several agents were charged with espionage. The trial was widely covered in the news, including regular commentary from FBI agent Leon Turrou, who was active in the investigation. Turrou's articles were sealed until after the trial and when Warner Bros. story editors finally got a chance to read them, the studio purchased the story rights. The script was fact-checked incessantly to insure the film was not a fancy fabrication. *Confessions of a Nazi Spy* was based on facts from the trial, which were widely documented in the press. The film was also endorsed by many civic, patriotic, and labor organizations. Warner brought with him over five hundred letters of support to prove the popularity of this film.

One piece of information that the subcommittee, particularly Senator Nye, did not expect to see, was a telegram from Nye to Ed Harrison of Warner Bros. advertising. Nye attended a screening of *Confessions of a Nazi Spy* on May 11, 1939, in Washington, DC, and after watching the film and speaking with Harrison, he sent the following telegram.

> The picture is exceedingly good. The cast is exceptionally fine. The plot may or may not be exaggerated but is one that ought to be with every patriotic American. As for myself, I hope there may be more pictures of a kind dealing with propaganda emanating from all foreign lands. Anyone who truly appreciates the one great democracy upon this earth will appreciate this picture and feel a new allegiance to the democratic cause.

Warner repeated that last line for emphasis before handing over similar dossiers on the other films criticized by the isolationist senators. As Nye's endorsement was read, Senator Worth Clark "went turkey red."[3] Warner also noted that out of the 140 films his studio had produced in the last two and a half years, only seven had been attacked as propaganda. Out of the nine thousand story ideas submitted each year, Warner added, only fifty films were made by Warner Bros. Presenting additional research, Warner showed how 70 percent of nonfiction books, 10 percent of novels, and a large amount of newspaper and radio coverage were dedicated to discussing the Nazi regime. Hollywood's films, even those at Warner Bros., only dealt with war-related issues in a small fraction of films.

Another charge denied by Warner was that Hollywood needed to defend Great Britain to hold on to their financial investment as a means to stay afloat. Warner candidly told the subcommittee that his studio made about five million dollars a year on films exhibited in Great Britain and was not worried about losing those profits. In 1933, Warner Bros. took the first stand against Hitler in Hollywood. The studio's decision to boycott Germany was prompted by the assault of their employee, Phil Kaufman, at the hands of Hitler's men.[4] "We voluntarily liquidated our business in Germany," Warner explained. "Business is based on keeping contracts, and Hitler does not keep his contracts with men, or with nations." Warner noted that he would have no problem pulling their films out of Britain if the Nazis took over.

The mogul concluded by assuring the senators of his patriotism: "Our country has become great because it is, in truth, a land of freedom." The unity found in the United States, for Warner, was "because of the freedoms of the individual." Taking this freedom as a responsibility, Warner added, "I will not censor the dramatization of the works of reputable and well-informed writers to conceal from the American people what is happening in the world." Warner's final argument was that "freedom of speech, freedom of religion, and freedom of enterprise cannot be bought at the price of other people's rights." Warner concluded, "I believe the American people have a right to know the truth." The statement was met with a raucous ovation.

Senator McFarland stepped in and asked Warner to include the other case studies he was submitting to the subcommittee. Warner provided an overview of *Sergeant York*, which had been an adaptation nightmare for any studio since the end of World War I because Alvin York, himself a strong antiwar figure, did not want to gain from his war legacy. Finally, with the help of Jesse Lasky, the film was being made with York's supervision. Warner informed the senators of the film's many positive reviews, reading excerpts from the *New York Times*, the *Hearst Journal-American*, and the *Washington Post*.

Underground, which premiered on June 23, 1941, features an illegal radio station travelling around Germany and informing the resistance. Knowing that such films had been questioned for legitimacy, Warner noted that "we shall be glad to present witnesses who have lived in Germany to prove that our dramatization does not exaggerate, in its plate, actual happenings under Nazism." In addition, Warner assured the subcommittee that this film easily understated the situation in Germany. If further proof was needed, Warner encouraged the senators to review the last few years of news coverage regarding the rise of fascism in Germany. Many of Warner's letters of support were regarding *Underground*, a film that "grossed more than the cost of production in the first 11 weeks of its showing."

The film also got a positive review in the *Los Angeles Times* and received a standing ovation at its premiere.[5] The *New York Times* was critical of the story, but not because of its anti-Nazi slant.[6] The isolationist senators may have been prompted by a review in the *Chicago Daily Tribune*, which called *Underground* "propaganda" but also called it an "engrossing story."[7]

International Squadron, which was yet to be released, chronicled the Lafayette Escadrille, a team of American fighter pilots during World War I who volunteered to fight for France during a crucial time in their country's defense. Again, drawn from a real story—Warner offered to screen the film for the senators as an additional gesture to prove the studio's and the film's dedication to truth and realism.

Warner's testimony was a well-crafted, thoughtful, and passionately delivered denunciation of the propaganda accusations. If any previous testimony showed cracks in the isolationists' wall, Warner had just blown the barrier to bits just in time for lunch.

After the lunch recess, Senator Tobey opened by taking exception to Warner's list of accused films and admitted he could not find any reason to see *Dive Bomber* as propaganda. Tobey pressed Warner on his views about "freedom of the seas," to which the mogul deferred to the elected officials to decide the limits of the policy. Regarding questions about where to send aid or food, Warner said he would be in favor of sending food to anyone in need anywhere in the country. The one stipulation, however, would be that it not reach the enemies of freedom.

For Warner, Great Britain was fighting on behalf of all free nations. Therefore, the United States should aid them in that fight. Warner was a very loyal man, as evidenced by his thirty-four-year marriage in an industry notorious for its high divorce rate. Senator Tobey fired back, "I can go you five better," and the room broke into applause. "I am no different than any other human being," said Warner, "though having been married 34 years I still like to look at a good-looking girl, even though my wife may be around." "I suppose you use the Psalmist's statement, 'my eye is not dimmed to my natural force of vision,'" Tobey replied to another round of laughter. Warner shot back once more, "My father taught me that when you quit seeing, you quit living," as laughter continued bouncing through the room.

Tobey's next line of questioning was in regard to a 1933 film titled *Captured*, starring Leslie Howard and Douglas Fairbanks. The film was examined because, according to Aubrey Blair, an executive secretary of the Screen Actors Guild, *Captured* used "personnel and planes of the Federal Government at March Field" and "84 noncommissioned officers and soldiers, 28 pilots, 14 Keystone bombers, and 5 or 6 other planes." The Screen Actors Guild telegrammed Darryl Zanuck (who was then a producer at Warner Bros.) the next day, September 26, to inform him that Blair was not an executive secretary but was an assistant working on membership (nothing to do with productions) and was fired in 1939.[8] Blair briefly worked for Central Casting before getting fired in 1940 and now worked for the Central Labor Council of Los Angeles.

Additional accusations included planes being repainted for the film and fueled by government dollars, and actors being housed in government facili-

Harry Warner testifies in 1941

ties. Tobey's problem was that "money of the taxpayers of America has been used illegally in the production of pictures for profit, and these same taxpayers are charged for the privilege of seeing those pictures." Blair would eventually release a statement clarifying that he had made these charges, but they were made in 1937 and "had nothing to do with the present Senatorial investigation."[9]

Warner could not even remember the film; in fact, he did not even think it was made by Warner Bros. at all. Tobey was not fully informed either, as he thought the film was produced in 1936. Darryl Zanuck had not heard of the film, but it was produced by Edward Chodorov at Warner Bros. Like Schenck before him, Warner told the subcommittee that he did not follow the day-to-day production process. Tobey also took issue with the notion that American servicemen were dressed as enemy soldiers for the purposes of the film and asked Warner if such actions were justified. Warner refused to answer because the accusations had not been proven and he needed time to consider the situation.

Tobey also had it in his mind that planes were destroyed during filming and, therefore, the studio was guilty of ruining government property. Another film, *West Point of the Air* (1935), found the same allegations hurled at it. However, the MGM representatives in the room told the subcommittee that no planes were wrecked during production.

While the industry men denied Tobey's accusations, the senator produced a letter from J. W. Buzzell of the Central Labor Council of Los Angeles, who claimed "at least 100,000 man-days of service had been rendered to motion-picture producers by the United States Government, free of charge, and that upward of a million dollars in wages had been taken away from the regular employees of the motion picture industry." These dollars were allegedly spent on gas, engine maintenance, and oil in addition to hours worked. The war department, however, refused to furnish a list of films they had assisted. Buzzell, along with the entire Central Labor Council of Los Angeles, would also stand against the continuation of the Senate investigation in the coming weeks.[10]

When Tobey pressed Warner for his viewpoint on war and intervention, Warner expressed his deep support for the Allied cause but noted that we could support the Allies without sending our own troops. "I think there are plenty of men in this world today who are willing to fight for that liberty that they have," said Warner, who felt all the United States needed to do was send the material Britain needed to defend itself. "It is more important today for unity to exist in our country," Warner added, "so that people can go to work and produce those things so that they can be sent over there than it is for you and me to argue." Warner's main argument was that if we send goods into a war, we can then prevent our own people from having to fight in that war. Responding to Warner's plea to keep US children away from war, Tobey agreed and reminded Warner that it was Congress, not the president, who had the power to declare war on another nation. Tobey was given a round of applause; Warner agreed, and declared his loyalty to any decision Congress made as elected officials.

After McFarland and Warner agreed on a nation's right to defend itself both during and prior to any international conflict, Senator Brooks jumped in with admiration for Warner's personal story. "I have been very greatly impressed by your testimony," said Brooks, who felt Warner's rags-to-riches story was "one of the great stories of American life." Brooks added that he did not see any propaganda in Warner Bros.' *Sergeant York*, and if the studio's other films were similar, it would "prove to be a cleansing of any charges made against you for your conduct." Warner thanked Brooks for his candor and suggested that if the senators watch any of his studio's films, that they see *Underground*, as it showed "a story in sympathy with the German people who are fighting for the very thing [freedom] you have just recited that you and I have today."

Senator Worth Clark then pushed Warner on the issue of propaganda in regard to *Underground*. Having not seen the film, Worth Clark asked if the film depicted Nazi atrocities. Warner argued that *Underground* shows the strength of Germans who did not support the Nazis. When Clark pushed again to get Warner to admit that the film showed "great brutality," Warner quipped back, "yes, well, do you think we should have made a picture that showed the Nazis kissing them or in love with them, or what?" Worth Clark continued to argue that *Underground* was a hate film. Warner shot back, "I think it is entirely wrong to produce pictures that produce hate against anybody." Worth Clark took issue with Warner's mindset to do anything possible to destroy Nazism by asking,

"Even if you plunge your country into this war and wreck it forever?" The senator's hyperbolic criticisms did not go anywhere with Warner. Worth Clark's next line of attack was to bring up the *Harrison's Report* on *Underground*, which stated that the film was "so depressing and harrowing that it leaves one not only in an extremely unhappy frame of mind, but in a nervous state as well." The report also described scenes of torture as "sickening." Warner responded to the stern reading by arguing, "If you portray the truth, it may hurt you, but, unfortunately, that is the truth." Warner again pushed the senator to actually see the film so that he would realize the film could only provoke Nazis. "It will not incite you. It will only portray to you what actually exists. You will see, for one thing, what you have kind of missed, my dear Senator." An increasingly agitated Worth Clark asked if the film would provoke viewers to hate the German people. "I do not know what people would think," said Warner. "I can't talk for the rest of the world. I think in America we have our own minds and we use them." Ignoring the applause following Warner's last statement, Worth Clark continued firing questions about Warner Bros. films provoking hatred. "I answered that several times," Warner said. "You did not," fired back Clark. "Well, then, you and I can't agree," Warner admitted firmly.

Warner and Worth Clark continued to go back and forth regarding the definition of war propaganda. The senator defined war propaganda as any film made to push a country into war, which Warner saw as a broad definition. Warner, on the other hand, argued that if Germany was producing films in the United States that were supporting Nazism, it would be war propaganda. Ignoring Warner's counter, Worth Clark reminded the mogul that Will Hays had stated that there should be no war propaganda in Hollywood films (but ignored Hays's comments about the responsibility of films during times of war). Warner agreed with Hays and argued that his company's films were entertaining, though not everyone might see them that way.[11] "We are making pictures of facts," Warner asserted. "That is the whole story in a nutshell." Warner's claim was strongly backed by the studio's deep history of ripping from the headlines to make gritty, realistic films.

Worth Clark responded to Warner's "facts" by bringing up the Production Code: "Some years ago you made a good many pictures of facts, and then the American people rose up and almost clamped a censorship on you." Of course, the story was not as generalized as Worth Clark thought because censorship threats directed at Hollywood usually came from specialized groups. For instance, the 1934 enforcement of censorship was largely due to the influence of the Catholic Legion of Decency, who did not represent the entirety of the American people.[12] Warner corrected the senator about why Hollywood took on censorship changes—largely to avoid government intervention—and the end result affected more of what could be shown on screen than what topics a film presented.

However, Worth Clark gained momentum as he received applause for arguing that England was fighting the same battle it had been fighting for hundreds of years—in other words, why should we be interested now? The senator reasoned that any war could plunge the United States into economic turmoil that could rival what Germany had seen in the past decade recovering from World War I. As Worth Clark received continued applause, Warner stated unequivocally that he was against any direct involvement in war. Worth Clark argued, equating Hitler's intentions with those of England, that the United States could not trust England because the country did not repay their debts from the First World War. "I do not think it is the intention of England to destroy the rest of the world," said Warner. "I am positive that is the intention of Hitler."

As the sparring wound down, Willkie landed some jabs at Worth Clark. At one point, Worth Clark was going to cite the campaign addresses of the recent presidential hopefuls (one of whom was Willkie), but Willkie interposed, "Suppose you check them before you cite them." Willkie added, inciting more laughter and applause, "You have made statements all over this country as being what I said and they bore no semblance to the facts." The verbal battle between Willkie and Worth Clark would no doubt grab headlines, as Willkie predicted: "This side show is what is played up in the papers."[13] However, Willkie told the press, "Compared to Mr. Warner's great defense of free speech this squabble to me seems the unimportant thing."[14] Warner's address was undoubtedly the strongest defense of Hollywood thus far and left the isolationist senators scrambling for a lone straw man to prop up.

Jack Moffitt described Warner's testimony in the *Hollywood Reporter* as "a citizen [who] got loose among a bunch of United States Senators and talked them all down." Moffitt labeled the day's applause as largely in support of Warner's words. With the senators praising many films on this day, Moffitt predicted that "unless a new method of attack is thought of, I believe this investigation will crawl up in some alley and die."[15] Moffitt called Warner's testimony historic, correctly foreseeing that scholars would study Warner's words. "Instead of backing the movies into a strait jacket," wrote Moffitt, "the committee may end up wearing one."[16] "If it does, Harry Warner is the guy that buckled it on," he concluded.[17] It could be added that Warner's presentation of Nye's letter in support of *Confessions of a Nazi Spy* should have stopped the investigation dead, but the isolationists on the subcommittee would continue, ignorantly undeterred.

Motion Picture Daily reported that Warner's testimony was a "brilliant performance" and the mogul "bested the subcommittee members at every turn.[18] The senators planned to take the following week to watch the films in question. In addition, a growing protest to the Senate investigation was planned at the Martin Beck Theatre in New York, where union leaders would discuss their plan to "demand discontinuance of the current investigation."[19] The event was ultimately held on September 29 and had representatives from about one hundred different unions and featured a dozen speakers that spoke out against the Senate investigation.[20] The increasing union opposition to the subcommittee would continue to grow in the coming weeks.

Senator McFarland was also uncharacteristically quiet on Thursday, perhaps because Warner commanded the floor with such force and could defend himself better than anyone else previously subpoenaed to the subcommittee. While it appeared as though the investigation was about over, there would be one more day of testimony. Friday would be shrouded in desperation. Hollywood had Darryl Zanuck and Barney Balaban on deck. The isolationists had something less.

CHAPTER ELEVEN

Zanuck, Balaban, and the Wild Finish

Day Eight: Friday September 26, 1941

Friday morning's session opened with Senator McFarland's inquiry into a claim made the day before. On Thursday, Senator Tobey described what he was told were the policies of the British war offices who would not hire anyone Irish, German, or Jewish. The alleged prejudice was briefly noted in an attempt to rouse Harry Warner, but the stoic mogul just showed disgust and vowed to look into it. McFarland presented it to the floor because he was fed up with the type of claims being made during these hearings without proper documentation or proof. For McFarland, such claims made from a senator did more damage to international relations and to the reputation of the United States than any film they were supposed to be investigating. In addition, McFarland made his own phone calls to the British war office, who confirmed that no such policy existed. Senator Tobey assured McFarland that his unnamed witnesses could elaborate on the situation would be called.

After days of flimsy arguments associated with dicey information, it was abundantly clear that Senator McFarland believed this investigation was a "smear" on Hollywood.[1] Increasingly unsatisfied with the subcommittee, McFarland promised to figure out who had supplied Senator Nye with information that the government was dictating movie content. Senator Worth Clark, trying to sympathize with McFarland's complaints, said, "I think people never 'holler' unless they are pretty badly hurt."[2] Not backing off, McFarland promised Clark that these issues needed to be brought to the Senate floor and the Dies Committee. "Talk about my being hurt," McFarland said, "you are the one who is going to be hurt before this thing is over." Worth Clark tried to respond but the applause from the audience drowned him out. The heated exchange between McFarland and Clark would simmer until exploding again in the afternoon.[3]

The subcommittee quickly moved to the first testimony of the day, James G. Stahlman, president of the *Nashville Banner*.

Testimony of James G. Stahlman

Stahlman inquired about the claim that MGM pulled advertising from the *Nashville Banner*, though he could not find any evidence of it. He went as far as to meet with Will Hays to discuss the matter, and both of them agreed that there was no reason to pursue the situation any further. Stahlman had dropped the issue and told Tobey that if it had not been brought up by Fidler, no one would be talking about it now. Stahlman also denied ever having spoken to Howard Dietz until the last week when he called to inquire about the subcommittee investigation. The only element of Fidler or Dietz's testimonies that Stahlman could corroborate was that MGM was unhappy with the coverage of *Marie Antoinette*, and at some point, MGM pulled advertising with the *Nashville Banner* before reinstating it shortly thereafter. Perhaps the isolationists predicted more fireworks from Stahlman, but it turned out to be a nonevent.

Testimony of Darryl F. Zanuck

Zanuck, vice president of production at Twentieth Century Fox, began his career with Warner Bros. in the 1920s. After years of producing headline-driven material that solidified the studio's early house style, he left the company over a dispute over salary cuts that exempted executives.[4] Zanuck then went into business with Joseph Schenck, brother of Nicholas Schenck, to create Twentieth Century, which would merge with Fox in 1935. Zanuck continued producing successful, engaging, and socially relevant films.[5] Zanuck asked to give his brief statement without interruption. He opened with an overview of his domestic birthplace as a way to acknowledge that origin had been important to the anti-Semites on the subcommittee. Rumors ran around Washington that the isolationist senators regretted subpoenaing Zanuck as soon as they learned he was not a Jew but instead a Methodist.[6] If any top Hollywood executive was an example of a non-Jewish outsider who was able to break into the business, it was Zancuk.

"Senator Nye," Zanuck said, "I am sure, will find no cause for suspicion or alarm in that background."[7] Getting his first round of applause for the day, Zanuck quickly made it clear that he was on to the Jew-baiting. Zanuck quickly took advantage of the isolationists' ignorance of the producer's background.

The Man I Married advertisement: June 20, 1940

Zanuck assured the senators that based on his experiences serving in World War I, he could only look at war with "abhorrence." In addition, Zanuck denied that any government official had asked him to make propaganda films. The studio's only work with the government, which had been previously discussed, was the training films "made at cost and without profit as a matter of patriotic duty."

Swiftly moving on to the allegations of propaganda films made at Twentieth Century Fox, Zanuck noted that *Man Hunt* was a popular book published by Little, Brown, & Co. and was also published as a series in the *Atlantic Monthly*. *The Man I Married* was adapted from a widely sold book titled *I Married a Nazi*, which was also serialized in *Liberty* magazine. "To condemn the motion-picture industry for dealing with subjects as timely, as vital, and as important as the current upheaval in the world is to subject the industry to an impossible censorship," argued Zanuck. Such strictures "would leave the American motion picture as worthless and sterile as those made in Germany and Italy."

Zanuck's production history had always focused on grabbing prominent headlines. When he was at Warner Bros., Zanuck produced the first gangster films that solidified the early genre cycle in the 1930s. Zanuck explained that when he made *The Public Enemy* (1931), the studio saw protests from the underworld gangsters. "I suppose the underworld thought this was unfair propaganda against the gangster," argued Zanuck, "just how some now feel our war pictures are unfair propaganda against Hitler." The room broke into applause once again as Zanuck slyly equated the isolationists with fascists. Zanuck's argument was simple: the studios did not create the gangsters, and they did not create the Nazis. They were just following what was in the newspapers.

The producer took aim at two claims from previous testimonies of Senators Nye and Champ Clark. One, that Twentieth Century Fox "deliberately sabotaged" a film titled *The Great Commandment* because it "preached peace and good will." Zanuck explained how the story was purchased for a large sum with plans to invest a lot of money into the production. However, after releasing a different religious film titled *Brigham Young*, the studio felt "the public was not in the mood to patronize a religious picture." *The Great Commandment*, explained Zanuck, had played in over a thousand theaters over a longer period of time. It did not get a massive release up front, but the studio had carefully rolled it out. The change in exhibition had everything to do with the performance of *Brigham Young*, and nothing to do with minimizing a positive message.

Next, Zanuck pushed back against Clark's claim that the film industry "was determined to wreak vengeance on Adolf Hitler by plunging this Nation into war in behalf of another ferocious beast, referring to Stalin." Zanuck pointed out that Hitler and Stalin were allied when some of the anti-authoritarian films in question were being made. Proud of his production record, Zanuck described himself as "a personal exhibit of one who was able to make among the best motion pictures as an independent producer," prompting another round of applause.

Senator Worth Clark proceeded to question Zanuck on the accuracy of his studio's films. "I believe that they very fairly represent the fact[s]," Zanuck answered, and explained that minor changes were often made (such as adding or subtracting a character), but the main details of their adaptations remain intact.

Worth Clark then trotted out the *Harrison's Report* once again, this time focusing on *Four Sons*, a film about a mother who loses all four of her sons to ideological warfare. The report called the film "extremely depressing" and said it had "no resemblance" to the story it was based on. When Worth Clark challenged Zanuck about the accuracy of the report, he replied, "I believe Mr. Harrison's viewpoints are so strained that he, perhaps, would look at a Shirley Temple picture and make it propaganda." Zanuck said the source material and film both dealt with a German family, but Clark assumed that the film dealt with a Russian (i.e. communist) family because *Harrison's Reports* referred to actress Eugenie Leontovitch by her real name and not the character's name, which was Frau Bern. Worth Clark had a difficult time comprehending how Zanuck could be correct and continued to put a great deal of faith in *Harrison's Reports*, which he called a "standard trade journal." "I should not place too much confidence on saying that is a standard trade journal," said Zanuck; "it has a very limited circulation." *Variety* observed that this exchange between Zanuck and Worth Clark was "lively" but ended in the senator turning "very red faced." Unsurprisingly, the discussion quickly moved on to another film.[8]

The next film in the isolationist's crosshair was *Man Hunt*, about a hunter charged with trying to kill Hitler. Worth Clark again started to read from *Harrison's Report*, which said the film was "not cheerful entertainment" but that there was some sympathy because "the hero is innocent of the crime." Zanuck accused Harrison of being wrong again, because at the end of the film the main character admits he did want to kill Hitler.

Zanuck encouraged Worth Clark to look at additional trade coverage of the so-called propaganda films, such as the *Film Daily*, which published its study of film critics' views on war pictures. Critics voted 103 to 7 that the current war films were not intended to influence the public on the European war. Also, the critics voted 103 to 9 that these films would increase the viewers' appreciation of democracy, and 109 to 4 voted that the films were appropriate for contemporary audiences. Most importantly, even with the minimal detractors in the previous votes, national critics voted unanimously, 113 to 0, that Congress should not take any action against the film industry to stop such productions from being made. Worth Clark dismissed these findings because the question of inciting war feelings was not directly asked (it was, however, in question one). Worth Clark asked Zanuck what he felt about propaganda pictures, to which the producer replied, "Well, that is a most difficult question. I usually find that when someone produces something that you do not like, you call it propaganda." This poke at the isolationist's double standard resulted in another series of roaring applause from the gallery.⁹ Zanuck argued that a filmmaker should be able to produce anything they want, within the strictures of the Production Code, and took full responsibility for how the public responded to his studio's films.

Zanuck was proud of his role in the film industry and shared a list of memories from watching the medium grow. "I look back and recall picture after picture," remembered Zanuck, "pictures so strong and powerful that they sold the American way of life, not only to America but to the entire world." Hollywood films "sold it so strongly that when dictators took over Italy and Germany, what did Hitler and his flunky, Mussolini, do? The first thing they did was ban our pictures, throw us out. They wanted no part of the American way of life." Zanuck encouraged the subcommittee to look at all of Hollywood films, not just the small percentage of them focusing on the war, but films like *Gone with the Wind* and *Grapes of Wrath*. It was because people watched these films, Zanuck argued, that Hollywood had grown into the powerhouse that it is.

"And Senator," concluded Zanuck, "you do not have to investigate us if you will look at all the pictures, our whole record—not just these Nazi pictures."¹⁰ These sentiments, which deviated from Zanuck's prepared statement and came from the heart, grabbed another "prolonged ovation."¹¹ According to the *Hollywood Reporter*, it was the "greatest hand that's been given to any speaker at these hearings."¹² Worth Clark described Zanuck as "a skillful salesman" and commended his ability to get applause and appreciation from all sides of the debate.

Zanuck's time in front of the subcommittee was brief compared to the others, but no less effective. The *Hollywood Reporter*'s Jack Moffit was not happy that Zanuck was given such a brief questioning period. "Having let John T. Flynn spend an entire day energizing upon the fantastic notions of studio operation held by the American Firsters," wrote Moffitt, "Senator Clark had but a scant hour to give the man who heads one of the world's biggest studios."¹³ Perhaps the time was so short because Zanuck defended the movie industry quite effectively. The testimony also followed the previous day's staunch Hollywood defense from Harry Warner. Perhaps the subcommittee moved on from Zanuck before things got ugly again. The desperate isolationist senators had to see the writing on the wall that their battle was coming to a close.

Barney Balaban, 1953. From *The Public is Never Wrong* by Adloph Zukor.

Testimony of Barney Balaban

Barney Balaban had been president of Paramount Pictures since 1936. Helping Paramount become the studio for screwball comedy, Balaban groomed stars such as Bob Hope and Bing Crosby. Overseeing 250 films a year, including features, B-films, newsreels, and documentaries, Balaban quickly received a reputation as a workhorse.[14] Balaban provided background on his company, which had controlling ownership of about 500 theaters and non-controlling stake in another 1,100. All of Paramount's agreements with theaters had included a cancellation clause, which Balaban noted was part of their contracts prior to the new consent decree.

When pressed about Hollywood's anti-Nazi films, Balaban showed that Paramount had not produced any. His reasoning was that they did not have the proper talent to deal with that kind of serious picture. While Paramount had previously discussed making war films after 1939, the studio decided to play it safe with the lighter films they were already producing. This was another good example of how the studios supported each other when something was working well. If Paramount did not have the ingredients to compete, let those studios have the war films while Paramount focused on their own talents. After all, most audiences did not want a diet of only war films—they would need the Paramount comedies to balance the offerings from the industry.

The subcommittee clearly was not going to get any dirt on Hollywood by questioning an employee from a company who had been producing lighthearted comedies while others dug into war-related material. When McFarland was asked if he had any questions, his reply was simply, "No, I was just thinking that we ought to be going to the football game." As the subcommittee found nothing more to discuss, Balaban was thanked for his time and dismissed. It is unclear what the subcommittee thought they would get out of the first three witnesses. The isolationist senators were simply sinking deeper into their own hole while McFarland continued to distance himself from them.

Tobey's Desperate Final Effort

Senator Tobey, who had remained largely quiet during the previous sessions, reopened the discussion about the prejudice happening in the British offices discussed earlier in the morning and promised that his witnesses would soon be arriving to testify. McFarland had been getting increasingly frustrated with Tobey, who had made several blanket statements that the British were guilty of "race prejudice."[15] Things got worse as McFarland realized Tobey's evidence to prove hearsay was limited to gossip from personal colleagues.

McFarland objected to the fact that Tobey would not reveal who his witnesses were, even to those on the subcommittee. "It is unfair for me to cross-examine a witness whom I know nothing in the world about," complained McFarland. "I ask for a poll on the proposition right now, if we are going to have this kind of procedure in this meeting," continued McFarland as the room broke into a combination of applause and boos. McFarland pointed out that the discussion of prejudice at the British war offices, while interesting and important to the Dies Committee, had nothing to do with the purpose of the current subcommittee investigation—an argument that, again, was rewarded with applause. McFarland asked for at least a twenty-four-hour notice before each new witness, but Senator Worth Clark would not allow McFarland to pressure Tobey any farther.

The first of Tobey's witnesses was Robert D. L'Heureux, who was Senator Tobey's secretary. L'Heureux stated that this claim of prejudice was actually from the British Purchasing Commission and came from one of L'Heureux's neighbors. The topic came up because L'Heureux's wife was recently hired by Boyd's Employment Service and was told the British offices wanted more employees, unless they were German, Irish, or Jewish. In short, Tobey's "bombshell" claim was based on unsubstantiated hearsay.

McFarland pointed out that none of these statements came from the British embassy or anyone connected to the previous claims. With his sentiments ignored, McFarland fumed and promised to challenge the isolationist senators on the Senate floor regarding the justification of any further investigation.[16] The discussions of potential prejudice in a foreign war office was so far from the initial purpose of investigation into motion-picture propaganda that McFarland would do everything he could to make sure his fidelity to the committee was officially over. As the *Los Angeles Times* noted, "Senatorial courtesy was almost obliterated by McFarland's numerous counter attacks."[17]

The next witness was the neighbor's wife, Penny Adams, who said her boss (described as Miss Black) was told by the British offices to recruit new girls with the aforementioned racial restrictions. An incensed McFarland pointed out that this was still hearsay, and no evidence had been presented. Again, the Arizona senator was ignored and Miss Black was called to testify.

Miss Black, whose real name was Charlotte Paero Oehman, had worked in secretarial placement at Boyd for four years. Oehman claimed that the British offices were replacing men who were being called into the service, and they wanted new employees, aged between seventeen and twenty, who had at least three generations removed from Germany, Ireland, or being Jewish. However, it was soon realized that there were no direct orders given from the British offices, only questions about the recruits' backgrounds. While still a questionable move worthy of investigating, the discussion remained irrelevant to the subcommittee's charge of exploring film propaganda or possible monopolistic practices.

Tobey, McFarland, and Worth Clark continued to go back and forth to get the facts of the matter, but ultimately, as McFarland again pointed out, the situation boiled down to "hearsay." Frustrated that this discussion took the focus away from the intention of the hearings, McFarland argued that "such flimsy statements as these" should not be thrown out against one of our great allies. Gaining applause once again, McFarland stated that the discussion was useless because the subcommittee had no time to quantify the integrity of these last witnesses. Tobey shot back, arguing that Willkie's lack of integrity "brought race prejudice here in a charge of race prejudice." Willkie quickly replied, "Senator Tobey, I want to suggest to you that I will loan you Darryl Zanuck and put on a real trumpet for you."[18]

Tobey ignored Willkie's comment and called up another witness, his son Charles Tobey Jr., who was a secretary for his dad. The only topic of Tobey Jr.'s testimony was that the State Employment Office in New York used symbols that signified whether the names were white and/or Christian. The witness read a transcript of a phone call he had with someone in that office, and no questions were asked. Not able to sit through the charade any longer, McFarland got up and left the room in disgust before the session was formally closed.[19]

After McFarland's exit, the largely quiet Senator Brooks weighed in on the current discussion of discrimination. "This interjection of racial prejudice is the most dangerous thing that can happen in America. I hope you can let it drop hereafter."[20] When the day's session closed, it was clear that tensions were high and, as the *Washington Post* reported, the Senate investigation ended like an "old serial" with the "plot still unsolved."[21]

The hearings were adjourned and another recess was planned, but Senator Worth Clark had at least ten more days of investigation on the books.[22] Jack Moffitt summarized the day in the *Hollywood Reporter*: "The campaign of this isolationist subcommittee seems to be breaking up into a thousand silly fragments."[23] Moffitt described the day's end as "a cascade of trivialities."[24] The *Los Angeles Daily News* called the afternoon's events "one of the silliest spectacles ever to take place in the capital."[25] An additional indication that the investigation was closing in on itself was not the question of legality that continually surfaced but the question of fiscal responsibility. Previous tradition was to approve Senate investigations with a check for expenses. However, with expenses building up for the many witnesses shipped from the west coast, Senator Lucas of Illinois (who handled the Senate's purse strings) was about to close the bank.[26]

Adding another nail in the coffin of the Senate investigation, Willkie issued a statement that cited the best-selling books that were made into feature films. Willkie also added,

> Unless the day comes in this country, as in Germany, when the public is denied the force of its own opinion and is compelled to witness praise for all that is contrary to its fundamental concepts of freedom and justice, the "other side" of Nazism will never be accepted literature and will never be produced for exhibition by American picture companies.[27]

The senators had planned a recess viewing of several accused propaganda films, including *Convoy, Flight Command, Escape, That Hamilton Woman, Man Hunt, The Great Dictator*, and *Sergeant York*. After eight days of testimonies, Senator Worth Clark told the press he was still unsure if Hollywood was guilty of warmongering, but he was confident that the American film industry was controlled by a select few.[28] The shift towards a monopoly argument was too late, as the senators had already embarrassed themselves with a monumental ignorance regarding the industrial structure of Hollywood.

The *Washington Post* began to write off the investigation because it had become abundantly clear that the real purpose of the subcommittee was to undermine aid to Great Britain.[29] The *Hollywood Reporter* publisher, Billy Wilkerson, also predicted the death of the investigation because after strong testimony, "the worm has turned," and Hays would no longer be allowed to appease his political friends in Washington by allowing such investigations to go forward.[30] For Wilkerson, it was clear after the eighth day's afternoon shenanigans that the senators' "effort to keep the publicity pot boiling" had turned against them.[31] It certainly had.

On September 25, the *Sun* reported that the FBI seized a truck full of unaddressed envelopes that featured postage from isolationist members of Congress. The FBI was actively investigating Nazi agents in the United States and the contents of the truck were being sent to the America First Committee from two Nazi-influenced organizations—the Make Europe Pay War Debts Committee and the Islands for Debts Committee.[32] Such coverage would only further hinder the reputation of the isolationist senators and create more skepticism about the true purpose of the motion-picture propaganda investigation.

Senator Nye, however, remained steadfast in his confidence that the investigation had proven their allegation that Hollywood had made a concerted effort to create motion-picture propaganda as a means to push the United States into war.[33] Still without ample proof for the assertion, Nye felt the investigation had "demonstrated that picture producers threatened exhibitors with action from Washington if they refused to show certain pictures."[34] The senator was certain that "the investigation up to now—and a continuation of the inquiry—have been amply justified."[35] Even though Nye's claims had all been eviscerated, some by his own words, the senator was still a true believer in his cause until the end. The investigation was scheduled to reconvene on October 6.

Second Recess, National Unity, and the End of the Investigation

The second recess began with the plan to resume the hearings in October after watching a series of films discussed during the investigation. However, the mounting criticism would make it difficult to predict a victory for the isolationist senators.[1] Because the films had not yet been screened, and with the growing divide within the subcommittee with Senator Tobey's antics on the last day, the *Los Angeles Times* predicted the end of the investigation was near.[2] Additional reports came in claiming Senator Worth Clark was "undecided" on the issue of motion-picture propaganda.[3] Plans were still in the works to subpoena MPPDA president Will Hays and Hollywood comedian Charlie Chaplin, though Worth Clark became hesitant to call Chaplin.

The isolationist senators were accused of "following the Nazi line" in James Morgan's column in the *Daily Boston Globe*.[4] Wheeler was hammered for maneuvering around the traditional approval process for a Senate inquiry by opening an investigation to see if there should be an investigation. The purpose was clear: move fast and grab headlines. Nye was attacked for finger-pointing at Hollywood Jews as the basis for his smear campaign. Morgan also observed that the propaganda investigation was a "strange terroristic inquisition" and followed "the familiar Hitler pattern for dividing to conquer."[5] Additional examples were given, such as Lindbergh's imperialistic rhetoric over the past year, which was echoed by Senator Worth Clark. Morgan saw the country as dangerously divided as it became clear "Americans are capable of running to extremes."[6]

Henry McLemore, the Hearst reporter who would soon become infamous for his advocacy of Japanese internment camps in the United States after the attack on Pearl Harbor, wrote a series of articles critical of the Senate investigation. McLemore took shots at Worth Clark for his inability to pronounce "denouement" and for praising his own ignorance of movies.[7] Additional essays criticized the subcommittee for their lack of focus, as McLemore observed: "Every half an hour or so someone remembers that the investigation has to do with movie propaganda."[8] McLemore also reported that his "well-informed Washington snoops" told him that the isolationist senators feel "double-crossed" by Senator McFarland, who "was supposed to be quieter than a mouse, as subdued as a husband coming home at five in the morning."[9] Of course, McFarland became the most combative and vocal member of the subcommittee, showing that he would not be muzzled by senior colleagues.

On October 1, 1941, the *Film Daily* ran another series of quotes from newspaper editors around the country.[10] Totaling thirty-two newspapers, the criticisms ranged from seeing the senators as working out of spite to accusing them of supporting Hitler. Many echoed Hollywood's free speech rights and defended the movies by way of the moviegoers who patronize the industry. While the Hollywood press was certainly vocal during the investigation, the *Film Daily* once again showed that it was not just those in Hollywood who stood against the senators. Voices from all around the country, with no monetary interest in movies, were also able to see the investigation for what it truly was.

Senator Wheeler spoke to an America First Rally at the Olympic Auditorium in Los Angeles on October 3, 1941. In front of a crowd of nine thousand, Wheeler called the Hollywood press and the studio's press managers "past masters in the arts of hocus pocus," who were "paid with stockholder's money" to attack the investigation.[11] Unwilling to back down and unafraid to speak out against Hollywood from within the city of Los Angeles, Wheeler promised that "the investigation will not be undermined" and it "will be continued until that task is done."[12] Not everyone in attendance was in support of the investigation, however. Wheeler was shouted down at one point when he charged that "the modern Benedict Arnold is the silver screen."[13] When one attendee stood up and shouted, "You're just a bunch of Nazis, Wheeler's inciting race prejudice," others around him moved in and the group began "exchanging blows."[14]

On the same evening, the Stop Film Censorship Committee held a conference at the Martin Beck Theatre in New York City. The main event was a speech from actress Mady Christians, whose words were transcribed and published in the next day's issue of the *Hollywood Reporter*. Christians's history as an actress in Germany and now in the United States was of special interest as she recalled seeing Germany in the 1920s as an "honest, democratic republic" which "produced great theatre, great writing, [and] great pictures."[15] However, by the early 1930s, all of the arts industries fell under state control. Christians argued that she still did not believe "it can happen here," but "having seen it happen, in a sane, democratically-governed country, with my own eyes, I wanted to speak up today to say—here are the storm signs."[16]

Still not backing down, Senator Worth Clark gave an address over the radio on October 4, 1941, titled "Monopoly and Propaganda in the Movie Industry," which was carried across Columbia's airwaves. Worth Clark complained that as soon as the subcommittee convened, "There was unloosed against it a veritable avalanche of vituperation and abuse" meant to "frighten it into inactivity."[17] The main thesis of Worth Clark's address was that the definition of freedom of speech needed to be amended to consider the great power of our mass media, especially motion pictures. The senator explained how earlier politicians would have to spend a great deal of time on the road speaking to smaller groups as a means to eventually reach a large number of citizens. Today, however, the competition between any single person and a motion picture was unfair. "The man who owns these machines," Worth Clark declared, "now exercises over the freedom of discussion a power which no government could ever exercise."[18]

If Worth Clark's jealousy over the power of movies had not already been made clear, this speech sealed the deal. The real problem for Worth Clark was that the studio moguls "are not public officials, they are not elected to office, they are not authorized public censors, they are not chosen by the people."[19] In other words, if a government official could not match or exceed the voice of a film, then the medium should be restricted. In addition, this control, according to the senator, was proof of a dangerous monopoly in Hollywood. The Senate investigation was necessary to draw out more information, Worth Clark argued, and it would not be stopped any time soon. The investigation was planned to continue on October 13, 1941; however, the subcommittee was still vulnerable because the Senate had not approved the travel expenses for future witnesses.[20]

Nevertheless, Worth Clark told the press that the investigation was sure to continue. "We intend to proceed with the slender resources at our command," assured Worth Clark in a prepared statement over the CBS airwaves, "regardless of criticism and regardless of threats."[21] Worth Clark was sure that the investigation would get congressional approval to continue because, in his view, allegations of a "tightly held monopoly" in Hollywood had been proven.[22] From Worth Clark's perspective, the eight companies discussed during the investigation were "closely associated," and the five majors were simply "satellites" of each other.[23] This vertically integrated system of production, exhibition, and distribution would be referred to by historians as a "mature oligopoly" and would eventually find itself a victim of additional regulations.[24]

Support for the Senate investigation was still found in expected quarters, such as the pages of Father Coughlin's *Social Justice*. One editorial called Hollywood's self-defense "good theater" and argued that the film industry "monopoly" was "rooting for war."[25] Another editorial took aim at California

Governor Culbert L. Olson for defending Hollywood as reimbursement for funding his gubernatorial campaign.[26]

On October 6, the Los Angeles Labor Council adopted a resolution to oppose the Senate inquiry. "This council believes that this investigation is a threat to organized labor because it attacks the fundamental liberties of freedom of speech and of expression, which are among the most priceless of labor's right."[27] The resolution was signed by J. W. Buzzell, the secretary of treasury of the LA Labor Council, and then sent to Senator Wheeler on October 10, 1941. Similar letters came to the senators from hundreds of unions from around the country.

With the momentum on Hollywood's side, Worth Clark continued to play damage control by releasing another statement on October 9 assuring the public of the subcommittee's future.[28] By this time the press knew that the investigation had ran its course, and the subcommittee was ready and waiting for the chairman to call the next session. McFarland refused to comment on Worth Clark's statement, likely because he knew the embarrassment of the final day's session resulted in irrevocable damage. The *Los Angeles Times* predicted the subcommittee's demise, citing that growing criticism had mounted in the press since the second recess.[29]

McFarland's recent silence did not deter the *Washington Post* from writing a puff piece titled "Dresses Like Banker, Looks Like Judge, Talks Like Cowboy."[30] The Arizona senator's performance during the propaganda investigation certainly laid an impression on the masses. "Judge Mack," as he was known in Arizona, was raised on a farm by "covered-wagon pioneers" and by age thirteen knew what it meant to "put up or shut up."[31] "It is not customary for bib-and-tucker Senators to sass their seniors," mused the *Washington Post*, "but that does not deter McFarland."[32] Back in Arizona, McFarland was known as a strong defender of blue collar workers and farmers. The isolationists in the Senate had assumed McFarland voted against aid for Britain and the Lend-Lease program, but they quickly realized how wrong they were.

Wendell Willkie continued to slam the Senate investigation in an interview with Terry Ramsaye on October 18, 1941. Willkie observed that although Hollywood was set up with a strong disadvantage in these hearings, "I am proud of the showing that our four principal witnesses have made in Washington for themselves and for their industry. They have proved it is an industry. They have proved how well founded and how well built an industry it is. They have demonstrated their own long considered and constructive approach to the work of their industry."[33] Willkie believed that the strong testimonies of Schenck, Warner, Zanuck, and Balaban had served the film community well and shed positive light on Hollywood. Contrary to Nye, Willkie was convinced that the moguls had proven there was no monopoly.

All pictures by Morris & Ewing

NICHOLAS M. SCHENCK   *HARRY M. WARNER*   *DARRYL F. ZANUCK*   *BARNEY BALABAN*

Hollywood defendants

The film industry was in the headlines again on October 20 when First Lady Eleanor Roosevelt responded to a story about German girls who were told it was "their duty to have children by German soldiers regardless of whether they were married."[34] The actual story, printed in the *New York Times*, stated, "A girl evading her duty is a traitor just like a soldier deserting his flag . . . for pure-blooded German girls there exists a war duty outside marriage and which has nothing to do with marriage."[35] Having also heard similar stories from friends returning to the United States, Roosevelt used her weekly NBC radio broadcast to denounce the mistreatment of German women and to defend Hollywood's anti-Nazi films. The First Lady argued that Hollywood had the "right to present their views through the plays they produce," just like the rights of "Senator Nye, Senator Wheeler, and Mr. Lindbergh to present their views to the world."[36] In addition, she argued, "Why is one propaganda any different from any other? Freedom of speech should be accorded to all. . . . Freedom for one side only is not true freedom."[37] Once the First Lady began attacking the propaganda investigation, it was a clear sign that the subcommittee had a short future.

Rumors circulated about Willkie receiving a top post in Hollywood for his efforts.[38] Hollywood's moguls, along with 160 of their associates, met on Halloween for a dinner at Toots Shor's iconic restaurant in New York City. Willkie told the group that Hollywood was stronger than ever after coming through the Senate investigation. "No industry which has been investigated by a Congressional committee in the last ten years has come through it with the same quality of spirit as the motion picture industry," boasted Willkie, who believed Hollywood had earned a new level of respect from Washington.[39]

Meanwhile, others came out to support the industry, such as Garson Kanin, a Hollywood writer-director who was working with the Division of Information of the Office of Emergency Management. Kanin commended Hollywood for making films about the world as it was: "Making pictures about our contemporary history" will be "a great favor toward national defense."[40] However,

Kanin encouraged filmmakers to continue to grow and engage in world events. Movies "must become an art form that will be an integral part of American life." Kanin concluded by calling the Senate investigation into motion-picture propaganda a "farce" because there were so few films in the discussion of propaganda. Kanin argued that Hollywood should have been making many more national defense films.

In November, the *American Journal of Sociology* published an article by Walter Wanger titled "The Role of Movies in Morale." Wanger argued that national morale is built by elucidating one's purpose, rousing them with confidence in the values of democracy, and by sheltering them from crisis situations. "Those who wish to build a strong and lasting morale in a democracy," argues Wanger, "must realize that their function is threefold: to clarify, to inspire, and to enter-tain."[41] What the communists and Nazis did well was give their people a sense of purpose (even if it was a corrupted one). Wanger's main concern was that "the tragic error in democratic education is the failure of democracy to explain itself to those who live and work in a democratic system. It is not surprising that indifferentism and defeatism overwhelm the citizens of a democracy."

For Wanger, the Nazis became so powerful because they were able to capitalize on "the confusion and the disenchantment of the people in the countries which had failed to give their people clarity and emotion about political principles." People need a sense of "mass spirit," which is where the movies come in, by providing "recreation for the millions." Movies could serve popular tastes but they could also play a role to educate and enlighten audiences as well. "Our political thinkers must formulate basic purposes, ideals, and concepts around which Americans can orient themselves. Movies can and will dramatize these concepts." Wanger did not mean that filmmakers should become politicians; he instead wanted filmmakers to rely on trustworthy national leaders and social scientists for engaging content. Even after the Senate Investigation into Motion Picture Propaganda, Wanger encouraged more movies to be socially relevant to maximize audience engagement.

A memo in support of Hollywood from the Washington Department of Commerce was sent for release on December 6, 1941. If the events of the next day had not occurred, this memo may have been the death knell for the sub-committee. The article stated that "the American motion picture industry has gone 'all out' in its cooperation with the national defense program."[42] Based on research from Nathan D. Golden, motion-picture consultant of the Depart-ment of Commerce, the article highlighted the Motion Picture Committee Cooperating for National Defense. Members included presidents of thirty different organizations from around the film industry. Golden noted that the film studios made these films at their expense and collect no profit. These films "have aided materially in disseminated American culture and in establishing international good-will."[43] Many of the films went beyond the recruitment films, and included subjects like "personal hygiene, types of disease, military courtesy, anti-aircraft activity, searchlights, instruction of the individual infantry soldier," in addition to "many other phases of the armed services."[44] Motion pictures, in summary, were a "recognized medium for the promotion of both civilian and military morale."[45]

Just days after the December 7 attack on Pearl Harbor, President Roosevelt called upon Hollywood to help rally the public and increase awareness of the new war effort. On December 13, the cover of the *Motion Picture Herald* featured a statement from Will Hays promising the film industry's "service and support to the President and the nation" while assuring Hollywood would continue the "flow of wholesome entertainment as an essential contribution to military and civilian morale and national spirit."[46] Martin Quigley, editor and publisher of the *Motion Picture Herald*, assured readers that films would play an essential role in reducing stress that comes along with wartime living. "If the motion picture is what we think it is and what we represent it to be," wrote Quigley, "it obviously has responsibilities beyond those which are inherent in merely a commercial operation."[47] Much was said around Hollywood in regard to morale and unity. Emphasis was put on supporting the war effort, film studios only worked daylight hours (to deter from a possible night air raid), and government censors debated releasing newsreel footage of the Pearl Harbor attack.[48]

In order to keep the public entertained and engaged, theaters kept their regular hours and some provided detailed safety instructions to patrons. *Variety* published one example from the Paramount in New York written by Robert M. Weitman, who was the theater's managing director and an alternate air warden for Times Square. Weekly drills were practiced, potential air raid situations were discussed, doctors and nurses were put on staff, screens were installed inside windows so they would not shatter inward, and each member of the staff was trained in a specific emergency response duty. In the event of a crisis, Weitman hoped to avoid having a "taut crowd" turn into "a savage pack of animals."[49] Such precautions were a logical compromise instead of engaging in an industry or city-wide blackout, though the air raid discussions did scare away many weary citizens.[50]

While the American people would see a large influx of war films, such as the recent release of *They Died with Their Boots On* and *You're in the Army Now* from Warner Bros., several comedians and singers found themselves on the list of most profitable stars of 1941, including Bob Hope, Mickey Rooney, Judy Garland, and Abbott and Costello. With the war now officially on, newsreels were also rolling. *March of Time* promised their "camera crews are mobilized and at their war stations!"[51]

In the *New York Times*, Bosley Crowther encouraged restraint from Hollywood now that the country was embroiled in war. Crowther saw movies as full of "psychological potency" that affected "millions of impressionable viewers," which meant that movies "will carry a burden of responsibility more grave and vital than any they've borne in the past."[52] Crowther was careful to note that movies should not fall into government control, and that they should still flourish in their current freedoms, but that producers needed to "carry a burden of responsibility."[53] Noting that the type of hatred that wreaked havoc on Pearl Harbor could not be provoked by a single film, Crowther encouraged "emotional balance" as a "safeguard against hysteria" by producing the same fare the industry would release during peacetime.[54]

The Senate subcommittee on Motion Picture Propaganda was finally disbanded on December 18, 1941, in a letter to Senator Wheeler from the chairman.[55] The report noted that "In view of the fact that our country is now at war and hence some matters covered by S. Res. 152 are now moot, in view of the further fact that other matters covered by S. Res. 152 and amendments thereto are quite controversial, it is believed by your subcommittee that in the interest of national unity it would not be desirable to report in detail upon them at this time."[56] With that, the final words were written: "Your subcommittee suspends operations and dissolves."[57] The subcommittee would never reconvene as Hollywood, along with the rest of the country, had become wholeheartedly dedicated to the war effort. The isolationists had no choice but to go along for the ride.

On December 28, the *New York Times* wrote a piece about Hollywood's "battle scars," stating that "in 1941, the motion picture industry experienced a variety of trials, court and otherwise, but came up smiling."[58] Besides the Senate investigation, Hollywood was forced to conform to the new consent decree and faced a new attack from the Legion of Decency who condemned George Cukor's *Two-Faced Woman* (1941), labor troubles with mobster Willie Bioff, and the income tax charges against Joseph Schenck. The *New York Times* explained that the nation's press largely backed Hollywood during the propaganda hearings, "which brought a lot of rattling skeletons out of the closet but produced no concrete evidence that the producers were motivated in making war films for other than reasons of commercial expediency."[59]

1942 and Beyond

Discussion of Hollywood's national role and influence continued to be a hot topic moving into 1942. While commentators like Crowther pushed for a balance of wartime productions, Billy Rose wrote a more reactionary perspective in a *Variety* column titled "Escapology Not the Answer; Showmen Must Sell

Aggressive Americanism to Everybody." Rose, like Crowther, saw movies as a source of morale building for the country. However, Rose argued that "Escape is a pleasant thing, but remember—you've always got to come back."[60] Similarly, Robert Joseph of the *New York Herald Tribune* called for a central "ministry of information" to "speed output of timely propaganda."[61] Calling movies "the greatest messenger of the universe," the *Hollywood Reporter*'s Wilkerson pushed specifically for movies about the treatment of American citizens in Japan after the attack on Pearl Harbor.[62]

With the war in mind as well as the industry's recent bout with the Senate subcommittee, Hollywood appointed a six-attorney team to serve as a strategic group with eyes on any potential threat to the film industry. The lawyers were Mendel Silberberg (Columbia Pictures), Maurice Benjamin (MGM), Herbert Freston (Warner Bros.), J. Robert Rubin (Loew's, Inc.), Austin C. Keough (Paramount), and Joseph Hazen (Warner Bros.). Moving forward, Hollywood would now have their legal experts serving as watchdogs to protect the industry from any future governmental harassment.

Keeping on the offensive, Harry Warner penned a piece in *Variety* on January 7, 1942, titled "Patriotism in Pictures." After having the film industry blasted for its nationalism, Warner explained that "no individual or profession has had or ever can have a corner on patriotism."[63] However, Warner saw no reason to exclude patriotism from films. He made clear that his studio has always depicted the happenings of the world, foreign and domestic. The newspapers do it, and so should the movies. "We have not sought to glorify war," Warner added, "we have only tried to honor our country and the men and women who stand ready, now as always, to defend it."[64] The mogul was determined to take another shot at the propaganda investigations by saying, "We were not the only voice, individual or collective, raised against the Nazi menace before we were actually at war. But the motion picture had to bear the brunt of much of the senatorial displeasure during the recent, rather ridiculous effort to show that, what we believe was good Americanism, was only 'propaganda' in disguise."[65]

The following month Willkie addressed the 1942 Academy Awards audience at the Biltmore Hotel. Now standing tall as a Hollywood messiah, Willkie was introduced by Walter Wanger. "When we were attacked and held to public trial by a group who tried to make American patriotism appear to be propaganda, and our call for American preparedness to be war-mongering, we called upon this man for leadership," gloated Wanger. "He tore away false issue as he might strip the shucks form his Indiana corn."[66] Willkie was welcomed as a hero and greeted by raucous applause from the audience.

Willkie spoke of the Senate subcommittee that attempted to "throttle this industry and suppress its freedom."[67] If the isolationists won and censured Hollywood, argued Willkie, "we should have lost not only something of great public value but we would have been establishing the very kind of Governmental suppression and autocracy which we are now opposing throughout the world."[68] Willkie took the gung-ho attitude towards the war, dissing a defense approach and instead pushing for our soldiers to go roaming for the enemy.

In May, Hollywood's war drive machinery was in full force. Many stars who did not go into active duty joined the USO effort. A Hollywood Victory Caravan was created that featured a long list of notable celebrities such as Dick Powell, Fred Astaire, Paul Henreid, Betty Hutton, Kay Kyser, Greer Garson, Judy Garland, Mickey Rooney, Harpo Marx, James Cagney, and Lucille Ball. In addition, Joseph Schenk chaired the Hollywood chapter of the Army and Navy Relief campaign. Film premieres began to double as war bond drives and Hollywood promised to raise at least $300,000 per week.[69]

By the fall of 1942, blatant propaganda was officially deemed ineffective even as some continued to call for a celluloid offensive on the Axis. *Variety* published a report in October that revealed, "Consensus seems to be that the hate motive, even when applied to Nazi and Jap barbarism, soon grows thin when continually projected on theater screens."[70] Five days later the Bureau of Motion Pictures (BMP), the film wing of the Office of War Information, released a dossier titled "Hollywood's War Effort; Here is Overall Picture." Published in *Variety* on October 19, the BMP discouraged propaganda films. The production manual stated:

> Every picture touching upon the war must be regarded purposefully and thoughtfully for what it can to do help win the war. It means that there should be fewer and better and more carefully selected war pictures—fewer blood-and-thunder combat thrillers and more serious works, which will help the public understanding of the war, its causes, the sacrifice and hard work it demands.[71]

The BMP did not want to see an influx of the wrong kind of war films and noted the importance of escapist pictures during times of heightened anxiety. Hollywood, therefore, should involve itself with the problems of the future. For example, movies should address questions such as why is the world at war, what can bring peace, who is our enemy and why? The BMP policy was that every film would help, in one way or another, the Allies win the war. Real-world drama should be depicted truthfully, honestly, and thoughtfully so that the narrative would age well as the war continued.

Those involved with the Senate investigation would continue to do their jobs and live their lives. Unlike other events in political history, this one would not have many ripple effects after December 7, 1941. Jimmie Fidler continued as a prominent radio personality and by 1950, his radio show reached forty million listeners across 486 different stations. Though he would never become Hollywood's favorite commentator, Fidler would continue his radio presence until retirement in 1983.

After the attack on Pearl Harbor, John T. Flynn urged the America First Committee to dissolve so that everyone could focus on the war effort. Becoming increasingly skeptical about the United States government, Flynn became a prominent supporter of Pearl Harbor conspiracy theories and penned a pamphlet titled *The Truth about Pearl Harbor* (1944), in which Flynn argued that the US government not only knew about the attack but actively worked to provoke it. Flynn's ideas became known as the Pearl Harbor advance-knowledge conspiracy theory. As Flynn's politics became more conspiratorial, he became an avid supporter of Joseph McCarthy in the 1950s.

The United States senators would see a mixed bag of career success. After serving in the Senate since 1938, D. Worth Clark was defeated in 1944 and would unsuccessfully run again in 1950. Ironically, Clark would eventually move to southern California (home of the Studios he once maligned) to invest in radio stations and banks. Gerald P. Nye carried his strong isolationism dating back to World War I all the way through World War II, but his career as a senator would end in 1944. He would eventually be appointed to the Federal Housing Administration in 1960 and served on the professional staff for the US Senate Committee on Aging in 1963. When Nye retired, a grand party was held and high-profile attendees included Robert and Ted Kennedy.

During World War II, Charles Tobey took on a more internationalist approach to politics. As an early critic of Joseph McCarthy, Tobey was labeled as weak on communism. The senator's career highlight would come during the 1951 Kefauver hearings on organized crime. Tobey went up against mobster Frank Costello in New York, pressing the crime boss on his responsibly as an American citizen. When Tobey pressured Costello to define his contribution as United States citizen, the mobster paused and famously quipped, "[I] paid my tax."[72]

Bennet Champ Clark served in the United States Senate from 1933 and lost his re-election bid in 1944. That same year, Champ Clark grabbed headlines after calling for Japanese emperor Hirohito to be hanged. Champ Clark was also the first senator to propose the GI Bill to Congress. In 1945, Clark was nominated by President Harry Truman to serve as a federal judge on the United States Court of Appeals for the DC Circuit.

Ernest McFarland is easily the most decorated of the senators who served on the subcommittee, quickly gaining a reputation as a strong liberal with a bipartisan ability to work with conservatives.[73] McFarland served on the US Senate from 1941 to 1953, became minority leader for the 82nd Congress, and was also one of the first supporters of the GI Bill. After leaving the Senate,

McFarland served as the governor of Arizona from 1955 to 1959, before sitting on the Arizona supreme court as chief justice in 1968. Finally leaving politics, McFarland continued to work in law.

Hollywood would undoubtedly continue to flourish. While Nicholas Schenck remained a strong movie mogul through the 1950s, he was a staunch opponent of the film industry investing in television. Going against the grain, Scheck lacked the foresight other moguls had to see a partnership with television as a new means of survival during changing times. After Louis B. Mayer began sparring with the new vice president of production, Dore Schary, Scheck fired Mayer and promoted Schary. Schary would make a name for himself by producing the message pictures Mayer protested against. Schenck would be replaced as studio president in 1955 and would remain as chairman of the board for less than a year.

Always a strong spokesman for the film industry, Harry Warner became a strong supporter of the Allies in World War II by using his studio to sell over $15 million in war bonds. The United States government would eventually name one of their Liberty Ships after the Warner brothers' father, Benjamin. Warner continued to enjoy studio success after the war, but not without the widely known disputes with his brother Jack. In 1956, Harry finally gave in to selling the studio only to learn that Jack took a back-door deal to stay on and replace Harry as president. To those close to him, Harry Warner was never the same after his brother's betrayal.

After replacing Adolph Zukor, Barney Balaban served as president of Paramount Pictures from 1936 until 1964. When the advent of television became a serious threat to the future of film production, Balaban negotiated a historic $50 million deal by selling the television rights of Paramount's pre-1948 film catalogue. Living a rather quiet life compared to other moguls, Balaban sat as vice chairman of the American Heritage Foundation and supported bond drives for Israel. Balaban is uncle to actor Bob Balaban, who came to fame during the New Hollywood years.

Howard Dietz was made head of MGM publicity, a position he kept until 1957. During World War II, Dietz worked with the US Treasury Department to sell war bonds in addition to shepherding stage performances for the Coast Guard. Dietz was also known as a talented songwriter and was eventually inducted into the Songwriters Hall of Fame. Dietz is most known as being cited as the creator of MGM's iconic Leo the Lion as well as the studio's mantra, Ars Gratia Artis (art for art's sake).

Darryl Zanuck served with the Army Signal Corps in World War II but returned to his duties as studio head of Twentieth Century Fox in 1943. During his tenure, Zanuck produced award-winning films such as *All About Eve*

(1950). Zanuck was an early advocate of widescreen technology, which shined in the studio's epic films. By 1956, Zanuck left the studio to produce independent films in Europe. Zanuck returned to serve as president of Twentieth Century Fox after Spyros Skouras nearly sunk the studio by allowing production costs to run wild, most notoriously with *Cleopatra* (1963) and star Elizabeth Taylor's inflated salary. Zanuck ran Fox until the 1970s.

After standing in defense of Hollywood during the Senate investigation, Wendell Willkie served as Twentieth Century Fox chairman of the board and penned a book titled *One World* (1943) that detailed his seven-week tour around the globe. Willkie's book inspired the World Federalist Movement, in which high profile supporters included Albert Einstein and Mahatma Gandhi. A staunch supporter of civil rights, Willkie worked with Walter White of the NAACP to push for better treatment of African Americans in movies (who were often portrayed as servants). When Willkie died in 1944, the NAACP named their headquarters after him.

Overshadowed by History

History has a way of overshadowing significant events with other meaningful news. It is the work of historians and scholars to shed light on the relevant past so that we can be reminded of where we came from and what was once important, and most importantly, so that we can see how we have changed (or not) over time. When a historical event becomes largely forgotten, it does not mean that the episode was inconsequential or unimportant in its day.

On November 22, 1963, two legendary writers passed. C. S. Lewis, the influential Christian apologist, and Aldous Huxley, the prophetic author of *Brave New World*, both died on the same day that United States President John F. Kennedy was assassinated. Lewis and Huxley had a much longer influence than Kennedy by this point, but that was not enough to overshadow the murder of the much-beloved leader of the free world. News of Lewis's death was published two days later on page eighteen of the *New York Times*.[1] Huxley's obituary did make the front page the day after he died; however, it was placed in the bottom left corner under a massive headline related to Kennedy's death.[2] All three stories would continue to travel around the world at their own pace. Each gathered its own historical significance as scholars of political history, theology, and literature wrote about these majors figures long after they passed.

For the 1941 Senate Investigation into Motion Picture War Propaganda, it is not as obvious why this part of history has not yet been given full attention. Certainly, there were world events looming that kept people distracted from the news of the Hollywood Senate investigation. Press coverage of the investigation both inside and outside of the film industry was constant in the fall of 1941, so it is clear that the public was informed. Of course, all coverage competed with the daily reports from Hitler's advances in Europe. The United States was also still digging out of the Great Depression, coupled with the growing concern about foreign invasion. While the public was undoubtedly cognizant of the Senate investigation, the December 7 attack on Pearl Harbor quickly refocused the country into a communal drive to win the war. Wedged between the Great Depression and the United States' entrance into World War II, the months leading up to the attack on Pearl Harbor were lost in the war's shadow. The attack on Pearl Harbor distracted the country (and the world) for enough years that when the war was over, everyone had moved on to new concerns. Suburbanization, baby booming, and new commercialization drove the postwar culture. The senators involved with Resolution 152 no longer had a connection to Hollywood criticism, and by the time they died or retired, their legacies were defined by other events. The film moguls moved on as well, making war films, expanding their studios, and investing in television, and by the time they were gone, their legacies were much larger than that single season in late 1941. Because the United States was engaged in a war less than six months after the hearings began, the immediate ripple effects were minimal. However, the historical implications can teach us how the events within and surrounding investigation outed and battled the seemingly accepted anti-Semitic prejudice in the United States.

The 1941 Senate hearings differed from the 1947 and 1952 House Un-American Activities (HUAC) hearings in Hollywood that would not only come to define many prominent figures in the industry but would be talked about for generations. The HUAC hearings have been immortalized in a way that the 1941 Senate Investigation never have. Hollywood moguls Jack Warner, Walt Disney, and Louis B. Mayer would be remembered (and criticized) for testifying as friendly witnesses in 1947. The *Hollywood Reporter*'s Wilkerson and Moffitt, who led the industry charge against the Senate inquiry, would provide full support to HUAC less than twenty years later. These blacklist years created a shadow that loomed over the industry for generations. Protests would be held as late as 1999, when Elia Kazan, who testified as a friendly witness in front of HUAC in 1952, was to be given a lifetime achievement award by the Motion Picture Academy.

While the 1941 Senate investigation had its share of fireworks, quips, arguments, and press coverage, it simply did not have the staying power of the anticommunist hearings of the 1940s and 1950s. Perhaps if Billy Wilkerson and Charlie Chaplin testified in 1941 as planned, they might have been enough star power to catapult the investigation into the history books sooner. Bringing in industry censor and anti-Semite Joseph Breen could have induced additional sparring that would have made the headlines sing. Instead, the Senate inquiry's focus on studio bosses gave it a different flavor. The 1947 HUAC hearings brought moguls, writers, stars, and critics to round out a wide range of Hollywood voices.

It is important to note the significance of the 1941 Senate Investigation's occurring before the attack on Pearl Harbor. Once a world war landed on US soil, it redirected tensions and prejudice towards the Axis powers of Japan, Germany, and Italy. There was not much use for going after anyone who encouraged defense against fascism after the United States found itself amidst another war. After Japan attacked the United States, any anti-Jewish fervor was overshadowed by hostility towards Japanese Americans, who were feared traitors and thrown into internment camps. The increased fear of the enemy in our midst continued and would peak after the war during the Red Scare. The 1941 Senate Investigation into Hollywood simply did not provoke the widespread "fear thy neighbor" attitudes that would become commonplace in postwar culture.

The 1947 HUAC investigation was able to accomplish what the isolationist senators could not quite nail down, which was to paint Hollywood as a bunch of turncoats. The changing face of World War II also led to a series of films that would not age well. Three prominent examples are *Mission to Moscow* (Warner Bros., 1943), *The North Star* (RKO, 1943), and *Song of Russia* (MGM, 1944). As film historian Thomas Doherty observes, these films "were ardently pro-Soviet, all were shamelessly dishonest in their depiction of the Communist system, and all seemed like a good idea at the time."[3] As Russia moved back into the enemy category, these films would be considered high-profile examples of Red propaganda. Martin Dies would retire from HUAC in 1944, and the subcommittee would go through a couple of chairmen before landing J. Parnell Thomas. It was Thomas's doing that turned a new Hollywood investigation into another national spectacle in 1947.

The HUAC trials on Hollywood remain a hot topic for historians and critics, so much so that the publishers of the *Hollywood Reporter* made an event out of apologizing for their publication's history of supporting HUAC and, ultimately, the blacklist.[4] Books continue to be written about the blacklist years, each providing differing views of what happened. The 1941 Senate investigation did not give historians much to debate—the senators bought into old-world Jewish stereotypes and sought to take away power that immigrant moguls gained by solidifying a new medium of entertainment. The press hung the xenophobic senators out to dry, and Hollywood stood in strong defense of its production trends and exhibition practices. Resolution 152 did not make or break careers like HUAC did; it only further solidified Hollywood as the communication powerhouse it already was.

However, what remains important is *why* the Senate investigation came to be and *what* specifically was debated in session, which is what I have hoped to detail in this book. Compared to the HUAC hearings, the moguls seemed to be on opposing sides of history. Throughout the 1941 Senate investigation, the moguls were arguing on behalf of their studios and defending free speech. By the time HUAC came to town in 1947, something changed, and the moguls began to throw their talent under the bus to avoid having studios appear to be traitor sanctuaries. In 1941, studio bosses stood by their movies and their messages while remaining unafraid to push back against the America First movement. Conversely, by 1947 studio bosses caved to the political winds of anticommunism by going along with a blacklist following the infamous Waldorf Statement.

But why has it taken so long for this event to finally be discussed at length? The historian R. G. Collingwood once described the difference between history and memory in the following terms. "Memory is subjective and immediate, [while] history [is] objective and mediate."[5] In other words, we remember what is most relevant in our own proximity. The same can be said for historians. There is always a reason for a book or article to be published; something makes it timely or useful to the zeitgeist. Since 1941, many United States politicians have singled out specific groups as threats to posterity. A great deal of scholarship has been dedicated to the HUAC hearings in 1947 and beyond, but relatively little has been directed at the 1941 Senate Investigation. The 1941 and 1947 events are indirectly connected. Of course, the 1941 investigation came from the Senate, and the 1947 trials originated from the House of Representatives—a common misconception when people incorrectly connect Joseph McCarthy (a Wisconsin senator) to the House committee. Questions of genesis aside, analogous tactics were used to smear Hollywood as an industry of influence in both cases.

We continue to see similar political prejudice in the twenty-first century as history repeats itself. Scores of young people have large gaps in their historical knowledge, for various reasons not all a fault of their own, which has historians worried. One study released in 2018 shows that four out of ten millennials do not understand the seriousness of the Holocaust.[6] Another 2018 study shows that 62 percent of Americans ages 18–34 are "drawn to socialism," and critics are concerned that the youth either do not know or care about socialism's murderous past.[7] History majors are in decline on college campuses, partially because of dwindling funding for history departments across the United States.[8] Lastly, and most terrifying, acts of anti-Semitism have been increasing at an alarming rate.[9]

When prejudice surges, there is often a correlation with a national movement that provides a platform for such attitudes. The isolationist senators and the myriad movements across the country leading up to 1941 provided a stage for bigotry and xenophobia. When anti-Semitic rhetoric went across the radio waves with fanatical white nationalist groups hanging onto every word, United States senators echoed the popular fearmongering by questioning the intentions of foreign-born Americans. The Hollywood episode allowed a powerful industry to stand eye to eye with the United States government to push back against a specific brand of streamlined and institutionalized prejudice. The Senate Investigation into Motion Picture War Propaganda is a reminder of the normalized prewar hatred that increased in intensity throughout the 1930s.

Much of our historical conversation about hate and prejudice are about the major boiling points such as the Civil War, both world wars, the Red Scare and the Cold War, the civil rights and Vietnam war era, the rise of gun violence, and so on. While these events certainly represent tension points worthy of continued study, it is also important to look at events that kept hatred simmering by justifying its place on the national stage. The America First movement, along with the German nationalist organizations, worked to standardize prejudice as a means of swaying the entire country against undesired groups—namely, the Jews. Such groups often play the long game by maintaining cultural fault lines, hoping they will irreversibly rupture during times of heightened conflict. As Sarah Churchwell has written in *Behold America: The Entangled History of America First and the American Dream*, this tradition of "America firsting" has continued while many are ignorant of its history.[10] Words like "isolationist" fell out of favor after World War II, but "America First" has continued despite its history of being co-opted by extremists. When younger generations inquire about the forces behind peaking cultural and racial tensions, one can often look into the past to explain the present.

The world will always be battling ignorance and bigotry, but never before have we had the immense communication machinery that every person has at their fingertips in the twenty-first century. Just like the Hollywood moguls pushed to depict reality in the late 1930s and early 1940s, we should also be driven to promote the truth and not the trendy political talking points of the day. Remember, anti-Semitism was not quite the social taboo in 1941 that it is in the twenty-first century—even though anti-Jewish hate crimes are increasingly regular.[11] Isolationists like Gerald Nye and Charles Lindbergh knew they could get away with such views (and they did for quite some time). If not for the platform of the motion picture, and with the growing pro-Nazi movements, the United States would have been subjected to an overwhelming amount of isolationist and nationalist sentiment on the radio and in the press. Hollywood and its defenders served as a stopgap between isolationists and interventionists during this time, when many watched Europe while thinking, "It can happen here."

The United States has a long history before and after 1941 of movies and popular culture being blamed for the social ills of the day. In the 1920s and 1930s, moral crusaders crashed down onto movies as the reason for teenage delinquency. HUAC would call attention to war films that had not aged well, such as Warner Bros.' *Mission to Moscow* (1943). The 1950s saw a social uproar over comic books seducing the innocent, in the 1960s rock n' roll was the devil's music, the 1980s had parents melting down over rap music, and the 1990s saw violent video games as the new architect of juvenile delinquency. In the twenty-first century, comedians and provocateurs are losing their jobs for being comedians and provocateurs. Whenever an aspect of popular culture gains social and political significance, particularly when it ruffles feathers, it runs the risk of pushback and censorship.

The 1941 Senate Investigation into Motion Picture Propaganda did not make, break, or define anyone. However, it served as a crowning point in United States history where a hotly debated topic over the European war centered on blaming movies for any interventionist attitude. For the isolationist senators, the goal was to defeat interventionism. For Hollywood, who was certainly supportive of Great Britain but not necessarily pro-war, the investigation was about defending the industry's freedom to make any film fit for public entertainment and engagement.

History has shown that as long as popular culture continues to flourish, the threats of politicians and self-appointed moral crusaders will continue. However, any argument to do away with the next feared form of popular culture will likely be as empty as those brought forth by the isolationist senators in 1941.

Notes

Introduction

1. Lippmann, Walter, *Public Opinion*, Pantianos Classics, 13.

2. Bernays, Edward, *Propaganda* (Brooklyn: IG Publishing, 2005 [reprint]), 60–61.

3. Bernays, 37.

4. Bernstein, Arnie, *Swastika Nation: Fritz Kuhn and the Rise and Fall of the German-American Bund* (New York: St. Martin's, 2013), 49.

5. Brinkley, Alan, *Voices of Protest: Huey Long, Father Coughlin, and the Great Depression* (New York: Vintage Books, 1983), 83.

6. Brinkley, *Voices of Protest*.

7. "Gov. Olson Pays Off," *Social Justice*, October 6, 1941.

8. Carr, Steven, *Hollywood & Anti-Semitism: A Cultural History up to World War II* (Cambridge: Cambridge University Press, 2001), 180.

9. Carr, *Hollywood & Anti-Semitism*.

10. "Edelstein Dies after Clash with Rankin in House over Anti-Jewish Speech," *Jewish Telegraphic Agency*, June 4, 1941.

11. Lindbergh, Charles, Des Moines Speech, September 11, 1941, https://rense.com/general32/speechw.htm

12. Lindbergh, Charles, Des Moines Speech, September 11, 1941.

13. "Sgt. York Raps 'York' Smear," *Daily Variety*, September 15, 1941, 1, 7.

14. The haunting night-for-night newsreel shots of the book burnings in Berlin on May 10, 1933, had already become motion picture metonymy for the cultural conflagrations in Nazi Germany.

15. "Sgt. York Raps 'York' Smear," *Daily Variety*, September 15, 1941, 1, 7.

16. *Variety* reported that several war objectors withdrew their objection and registered for selective service after watching *Sergeant York*. "Sgt. York Film's Influence On War Objectors," *Variety*, December 24, 1941, Media History Digital Library, http://www.archive.org/stream/variety144-1941-12#page/n239/mode/2up/search/Pearl+Harbor

17. Welky, David, *The Moguls and the Dictators: Hollywood and the Coming of World War II* (Baltimore: The Johns Hopkins University Press, 2008), 288.

18. Welky, David, *The Moguls and the Dictators*.

19. S. Res. 152, National Archives, Washington, DC, RG 46, box 2 of 2.

20. Stuart, Gary L., *Call Him Mac: Ernest W. McFarland, The Arizona Years* (Tuscan: Sentinel Peak, 2018).

21. Carr, Steven, *Hollywood & Anti-Semitism: A Cultural History Up to World War II* (New York: Cambridge University Press, 2001), 175.

Chapter One

1. Ross, Steven, *Hitler and Los Angeles: How Jews Foiled Nazi Plots Against Hollywood and America* (New York: Bloomsbury, 2018), 121.

2. Ross, 133.

3. Rosenzweig, Laura B. *Hollywood's Spies: The Undercover Surveillance of Nazis in Los Angeles* (New York: New York University Press, 2017), 19.

4. Rosenzweig, 20–23.

5. Ross, 7.

6. Rosenzweig, 26.

7. Ross, 43.

8. Ross, 67; Rosenzweig, 51–55.

9. Doherty, Thomas, *Hollywood and Hitler 1933–1939* (New York: Columbia University Press, 2013), 105.

10. Doherty, 100.

11. Doherty, 107.

12. Sinclair, Upton, "The Movies and Political Propaganda," *The Movies on Trial: The Views and Opinions of Outstanding Personalities Anent Screen Entertainment Past and Present* (New York: The Macmillan Company, 1936), 195.

13. Ross, Steven J. *Hollywood Left and Right: How Movie Stars Shaped American Politics* (New York: Oxford University Press, 2011), 61.

14. Sinclair, Upton, *Upton Sinclair Presents William Fox* (Los Angeles: published by the author, 19330; see also Kreeft, Vanda, *The Man Who Made the Movies: The Meteoric Rise and Tragic Fall of William Fox* (New York: Harper, 2017).

15. Goldstein, Sidney E, "The Motion Picture and Social Control," *The Movies on Trial: The Views and Opinions of Outstanding Personalities Anent Screen Entertainment Past and Present* (New York: The Macmillan Company, 1936), 230.

16. Maltby, Richard, "The Production Code and the Hays Office," *Grand Design: Hollywood as a Modern Business Enterprise*, ed. Tino Balio (Berkeley and Los Angeles: University of California Press, 1995), 56.

17. Giovacchini, Saverio, *Hollywood Modernism: Film and Politics in the Age of the New Deal* (Philadelphia: Temple University Press, 2001), 86.

18. Giovacchini, 87.

19. Allen, Frederick Lewis, *Since Yesterday: The 1930s in America* (New York: Harper & Row, 1939), 321.

20. Allen, 322.

21. Brinkley, Alan. *Voices of Protest: Huey Long, Father Coughlin, & The Great Depression* (New York: Vintage Books, 1983), 269.

22. Yogerst, 75.

23. Yogerst, 136; Welky, David, *The Moguls and the Dictators: Hollywood and the Coming of World War II* (Baltimore: The Johns Hopkins University Press, 2008), 93

24. Weinstein, Allen, and Alexander Vassiliev, *The Haunted Wood: Soviet Espionage in America—the Stalin Era* (New York: Random House, 1999), 143.

25. Ogden, August Raymond, *The Dies Committee: A Study of the Special House Committee for the Investigation of Un-American Activities, 1938–1944* (Washington: The Catholic University of America Press, 1945), 49.

26. "Washington's Red-Baiting Probes Regarded as a One-Ring Circus," *Variety*, August 24, 1938, 2

27. Roos, Joseph, Memo to the US Senate regarding the Attack on Motion Pictures, 1940, 16. CRC files, folder 17–30.

28. "Stars' Names and Donations Cited as Evidence That Hollywood Is Aiding Radicals in 'Boring' from Within," *Motion Picture Herald*, August 27, 1938, 29.

29. "Stars' Names and Donations Cited as Evidence That Hollywood Is Aiding Radicals in 'Boring' from Within," 30.

30. Ross, 106.

31. Article from August 16, 1938 was reprinted in Roos, 17.

32. Article from August 17, 1938 was reprinted in Roos, 19.

33. "Washington's Red-Baiting Probes Regarded as a One-Ring Circus," *Variety*, August 24, 1938, 2.

34. Ogden, August Raymond, *The Dies Committee: A Study of the Special House Committee for the Investigation of Un-American Activities, 1938–1944* (Washington: The Catholic University of America Press, 1945), 71.

35. "Anti-Nazi League Derides 'Red' Attack on Industry," *BoxOffice*, August 27, 1938, 34.

36. "Stars Called 'Reds' in Testimony to Dies Committee," *Motion Picture Herald*, August 27, 1938, 30.

37. "Anti-Nazi League Derides 'Red' Attack on Industry," *BoxOffice*, August 27, 1938, 34.

38. The film was nominated for writing and score.

39. Lorence, James L., "The 'Foreign Policy of Hollywood': Interventionist Sentiment in the American Film, 1938–1941"; *Hollywood as Mirror: Changing Views of "Outsiders" and "Enemies" in American Movies*, ed. Robert Brent Toplin (Westport: Greenwood Press, 1993), 98; Koppes, Clayton R. and Gregory D. Black, *Hollywood Goes to War: How Politics, Profits and Propaganda Shaped World War II Movies* (Berkeley and Los Angeles: University of California Press, 1987), 40–44.

40. Party invite from Harry Warner dated July 16, 1938 for a party on July 25, Community Relations Committee Collection, Warner Brothers Pictures Inc., 1938–1939, folder 17–47.

41. Letter from Harry Warner to Leon Lewis dated July 18, 1938. Community Relations Committee Collection, Warner Brothers Pictures Inc., 1938–1939, folder 17–47.

42. July 26 memorandum from Harry Warner's party on July 25, 1938, Community Relations Committee Collection, Warner Brothers Pictures Inc., 1938–1939, folder 17–47.

43. Lazaron, Morris, *Common Ground: A Plea for Intelligent Nationalism* (New York: Liveright Publishing Corporation, 1938), 51.

44. Lazaron, 319.

45. Lazaron, 324.

46. Roos, 22.

47. "JEWS ARE ORDERED TO LEAVE MUNICH," *New York Times*, November 11, 1938.

48. Doherty, 306.

49. Cooper, Graham, "Olympia in America, 1938: Leni Riefenstahl, Hollywood, and the Kristallnacht," *Historical Journal of Film, Radio, and Television*, October 1993.

50. Cooper, Graham, "Olympia in America, 1938: Leni Riefenstahl, Hollywood, and the Kristallnacht."

51. Doherty, 307.

52. Doherty, 307.

53. Lazaron, 51.

54. Kennedy, David M., *Freedom from Fear: The American People in Depression and War, 1929–1945* (New York: Oxford University Press, 1999), 410.

55. Letter from Carl Laemmle to Leon Lewis dated December 28, 1938, Community Relations Committee collection 2, folder 17–29.

56. Letter from Carl Laemmle to Lizzie P. Cohn dated December 5, 1938, Community Relations Committee collection 2, folder 17–30.

57. Letter from Carl Laemmle to Lizzie P. Cohn dated December 5, 1938, Community Relations Committee collection 2, folder 17–30.

58. Letter from Carl Laemmle to Lizzie P. Cohn dated December 5, 1938, Community Relations Committee collection 2, folder 17–30.

Chapter Two

1. Rosten, Leo, *Hollywood: The Movie Colony, the Movie Makers* (New York: Harcourt, Brace, and Company, 1941), 4.

2. Rosten, 67–68.

3. Giovacchini, Saverio, *Hollywood Modernism: Film and Politics in the Age of the New Deal* (Philadelphia: Temple University Press, 2001), 100.

4. Haynes, John Holmes, "The Movies and the Community," *The Movies on Trial: The Views and Opinions of Outstanding Personalities Anent Screen Entertainment Past and Present* (New York: The Macmillan Company, 1936), 197.

5. Bennett, Todd, "The Celluloid War: State and Studio in Anglo-American Propaganda Film-Making, 1939–1941," *International History Review*, Vol. 24, No. 1, March 2002, 64.

6. Nugent, Frank S, "The Warners Make Faces at Hitler in 'Confessions of a Nazi Spy'— 'Cisco Kid Returns' to Roxy," *New York Times*. April 29, 1939.

7. Nugent, Frank S, "The Warners Make Faces at Hitler in 'Confessions of a Nazi Spy'— 'Cisco Kid Returns' to Roxy."

8. Reprinted in Roos, 23.

9. Roos, 29. Capitalization in original document.

10. Roos, 29.

11. Roos, 30. Capitalization in original document.

12. Roos, 31. Emphasis mine.

13. Article reprinted in Roos, 32.

14. Roos, 34.

15. Roos, 35. The German Vice Consul was Herman Geistreich.

16. "War News Tangle," *Motion Picture Herald*, November 18, 1939, 8.

17. "War News Tangle."

18. Bennett, Todd, "The Celluloid War: State and Studio in Anglo-American Propaganda Film-Making, 1939–1941," *The International History Review*, Vol. 24, No. 1, March 2002, 64.

19. Bennett, Todd, "The Celluloid War: State and Studio in Anglo-American Propaganda Film-Making, 1939–1941."

20. "Art & Democracy." *Motion Picture Herald*. November 18, 1939, 8.

21. "Art & Democracy."

22. DeMille, William C. *Hollywood Saga* (New York: E.P. Dutton & Company, Inc., 1939), 311.

23. DeMille, 312.

24. DeMille, 312.

25. Thorp, a professor of American studies, also noted that the number of tickets sold was different from the total viewers, since many were repeat attendees. More specifically, movies likely drew from about twenty-five percent of the population. Thorp, Margaret, *America at the Movies* (New Haven: Yale University Press, 1939).

26. "80,000,000 Myth," *Variety*, September 17, 1941, 4.

27. "80,000,000 Myth," 163.

28. "80,000,000 Myth," 172.

29. "80,000,000 Myth," 174.

30. "Franklin Roosevelt's Neutrality Message, 1939," *America Between the Wars, 1919–1941* (Malden: Wiley-Blackwell, 2012), 213.

31. "Franklin Roosevelt's Neutrality Message, 1939."

32. See Doherty, Thomas, *Hollywood and Hitler 1933–1939* (New York: Columbia University Press, 2013); Ross, Steven, *Hitler in Los Angeles: How Jews Foiled Nazi Plots Against Hollywood and America* (New York: Bloomsbury, 2017); Yogerst, Chris, *From the Headlines to Hollywood: The Birth and Boom of Warner Bros* (Lanham: Rowman & Littlefield, 2016).

33. Quotes from Wanger's Liberty article titled "The Stars Call Them Leeches," September 9, 1939. Walter Wanger papers. Wanger/Fidler debate files. Wisconsin Center for Film and Theater Research.

34. Jimmie Fidler answers Wanger on the air, September 9, 1939. Walter Wanger papers, Wanger/Fidler file, Wisconsin Center for Film and Theater Research.

35. In the Superior Court of the State of California in and for the County of Los Angeles—Water Wanger Productions, Incorporated vs. James Fidler, also known as Jimmie Fidler. Walter Wanger papers, Wanger/Fidler file, Wisconsin Center for Film and Theater Research.

36. Silver to Wanger and Harry Kosiner, December 30, 1939. Walter Wanger papers, Wanger/Fidler file, Wisconsin Center for Film and Theater Research.

37. Hays, Will, "The Motion Picture in a Changing World, 1940," *America Between the Wars, 1919–1941* (Malden: Wiley-Blackwell, 2012), 229.

38. Hays, Will, "The Motion Picture in a Changing World, 1940," 230.

39. Selden, Walter, "Movies and Propaganda," *The Forum*, March 23, 1940, Motion Picture Association of America general correspondence files, microfilm roll 6, Margaret Herrick Library.

40. RKO contracts, #3554, Margaret Herrick Library.

41. Warner, Harry, "United We Survive, Divided We Fall!" Community Relations Committee Files, Series 2, folder 17–48.

42. Warner, 4.

43. Warner, 11.

44. Warner, 11–12.

45. Wekly, *Moguls and the Dictators*, 205.

46. Wekly, 206.

47. Crowther, Bosley, "THE SCREEN: 'The Mortal Storm,' a Deeply Tragic Anti-Nazi Film, at the Capitol—'Hot Steel' at the Rialto," *New York Times*, June 21, 1940.

48. Hollywood Museum Collection, Frank Borzage scrapbook, Margaret Herrick Library.

49. Hollywood Museum Collection, Frank Borzage scrapbook, Margaret Herrick Library.

50. Hollywood Museum Collection, Frank Borzage scrapbook, Margaret Herrick Library.

51. Hollywood Museum Collection, Frank Borzage scrapbook, Margaret Herrick Library.

52. "Salem Showman Sells 'Storm' Successfully," *Showman's Trade Review*, November 30, 1940, 9.

53. "Salem Showman Sells 'Storm' Successfully."

54. Welky, *Moguls and Dictators*, 214.

55. Crowther, Bosley, "THE SCREEN IN REVIEW; 'Brother Orchid' Finds Edward G. Robinson in an Excellent Farce at the Strand—'Four Sons' Opens at the Roxy—Three New Foreign Films Here," *New York Times*, June 8, 1940.

56. Clarence Erickson to Walter Wanger, January 25 1941. Reprinted in Lorence, 85.

57. Morteline, Dennis, "Personal History of a Foreign Correspondent," *Hollywood*, August, 1941, 35–36.

58. Crowther, Bosley, "THE SCREEN; At the Rivoli," *New York Times*, August 28, 1940.

59. "Foreign Correspondent (UA-Wanger) International Adventure," *Motion Picture Herald*, August 31, 1940, 52.

60. Welky, 226.

61. "Former Professor to Work with Producers on Defense Plan Activities," *Film Daily*, October 28, 1940, 1 and 4.

62. Ross, 135.

63. Ross, 136.

64. Roos has been credited with taking Lewis's operation to the next level. Ross, 139.

65. Ogden, August Raymond, *The Dies Committee: A Study of the Special House Investigation of Un-American Activities, 1938–1944* (Washington DC: The Catholic University of America Press, 1945), 211–213.

66. "An Oscar for Dies," *Variety*, February 21, 1940, 3.

67. "Dies' Articles on Film 'Reds' Are Attacked," *Motion Picture Herald*, February 17, 1940, 25.

68. "Motion Picture Industry Due for Probe by Dies," *Film Daily*, February 16, 1940, 6.

69. "Screen Writers Guild Asks Removal of Dies," *Film Daily*, March 6, 1940, 10.

70. Roos, 1.

71. Roos, 1.

72. Roos. 2.

73. Roos, 7.

74. Roos, 11.

75. Roos, 11.

76. Roos, 11.

77. Ross, 297.

78. Quoted in Ross, 297.

Chapter Three

1. Hays, Will, *Motion Pictures and Total Defense*, March 31, 1941, National Archives, Washington, DC, RG 46, box 2 of 2, 1.

2. Hays, 5.

3. Hays, 6.

4. Hays, 8.

5. Hays, 37–38.

6. Hays, 38.

7. Phelps, G. Allison, *An American's History of Hollywood: The Tower of Babel*, 1940, National Archives, Washington, DC, RG 46, box 2 of 2, 4.

8. Phelps, 4–5.

9. Phelps, 6–7.

10. Phelps, 8.

11. Phelps, 11.

12. Phelps, 25.

13. Phelps, 31.

14. Phelps, 35.

15. "Senator Clark Arrives in City," *Los Angeles Times*, June 19, 1941, ProQuest Historical Newspapers, Library of Congress.

16. "Senator Clark Arrives in City."

17. "Throng Hears Lindbergh in Fight on War," *Los Angeles Times*, June 21, 1941, ProQuest Historical Newspapers, Library of Congress.

18. "Lindbergh Warns U.S. Anew on War," *Baltimore Sun*, June 21, 1941, ProQuest Historical Newspapers, Library of Congress.

19. "Lindbergh Warns U.S. Anew on War," *Baltimore Sun*, June 21, 1941, ProQuest Historical Newspapers, Library of Congress.

20. "Lindbergh Warns U.S. Anew on War."

21. "Bowl Program Will Lure Many," *Los Angeles Times*, June 23, 1941, ProQuest Historical Newspapers, Library of Congress.

22. "Willkie Pleads for United Nation for Defense," *Christian Science Monitor*, July 24, 1941, ProQuest Historical Newspapers, Library of Congress.

23. "Willkie Pleads for United Nation for Defense."

24. "Willkie Pleads for United Nation for Defense."

25. Elton McMillan Jr., James, *Ernest W. McFarland* (Sharlot Hall Museum Press, 2004), 78.

26. Nye, Gerald P. "Our Madness Increases as Our Emergency Shrinks." Radio Address. August 1, 1941. See also Welky, 293–295.

27. Nye, Gerald P. "Our Madness Increases as Our Emergency Shrinks." Radio Address. August 1, 1941.

28. Nye, Gerald P. "Our Madness Increases as Our Emergency Shrinks."

29. Nye, radio address; Moser, John E, "Gigantic Engines of Propaganda: The 1941 Senate Investigation of Hollywood," *The Historian*, vol. 63, issue 4, June 2001.

30. Moser, John E, "Gigantic Engines of Propaganda: The 1941 Senate Investigation of Hollywood."

31. Moser, John E, "Gigantic Engines of Propaganda: The 1941 Senate Investigation of Hollywood."

32. Moser, John E, "Gigantic Engines of Propaganda: The 1941 Senate Investigation of Hollywood."

33. Moser, John E, "Gigantic Engines of Propaganda: The 1941 Senate Investigation of Hollywood," *The Historian*, vol. 63, issue 4, June 2001, 740.

34. "Nye Cites M.O.T. Short Subject," *Variety*, August 18, 1941.

35. "Nye Cites M.O.T. Short Subject."

36. "Nye Cites M.O.T. Short Subject."

37. Crippen, Harlan, "Wheeler: Patriot or Appeaser?" *U.S. Week*, August 16, 1941, National Archives, Washington, DC, RG 46, box 2 of 2.

38. Letter reprinted in Lorence, 86–87.

39. Letter reprinted in Lorence, 86–87.

40. Letter reprinted in Lorence, 86–87.

41. All quotes from Walter Wanger's address to the Annual Convention of the Variety Clubs of America. May 1941. Walter Wanger Papers. Wisconsin Center for Film and Theater Research.

42. Cole, Wayne, *America First—The Battle Against Intervention 1940–1941* (Madison: University of Wisconsin Press, 1951), 69.

43. Cole, 109; It should be noted that while Cole's book is well-researched, he is sympathetic to the America First Committee and blames both the weaknesses of America First as well as the "name-calling" of its opponents for the failure of the committee.

44. Birdwell, Michael E., *Celluloid Soldiers: Warner Bros.'s Campaign against Nazism* (New York: New York University Press, 1999), 156.

45. The statement was typed and distributed on September 2, 1941, Hunt, William, America First Statement, Community Relations Committee papers.

46. Ibid.

47. Ibid, 2.

48. Ibid, 3.

49. Ibid, 4.

50. Cole, Wayne, *Gerald P. Nye and American Foreign Relations* (St. Paul: University of Minnesota Press, 1962), 185.

51. Memo from John T. Flynn to Burton K. Wheeler dated August 6, 1941. National Archives, Washington, DC, RG 46, box 2 of 2.

52. Memo from John T. Flynn to Burton K. Wheeler dated August 6, 1941.

53. Glasgow, Andrew, "Promoting Unity Behind Defense," *New York Times*, August 31, 1941, National Archives, Washington, DC, RG 46, box 1 of 1.

54. Glasgow, Andrew, "Promoting Unity Behind Defense."

55. "Hays Strikes at Charges," *Los Angeles Times*, August 31, 1941, 3. ProQuest Historical Newspapers.

56. "Hays Strikes at Charges."

57. "Hays Strikes at Charges."

58. Letter from D. C. Phelps to Senator Wheeler, Dated September 1, 1941, National Archives, Washington, DC, RG 46, box 2 of 2.

59. Letter from D. C. Phelps to Senator Wheeler, Dated September 1, 1941, National Archives, Washington, DC, RG 46, box 2 of 2. Roosevelt's New Deal was referred to as the "Jew Deal" because of the large Jewish support that was given by Hollywood to the president's recovery programs during the Great Depression.

60. Memo from Lucy Salamanca to Baily Stortz, Clerk of the Senate Interstate Commerce Committee, dated September 3, 1941, National Archives, Washington, DC, RG 46, box 2 of 2.

61. Letter from Mary Kipling of the National Legion of Mothers of America to Senator Wheeler dated September 3, 1941, National Archives, Washington, DC, RG 46, box 2 of 2.

62. Letter from Furlow to Wood, September 4, 1941, National Archives, Washington, DC, RG 46, box 2 of 2.

63. The 1938 investigation of communism in Hollywood only gets a brief mention in Ogden, August Raymond, *The Dies Committee: A Study of the Special House Investigation of Un-American Activities, 1938–1944* (Washington DC: The Catholic University of America Press, 1945), 212–213.

64. Memo from Norr to Hays, written by Silberberg, February 1, 1940, Motion Picture Association of America general correspondence files, microfilm roll 6, Margaret Herrick Library.

65. Memo from Norr to Hays, written by Silberberg, February 1, 1940, Motion Picture Association of America general correspondence files, microfilm roll 6, Margaret Herrick Library.

66. Letter Edward Kendrick to Senator Wheeler dated September 4, 1941, National Archives, Washington, DC, RG 46, box 2 of 2.

67. Letter from Paul Kineiry to Senator Clark dated August 2, 1941, National Archives, Washington, DC, RG 46, box 1 of 1.

68. Letter from Russell Mack to Senator Clark dated August 2, 1941, National Archives, Washington, DC, RG 46, box 1 of 1.

69. Letter from John Chancellor to Senator Clark on August 3, 1941, National Archives, Washington, DC, RG 46, box 1 of 1.

70. Letter from Ruth Richardson to Senator Wheeler dated August 9, 1941, National Archives, Washington, DC, RG 46, box 1 of 1.

71. Letter from Mrs. H. Ladd McLinden to Senator Clark dated September 4, 1941, National Archives, Washington, DC, RG 46, box 1 of 1.

72. Letter from Helen Connell to Senator Clark (undated), National Archives, Washington, DC, RG 46, box 1 of 1.

73. Letter from Helen Connell to Senator Clark (undated), National Archives, Washington, DC, RG 46, box 1 of 1.

74. The radio addresses were delivered on August 10 and 24, respectively. National Archives, Washington, DC, RG 46, box 2 of 2.

75. Phelps Attack on Senate Investigation. September 8, 1941, Community Relation Committee papers.

76. The original resolution can be found at the National Archives, Washington, DC, RG 46, box 2 of 2.

77. Neal, Steve, *Dark Horse: A Biography of Wendell Willkie* (Garden City: Doubleday & Company, Inc., 1984), 213.

Chapter Four

1. "Willkie Hurls New Bombshell," *Hollywood Reporter*, September 9, 1941, Community Relations Committee Papers.

2. "Willkie Hurls New Bombshell," *Hollywood Reporter*, September 9, 1941. All previously mentioned articles also ran on September 9.

3. Willkie, *Hollywood Reporter*, September 19, 1941, Community Relations Committee Papers.

4. Willkie, *Hollywood Reporter*, September 19, 1941, Community Relations Committee Papers.

5. Willkie, *Hollywood Reporter*, September 19, 1941, Community Relations Committee Papers.

6. Willkie, *Hollywood Reporter*, September 19, 1941, Community Relations Committee Papers.

7. Willkie, *Hollywood Reporter*, September 19, 1941, Community Relations Committee Papers.

8. *Propaganda in Motion Pictures: Hearings Before a Subcommittee of the Committee on Interstate Commerce*. United States Senate, Seventy-Seventh Congress, First Session on S. Res. 152: A Resolution Authorizing an Investigation of War Propaganda Disseminated by the Motion-Picture Industry and of Any Monopoly in the Production or Exhibition of Motion Pictures. September 9 to 16, 1941. Digitized by Google for the University of Michigan. All quotes throughout this manuscript are from the aforementioned congressional record unless otherwise noted.

9. Jowett, Garth S., "A Capacity for Evil: The 1915 Supreme Court Mutual Decision," *Controlling Hollywood: Censorship and Regulation in the Studio Era*, edited by Matthew Bernstein (New Jersey: Rutgers University Press, 1999), 16.

10. Moffitt, Jack, "Nye Hold Floor All Day—Talks Los, Proves Nothing; Can't Point Out Propaganda," *Hollywood Reporter*, September 10, 1941.

11. Moffitt, Jack, "Nye Hold Floor All Day—Talks Los, Proves Nothing; Can't Point Out Propaganda."

12. Pearson, Drew, "Drew Pearson Says," *Hollywood Reporter*, September 10, 1941.

13. Phelps, G. Allison, *An American's History of Hollywood: The Tower of Babel*, 1940, National Archives, Washington, DC, RG 46, box 2 of 2, 22.

14. "Sen. Pepper Calls Nye Anti-Semite," *The Sentinel*, v.123, no. 12, 1941, 67.

15. Fox, George G., "From the Watch Tower," *The Sentinel*, v.123, no. 7, 1941, 9.

16. The *Hollywood Reporter*, August 22, 1941, National Archives, Washington, DC, RG 46, box 2 of 2.

17. Sternheimer, Karen, *Celebrity Culture and the American Dream: Stardom and Social Mobility* (New York: Routledge, 2011), 3. See also, Ross, Steven, *Hollywood Left and Right: How Movie Stars Shaped American Politics* (New York: Oxford University Press, 2011).

18. Welky, 291.

19. Letter to Burton K. Wheeler on August 1, 1941, from John P. Hutchings of Samuel Goldwyn, Inc., National Archives, Washington, DC, RG 46, box 2 of 2. The full letter read, "I resent your statement that studio employees were forced to attend the Wendell Willkie Unity Rally at the Hollywood Bowl recently. None of us at this Studio were forced to attend and many did not attend. If this is our idea of promoting publicity, then I think it's damanably [sic] cheap!"

20. "Borzage Denies Nye Charge of Ouster from 'Storm,'" *Variety*, September 15, 1941.

21. Letter from Ada Hanifin to Senator Clark dated September 9, 1941, National Archives, Washington, DC, RG 46, box 1 of 1.

22. Letter from Ada Hanifin to Senator Clark dated September 9, 1941, National Archives, Washington, DC, RG 46, box 1 of 1.

23. Letter from Ada Hanifin to Senator Clark dated September 9, 1941, National Archives, Washington, DC, RG 46, box 1 of 1.

24. Wendell Willkie statement to the press, September 10, 1941, 1941 War Film Hearings, File 52, Wendell L. Willkie Statements, Margaret Herrick Library.

25. "NYE BRANDS FILIMS 5TH COLUMN," *Variety*. September 9, 1941.

26. "NYE BRANDS FILIMS 5TH COLUMN."

27. "NYE BRANDS FILIMS 5TH COLUMN."

28. Golden, Herb, "Arizona Senator Takes Nye for Count in Word Dueling," *Variety*, September 10, 1941.

29. "Applause and Hisses, Both Sides," *Variety*, September 10, 1941.

30. Moffitt, Jack, "Nye Hold Floor All Day—Talks Los, Proves Nothing; Can't Point Out Propaganda," *Hollywood Reporter*, September 10, 1941.

31. "MUD-SLINGING THE PIX BIZ," *Variety*, September 10, 1941.

32. Willkie, Wendell, "Text of Willkie Statements in Defense of the Industry, *Motion Picture Herald*, September 13, 1941, 18.

Chapter Five

1. Attendance estimate from *Variety*, September 11, 1941.

2. Schenck was in legal trouble for tax evasion.

3. The anti-Semitism of the committee based on similar observations was noted in Dick, Bernard F., *The Star-Spangled Screen: The American World War II Film* (Lexington: University Press of Kentucky, 1985), 90.

4. Black, Gregory D., *Hollywood Censored: Morality Codes, Ethics, and The Movies* (Cambridge: Cambridge University Press, 1994), 149.

5. Moffitt, Jack. "Investigation in Deeper Bog," *Hollywood Reporter*, September 11, 1941.

6. "Willkie Makes Prompt Reply to Nye Charge," *Motion Picture Daily*, September 10, 1941, 4

7. Moffitt, "Investigation in Deeper Bog."

8. Wendell Willkie statement, September 11, 1941, 1941 War Film Hearings, File 52, Wendell L. Willkie Statements, Margaret Herrick Library.

9. "6 Man Monopoly in Films Seeks U.S. War, Says Senator," *San Francisco Examiner*, September 11, 1941.

10. "The Film Inquiry: Willkie Blasts Senators, Says They're Using Probe to Fight U.S. Foreign Policy," *San Francisco Chronicle*, September 11, 1941.

11. Multiple sources reported interjections from Willkie that did not appear in the congressional record. See "Clark Digs Up Trust Charge," *Variety*, September 11, 1941; Barkley, Frederick R., "Willkie Asks War Film Review by Senators Judging Propaganda," *New York Times*, September 11, 1941.

12. Willkie, Wendell, "Text of Willkie Statements in Defense of the Industry," *Motion Picture Herald*, September 13, 1941, 18.

13. Glenn, Charles, "Hollywood Vine," *People's World*, September 11, 1941. *People's World* is a left-wing publication in San Francisco.

14. Glenn, Charles, "Hollywood Vine." Glenn likely confused Clark of Missouri (who testified on this day) for Clark of Idaho (who was the chairman)

15. Glenn, Charles, "Hollywood Vine."

16. Glenn, Charles, "Hollywood Vine."

17. Carson, Lee, "Willkie Backs Accuracy of Films on War," *Los Angeles Examiner*, September 11, 1941.

18. Carson, Lee, "Willkie Backs Accuracy of Films on War."

19. McManus, John T., "Hollywood's Crime," *Washington Post*, September 10, 1941.

20. McManus, John T., "Hollywood's Crime."

21. Nover, Barnet, "On Propaganda," *Washington Post*, September 10, 1941.

22. Nover, Barnet, "On Propaganda." The current Merriam-Webster dictionary still support's Nover's claim, defining the term both historic and contemporary as: "(1) capitalized, a congregation of the Roman curia having jurisdiction over missionary territories and related institutions; (2) the spreading of ideas, information, or rumor for the purpose of helping or injuring an institution, a cause, or a person; (3) ideas, facts, or allegations spread deliberately to further one's cause or to damage an opposing cause; also: a public action having such an effect."

23. Nover, Barnet, "On Propaganda."

24. "What Is Anti-Semitism?" *New York Daily News*, September 10, 1941.

25. "What Is Anti-Semitism?"

26. "What Is Anti-Semitism?"

27. Ainsworth, Ed, "As You Might Say," *Los Angeles Times*, September 11, 1941.

28. Ainsworth, Ed, "As You Might Say."

29. Ainsworth, Ed, "As You Might Say."

30. Pegler, Westbrook, "Fair Enough," *Los Angeles Times*, September 15, 1941; This article was filed under the second day's press coverage even though it was dated September 15. There are no specific observations that key this piece to any specific day of the hearings, so I have decided to keep its coverage in line with how it was filed at the time.

31. Pegler, Westbrook, "Fair Enough."

32. Pegler, Westbrook, "Fair Enough."

33. "Isolationist Boomerang," *New York Herald Tribune*, September 10, 1941.

34. "Film Inquiry Senators Scored," *New York Times*, September 10, 1941.

35. "The Isolationists Put on a Show," *Christian Science Monitor*, September 11, 1941.

36. Lasky, Jesse, "Nye is 'Dared' to Investigate Sgt. York," *San Francisco Chronicle*, September 11, 1941.

Chapter Six

1. Lindbergh, Charles, "Des Moines Speech," September 11, 1941. http://www.charleslindbergh.com/americanfirst/speech.asp

2. Lindbergh, Charles, "Des Moines Speech."

3. "Chaplin Faces Senate Quiz on War Films," *Los Angeles Examiner*, September 14, 1941.

4. Attendance noted in O'Donnell, John, "Film Monopoly Glorifies War, Inquiry Told," *Times Herald*, September 12, 1941.

5. Morris, George H., "Skouras Urges Industry 'Moral Merger,'" *Film Daily*, June 7, 1941, 4.

6. Memo quoted at length in Doherty, 58.

7. Flynn only named those from RKO—*Ramparts We Watch, Americans All—Men from Many Lands, Britain's R.A.F., Australia at War, Peace Under Hitler, War in Europe, Men of the F.B.I., Gateways to Panama*, and *Crisis in the Atlantic*.

8. Hoffman, Irving, "Tales of Hoffman," *Hollywood Reporter*, September 12, 1941.

9. Hoffman, Irving, "Tales of Hoffman."

10. Hoffman, Irving, "Tales of Hoffman."

11. Bernstein, Arnie, *Swastika Nation: Fritz Kuhn and the Rise and Fall of the German-American Bund* (New York: St. Martin's, 2013), 277.

12. Hill, Cap, "Flynn Drools Same Drivel," *Variety*, September 11, 1941.

13. Hill, Cap, "Flynn Drools Same Drivel."

14. "Flynn's Puppet Show," *Variety*, September 11, 1941.

15. "Flynn's Puppet Show."

16. Moffitt, Jack, "Senate Hearing Still Big Yawn," *Hollywood Reporter*, September 12, 1941.

17. Moffitt, Jack, "Senate Hearing Still Big Yawn."

18. Moffitt, Jack, "Senate Hearing Still Big Yawn."

19. Moffitt, Jack, "Senate Hearing Still Big Yawn."

20. Pearson, Drew, "Drew Pearson Says," *Hollywood Reporter*, September 12, 1941.

21. Pearson, Drew, "Drew Pearson Says."

22. Pearson, Drew, "Drew Pearson Says."

23. "1-Man Hope in Film Probe," *PM*, September 12, 1941.

24. Mittauer, Frank, "Willkie Hits at Film Snipers," *Daily News*, September 12, 1941.

25. Mittauer, Frank, "Willkie Hits at Film Snipers."

26. Boddy, Manchester, "Views of the News," *Daily News*, September 15, 1941. See also, "Chaplin Called as Witness in Senate Film Investigation," *Los Angeles Times*, September 14, 1941.

27. Boddy, Manchester, "Views of the News," *Daily News*, September 15, 1941.

28. Boddy, Manchester, "Views of the News," *Daily News*, September 15, 1941.

29. O'Donnell, John, "Film Monopoly Glorifies War, Inquiry Told," *Times Herald*, September 12, 1941.

30. An overview and analysis of the Dreyfus affair can be found in Arendt, Hanna, *The Origins of Totalitarianism* (New York: Harcourt, 1968), 89–120.

31. Thompson, Dorothy, "On the Record—Collusion: Dorothy Thompson Says Nazi Party Line in U.S. Probes Movies as the Entering Wedge," *Cleveland Plain Dealer*, September 12, 1941.

32. Thompson, Dorothy, "On the Record—Collusion: Dorothy Thompson Says Nazi Party Line in U.S. Probes Movies as the Entering Wedge."

33. Thompson, Dorothy, "On the Record—Collusion: Dorothy Thompson Says Nazi Party Line in U.S. Probes Movies as the Entering Wedge."

34. "A 1941 Inquisition," *Yakima Daily Republic*, September 13, 1941.

35. "Willkie's Chance," *Grandview Herald*, September 11, 1941.

36. Johnson, Gen, Hugh S., "Freedom of Opinion Seems Involved in Proposed Film Propaganda Probe," *Philadelphia Inquirer*, September 12, 1941.

37. Lincoln, Gould, "The Political Mill," *Evening Star*, September 11, 1941.

38. Robb, Arthur, "The Fourth Estate," *Editor & Publisher*, September 13, 1941.

39. Robb, Arthur, "The Fourth Estate."

Chapter Seven

1. Memo from Francis Harmon to Will Hays, Febrary 9, 1940. MPAA general correspondence files, Roll 6.

2. Ward, Paul W., "Willkie Stays Away from Movie Hearing," *Baltimore Sun*, September 16, 1941, Motion Picture Academy Library, Jock Lawrence Papers, United States Senate—Clippings 1941, 1.f-12.

3. Letter from CBS to Senator Clark on September 15, 1941, National Archives, Washington, DC, RG 46, Box 2 of 2.

4. "Here and There," *Harrison's Reports*, September 20, 1941, Media History Digital Library, http://archive.org/stream/harrisonsreports23harr#page/n163

5. Fidler, Jimmie, "Jimmie Fidler," *Chicago Times*, September 21, 1941.

6. "McNailly, William J., "More or Less Personal," *Minneapolis Tribune*, September 23, 1941.

7. "McNailly, William J., "More or Less Personal."

8. McFarland first said England, mistakenly, and quickly corrected himself.

9. "Movies Biased? Editor Asks If Inquiry Is," *Washington Post*, September 15, 1941.

10. "Movies Biased? Editor Asks If Inquiry Is."

11. "Fidler Airs Woes at Probe," *Variety*, September 16, 1941.

12. "Fidler Airs Woes at Probe."

13. "Fidler Airs Woes at Probe."

14. "Fidler Airs Woes at Probe."

15. "D.A. Raps Senate Probe," *Variety*, September 16, 1941.

16. "D.A. Raps Senate Probe."

17. "D.A. Raps Senate Probe."

18. "Zanuck Tells Legion Films Guard Liberty," *Motion Picture Daily*, September 16, 1941.

19. "Zanuck Tells Legion Films Guard Liberty."

20. "Harry Brand and Russ Birdwell Pin Label of 'Liar' on Fidler," *Hollywood Reporter*, September 16, 1941.

21. "Harry Brand and Russ Birdwell Pin Label of 'Liar' on Fidler."

22. Stein, Herb, "An Open Letter to Hollywood's Lord-Haw! Haw!" *Hollywood Reporter*, September 17, 1941.

23. Stein, Herb, "An Open Letter to Hollywood's Lord-Haw! Haw!"

24. Stein, Herb, "An Open Letter to Hollywood's Lord-Haw! Haw!"

25. Pegler, Westbrook, untitled column, *Los Angeles Times*, September 13, 1941.

26. Pegler, Westbrook, untitled column, *Los Angeles Times*, September 13, 1941.

27. Pegler, Westbrook, untitled column, *Los Angeles Times*, September 13, 1941.

28. Bromfield, Louis, "Letters to the Editor: Behind the 'Investigation' of the Movies," *Washington Post*, September 16, 1941.

29. Bromfield, Louis, "Letters to the Editor: Behind the 'Investigation' of the Movies."

30. Bromfield, Louis, "Letters to the Editor: Behind the 'Investigation' of the Movies."

31. Schallert, Edwin, "Old War Movies Bold; Modern Conservative," *Los Angeles Times*, September 17, 1941.

32. Schallert, Edwin, "Old War Movies Bold; Modern Conservative."

33. "Red Propaganda Films Due for Release, Movie Probe Told," *Los Angeles Examiner*, September 16, 1941.

34. "New Laws for Film Industry Said in Offing," *Citizen-News*, September 16, 1941.

35. Tucker, Ray, "News Behind the News," *Citizen-News*, September 15, 1941.

Intermission

1. "Olson Protests Implications: Charges Probe Unjustifiable Attack on Movie Industry," Olson, Culbert L., *Los Angeles Examiner*, September 17, 1941.

2. "Olson Protests Implications: Charges Probe Unjustifiable Attack on Movie Industry."

3. "Olson Protests Implications: Charges Probe Unjustifiable Attack on Movie Industry."

4. Hatchen, Arthur, "Roosevelt Jeers War Film Charge," *Los Angeles Examiner*, September 17, 1941.

5. Moffitt, Jack, "Moffitt in Washington," *Hollywood Reporter*, September 17, 1941.

6. Moffitt, Jack, "Moffitt in Washington."

7. Moffitt, Jack, "Moffitt in Washington."

8. Wilkerson III, W. R, *Hollywood Godfather: The Life and Crimes of Billy Wilkerson*, Chicago: Chicago Review Press, 2018, 80.

9. Wilkerson III, W. R, *Hollywood Godfather*.

10. "Film Probers to Ignore F.D.R. Denial," *Hollywood Citizen News*, September 17, 1941.

11. "Labor Attacks Fifth-Wheelers," *Hollywood Reporter*, September 17, 1941.

12. Pearson, Drew, "Drew Pearson Says," *Hollywood Reporter*, September 17, 1941.

13. Wilkerson III, W. R., *Hollywood Godfather: The Life and Crimes of Billy Wilkerson*, Chicago: Chicago Review Press, 2018, 51–2.

14. Wilkerson III, W. R, *Hollywood Godfather*.

15. Wilkerson III, W. R, *Hollywood Godfather*.

16. "Editorial Comment: The Editor's Column," *Hollywood Citizen-News*, September 17, 1941.

17. Othman, Frederick C., "Pure Propaganda is Box Office Poison," *Los Angeles Daily News*, September 18, 1941.

18. Othman, Frederick C., "Pure Propaganda is Box Office Poison."

19. Othman, Frederick C., "Pure Propaganda is Box Office Poison."

20. "The Inquiry and the Answer," *Motion Picture Herald*, September 20, 1941.

21. "The Inquiry and the Answer."

22. "Film Inquiry Legal, Says Senator Clark," *San Francisco Chronicle*, September 20, 1941.

23. "Film Inquiry Legal, Says Senator Clark."

24. "Producers of Atrocity Films Hire Willkie," *Free American*, September 18, 1941.

25. "Die Staatsfeinde," *Free American*, September 18, 1941.

26. "Die Staatsfeinde."

27. "Die Staatsfeinde."

28. McFarland, Ernest, Speech at an Ohio Democratic Rally, September 21, 1941, *The Ernest W. McFarland Papers: The United States Senate Years 1940–1952*, James E. McMillan (ed.), 52.

29. McFarland, Ernest, Speech at an Ohio Democratic Rally, September 21, 1941, *The Ernest W. McFarland Papers: The United States Senate Years 1940–1952*, James E. McMillan (ed.), 53.

30. National Archives, Washington, DC, RG 46, box 2 of 2.

31. National Archives, Washington, DC, RG 46, box 2 of 2.

32. "War Films Face Boycott Threat," *New York Times*, September 20, 1941.

33. "War Films Face Boycott Threat."

34. "Fact, If in Film Form, Annoys That Committee," *Washington Post*, September 23, 1941.

35. Winchell, Walter, "Walter Winchell on Broadway," *Washington Times Herald*, September 22, 1941.

36. "Police Block Pickeet War as Nye Talks," *Sunday Mirror*, September 21, 1941, Jock Lawrence Papers, United States Senate—Clippings 1941, 1.f-12, Margaret Herrick Library.

37. "Police Block Pickeet War as Nye Talks."

38. Pearson, Drew, "Drew Pearson Says," *Hollywood Reporter*, September 22, 1941.

39. "Warmongering by the Books," *San Francisco Chronicle*, September 19, 1941.

40. "Inquiry and Invective," *Newsweek*, September 22, 1941.

41. "Hollywood Fights," *New Republic*, September 15, 1941.

42. Anderson, John, "The Drama by John Anderson," *New York Journal-American*, September 21, 1941.

43. "Hollywood in Washington," *Time*, September 22, 1941.

44. "Hollywood in Washington."

45. "Hollywood in Washington."

46. "Hollywood in Washington."

47. "Critic Assists Senate Film Probe," *Social Justice*, September 22, 1941.

48. Screen Actors Guild resolution dated September 22, 1941, National Archives, Washington, DC, RG 46, box 2 of 2. The memo was sent from Kenneth Thomson, executive secretary of the SAG to Wheeler.

Chapter Eight

1. Pearson, Drew and Robert S. Allen, "Hollywood Aids Film Quiz," *Tucson Daily Citizen*, Septmeber 23, 1941.

2. Gomery, Douglas, *The Hollywood Studio System: A History* (London: British Film Institute, 2005), 32.

3. Gomery, 104.

4. Gomery, 105.

5. Carr, Seven, *Hollywood & Anti-Semitism: A Cultural History up to World War II* (Cambridge: Cambridge University Press, 2001), 173.

6. "Producer Say Screen Monopoly Impossible," *Los Angeles Times*, September 23, 1941.

7. Muscio, Giuliana, *Hollywood's New Deal* (Philadelphia: Temple University Press, 1997), 47.

8. Hume, Oscar, "Downey Rips Probe Charges," *Film Daily*, September 24, 1941.

9. Hume, Oscar, "Downey Rips Probe Charges."

10. "Underground Biz Spurred by Inquiry," *Film Daily*, September 23, 1941.

11. "Critics Nix Senate Charges," *Film Daily*, September 23, 1941.

12. "Critics Nix Senate Charges."

13. "Critics Nix Senate Charges."

14. Moffitt, Jack, "Scheck Turns Tables on Solons, Teaches Inquisitors Some Common Facts About Pix; Wins Over His Audience," *Hollywood Reporter*, September 23, 1941. The Rex Moffitt refered to here was a prominent horse that was found in Western film serials of the 1920s and 1930s, the first of which was titled *The King of the Wild Horses* (1924).

15. Moffitt, Jack, "Scheck Turns Tables on Solons, Teaches Inquisitors Some Common Facts About Pix; Wins Over His Audience."

16. Moffitt, Jack, "Scheck Turns Tables on Solons, Teaches Inquisitors Some Common Facts About Pix; Wins Over His Audience."

17. Moffitt, Jack, "Scheck Turns Tables on Solons, Teaches Inquisitors Some Common Facts About Pix; Wins Over His Audience."

18. Moffitt, Jack, "Scheck Turns Tables on Solons, Teaches Inquisitors Some Common Facts About Pix; Wins Over His Audience."

9. "Schenck Throws Quiz for Loss," *Variety*, September 24, 1941.

20. "Schenck Throws Quiz for Loss."

21. "N.Y. Labor Federation Declares All-Out War on Fifth-Wheelers," *Hollywood Reporter*, September 23, 1941.

22. Frakes, Margaret, "Why the Movie Investigation," *Christian Century*, September 24, 1941.

23. Frakes, Margaret, "Why the Movie Investigation."

24. Frakes, Margaret, "Why the Movie Investigation." It is also worth noting that in the original text, Frakes's use of "Nazi" was not capitalized, writing instead "nazi." This could be a simple copyediting error, but it could be a purposeful error to minimize the importance of the Nazi regime.

25. Hynes, Betty, "Sen. Reynolds, Fiancée Eclipse Film Moguls at Pearson Party," *Washington Times Herald*, September 24, 1941.

Chapter Nine

1. Moffitt, September 35, 1941.
2. "War-Whooping Denied by Schenck," *Variety*, September 25, 1941.
3. "Dietz Says Fidler 'Liar'" plus Press Gag Attempt Denied," *Variety*, September 25, 1941.
4. Phelps, G. Allison, *An American's History of Hollywood: The Tower of Babel*, 1940 (National Archives, Washington, DC), 13.
5. "War-Whooping Denied by Schenck," *Variety*, September 25, 1941.
6. "War-Whooping Denied by Schenck."
7. "War-Whooping Denied by Schenck."
8. "War-Whooping Denied by Schenck."
9. Moffitt, Jack, "Propaganda Charge Squelched," *Hollywood Reporter*, September 25, 1941.
10. Moffitt, Jack, "Propaganda Charge Squelched."
11. Moffitt, Jack, "Propaganda Charge Squelched."
12. Hays, Will, *Motion Pictures and Total Defense*, March 31, 1940, National Archives, Washington, DC, RG 46, box 2 of 2.
13. "Miss Hellman Calls Film Quiz a Disgrace," *Washington Post*, September 25, 1941.

Chapter Ten

1. "U.S. Dailies Editorially Rake Senate Witch Hunt," *Film Daily*, September 25, 1941.
2. The ad for Sergeant York appeared in the September 22 issue of the *Hollywood Reporter*. National Archives, Washington, DC, RG 46, box 2 of 2.
3. Pearson, Drew, "Senators' Case Bogs to Zero," *Hollywood Reporter*, September 26, 1941.
4. Doherty, Thomas, *Hollywood and Hitler 1933–1939* (New York: Columbia University Press, 2013), 35–36.
5. Yogerst, Chris, *From the Headlines to Hollywood: The Birth and Boom of Warner Bros.* (Lapham: Rowman & Littlefield, 2016); Scheuer, Philip K., "Nazi Gestapo Kayoed in Hard-Hitting Underground," *Los Angeles Times*, June 23, 1941.
6. "Underground, a Film Dealing with Radio Anti-Nazi Activities, Seen at the Globe," *New York Times*, June 23, 1941.
7. Smith, Cecil, "Underground is Propaganda but has Engrossing Story," *Chicago Daily Tribune*, August 15, 1941.
8. "Status of Aubrey Blair Denied," *Variety*, September 26, 1941.
9. "Blair Answers Tobey Charge," *Variety*, September 30, 1941.
10. Resolution signed by J. W. Buzzell, the Secretary of Treasury, LA Labor Council, on October 6, 1941. Resolution was sent to Senator Wheeler on October 10, 1941. National Archives, RG 46. Box 2 of 2.
11. Hays also vaguely defined films as a primary means of entertainment in his 1941 dossier on the industry; Hays, Will, *Motion Pictures and Total Defense*, March 31, 1941, National Archives, RG 46 box 2 of 2.
12. Doherty, Thomas, *Pre-Code Hollywood: Sex, Immorality, and Insurrection in American Cinema 1930–1934* (New York: Columbia University Press, 1999), 320.

13. Moffitt, Jack, "New Charges in Film Quiz Hurled," *Hollywood Reporter*, September 25, 1941.

14. Moffitt, Jack, "New Charges in Film Quiz Hurled."

15. Moffitt, Jack, "New Charges in Film Quiz Hurled."

16. Moffitt, Jack, "New Charges in Film Quiz Hurled."

17. Moffitt, Jack, "New Charges in Film Quiz Hurled."

18. "Warner Defends Picture Policy," *Motion Picture Daily*, September 26, 1941, 4. http://www.archive.org/stream/motionpicturedai50unse#page/n569/mode/2up/search/wendell+willkie

19. "Warner Defends Picture Policy."

20. "Defensive Alliance Formed," *Variety*, September 30, 1941.

Chapter Eleven

1. Carson, Lee, "Film Quiz Accused as Smear by Senator," *Los Angeles Examiner*, September 27, 1941.

2. All session quotes in this chapter are from *Moving-Picture and Radio Propaganda*, pages 393–449

3. "Senate Vote on Film Sift Asked," *Hollywood Citizen-News*, September 26, 1941.

4. Yogerst, Chris, *From the Headlines to Hollywood: The Birth and Boom of Warner Bros.*, (Lanham: Rowman & Littlefield, 2016), 72.

5. Gomery, Douglas, *The Hollywood Studio System: A History* (London: British Film Institute, 2005), 118.

6. Moffitt, Jack, "Darryl Zanuck Thrills Hearing," *Hollywood Reporter*, September 27, 1941.

7. Trussell, C. P., "McFarland Accuses Tobey at Movie Inquiry of Act Prejudicial to U.S.," *Baltimore Sun*, September 27, 1941, ProQuest Historical Newspapers, Library of Congress, Washington, DC.

8. "Probe to Muddle Onward," *Variety*, September 29, 1941.

9. Trussell, C. P., "McFarland Accuses Tobey at Movie Inquiry of Act Prejudicial to U.S.," *Baltimore Sun*, September 27, 1941, ProQuest Historical Newspapers, Library of Congress, Washington, DC.

10. Trussell, C. P., "McFarland Accuses Tobey at Movie Inquiry of Act Prejudicial to U.S.," *Baltimore Sun*, September 27, 1941, ProQuest Historical Newspapers, Library of Congress, Washington, DC.

11. Donovan, Hedley, "Movie Probe Episode Ends Like Old Serial," *Washington Post*, ProQuest Historical Newspapers, Library of Congress, Washington, DC.

12. Moffitt, Jack, "Darryl Zanuck Thrills Hearing," *Hollywood Reporter*, September 27, 1941.

13. Moffitt, Jack, "Darryl Zanuck Thrills Hearing."

14. Gomery, Douglas, *The Hollywood Studio System: A History*, (London: British Film Institute, 2005), 83.

15. Francis, Warren B., "Bitter Words at Film Investigation," *Los Angeles Times*, September 27, 1941, ProQuest Historical Newspapers, Library of Congress, Washington, DC.

16. Andrews, Bert, "Film Inquiry Forgets Hollywood to Air Gossip on British Mission," *New York Herald Tribune*, September 27, 1941, ProQuest Historical Newspapers, Library of Congress, Washington, DC.

17. Francis, Warren B., "Bitter Words at Film Investigation," *Los Angeles Times*, September 27, 1941, ProQuest Historical Newspapers, Library of Congress, Washington, DC.

18. The congressional records uses the word "trumpet" here, but Jack Moffitt's quotation in the *Hollywood Reporter* and C. P. Trussell of the *Baltimore Sun* report that the word was "comedy."

19. Mattauer, Frank, "Zanuck Denies Shelving of Peace Film," *Los Angeles Daily News*, September 27, 1941.

20. Mattauer, Frank, "Zanuck Denies Shelving of Peace Film."

21. Donovan, Hedley, "Movie Probe Episode Ends Like Old Serial," *Washington Post*, ProQuest Historical Newspapers, Library of Congress, Washington, DC.

22. "Movie Probe End Sighted," *Hollywood Citizen-News*, September 27, 1941; "Film Inquiry Halt Denied," *Los Angeles Times*, September 28, 1941, ProQuest Historical Newspapers, Library of Congress, Washington, DC.

23. Moffitt, Jack, "Darryl Zanuck Thrills Hearing," *Hollywood Reporter*, September 27, 1941.

24. Moffitt, Jack, "Darryl Zanuck Thrills Hearing."

25. Moffitt, Jack, "Darryl Zanuck Thrills Hearing."

26. "Wash. Reports Hays Will Wind Up the Fifth-Wheel Inquiry," *Hollywood Reporter*, October 1, 1941.

27. "Picture Inquiry Censorship Step, Says Willkie," *Los Angeles Examiner*, September 27, 1941.

28. "Senators to See 6 Films in Test on Propaganda," *New York Herald Tribune*, September 28, 1941.

29. "Movie Quiz," *Washington Post*, September 28, 1941.

30. Wilkerson, W. K., "Tradeviews," *Hollywood Reporter*, September 30, 1941.

31. Wilkerson, W. K., "Tradeviews."

32. Clippings from the *Baltimore Sun*, September 25 and September 26, 1941, Jock Lawrence Papers.

United States Senate—Clippings 1941, 1.f-12, Margaret Herrick Library.

33. "Nye Claims Movie Propaganda is Proved by Senate Inquiry," *Baltimore Sun*, September 29, 1941, ProQuest Historical Newspapers, Library of Congress, Washington, DC.

34. "Nye Claims Movie Propaganda is Proved by Senate Inquiry."

35. "Nye Claims Movie Propaganda is Proved by Senate Inquiry."

Game Over

1. "Seeing Films Will Decide for Senators," *Hartford Courant*, September 28, 1941, ProQuest Historical Newspapers, Library of Congress, Washington, DC.

2. "Film Inquiry Halt Denied," *Los Angeles Times*, September 28, 1941, ProQuest Historical Newspapers, Library of Congress, Washington, DC.

3. "Films Hold Key to Verdict, Clark Says," *Washington Post*, September 28 1941, ProQuest Historical Newspapers, Library of Congress, Washington, DC.

4. Morgan, James, "Weak Spot in the Opposition," *Daily Boston Globe*, September 28, 1941, ProQuest Historical Newspapers, Library of Congress, Washington, DC.

5. Morgan, James, "Weak Spot in the Opposition."

6. Morgan, James, "Weak Spot in the Opposition."

7. McLemore, Henry (article has no title), *Los Angeles Times*, September 29, 1941.

8. McLemore, Henry, "Movie Investigation Proves Everything Else," *Evening Star*, September 29, 1941.

9. McLemore, Henry, "Film Quiz Disappoints Burle-Q Fans," *Evening Star*, October 1, 1941.

10. "Nation's Editors Press Fire on Propaganda Probe," *Film Daily*, October 1, 1941.

11. "Wheeler Blasts Film Industry," *Variety*, October 3, 1941.

12. "Wheeler Blasts Film Industry."

13. "Wheeler Blasts Film Industry."

14. "Wheeler Blasts Film Industry."

15. "Mady Christians Warns U.S. Not to Let It Happen Here," *Hollywood Reporter*, October 3, 1941.

16. "Mady Christians Warns U.S. Not to Let It Happen Here."

17. Text of Clark's radio address, CRC files, 31–08, California State University–Northridge.

18. Text of Clark's radio address, CRC files, 31–08, California State University–Northridge.

19. Text of Clark's radio address, CRC files, 31–08, California State University–Northridge.

20. Francis, Lorania K., "Film Inquiry Foes Flayed," *Los Angeles Times*, October 5, 1941; "Clark Says Film Quiz to Continue," *Los Angeles Examiner*, October 4, 1941.

21. "Chairman Says Film Inquiry Will Go Ahead," *New York Herald Tribune*, October 5, 1941, ProQuest Historical Newspapers, Library of Congress, Washington, DC.

22. "Chairman Says Film Inquiry Will Go Ahead."

23. "Chairman Says Film Inquiry Will Go Ahead."

24. Balio, Tino, *The American Film Industry* (Madison: The University of Wisconsin Press, 1985), 253.

25. "Movie Monopoly Rooting for War," *Social Justice*, October 6, 1941.

26. "Gov. Olson Pays Off," *Social Justice*, October 6, 1941.

27. National Archives, RG 46, box 2 of 2.

28. Francis, Lorania K., "Investigation of Films May Be Abandoned," *Los Angeles Times*, October 9, 1941, ProQuest Historical Newspapers, Library of Congress, Washington, DC.

29. Francis, Lorania K., "Investigation of Films May Be Abandoned."

30. Weller, Frank I., ""Dresses Like Banker, Looks Like Judge, Talks Like Cowboy," *Washington Post*, October 15, 1941, ProQuest Historical Newspapers, Library of Congress, Washington, DC.

31. Weller, Frank I., ""Dresses Like Banker, Looks Like Judge, Talks Like Cowboy."

32. Weller, Frank I., ""Dresses Like Banker, Looks Like Judge, Talks Like Cowboy."

33. Bell, Nelson B., "Mr. Willkie Has a Word about that Trial by Fury," *Washington Post*, October 21, 1941, ProQuest Historical Newspapers, Library of Congress, Washington, DC.

34. "Nazi Words to Girls Shocks First Lady," *New York Times*, October 20, 1941, ProQuest Historical Newspapers, Library of Congress, Washington, DC.

35. Quoted in "Mrs. Roosevelt Condemns Nazi Order to Girls," *New York Herald Tribune*, October 20, 1941, ProQuest Historical Newspapers, Library of Congress, Washington, DC.

36. "Nazi Words to Girls Shocks First Lady."

37. "Nazi Words to Girls Shocks First Lady."

38. Heffernan, Harold, "Hollywood Highlights," *Hartford Courant*, November 5, 1941, ProQuest Historical Newspapers, Library of Congress, Washington, DC.

39. "Willkie Tells Picture Pioneers Industry Gained New Stature in Washington," Motion Picture Herald, November 8, 1941, Media History Digital Library, http://www.archive.org/stream/motionpictureher145unse#page/n87/mode/2up/search/wendell+willkie.

40. "Film Men Called Derelict in Crisis," New York Times, November 15, 1941, ProQuest Historical Newspapers, Library of Congress, Washington, DC.

41. Wanger, Walter, "The Role of Movies in Morale," American Journal of Sociology, November 3, 1941, 378–383. Walter Wanger Papers, speeches file, Wisconsin Center for Film and Theater Research.

42. Press release from the Department of Commerce in Washington. NA, RG 46, box 2 of 2.

43. Press release from the Department of Commerce in Washington. NA, RG 46, box 2 of 2.

44. Press release from the Department of Commerce in Washington. NA, RG 46, box 2 of 2.

45. Press release from the Department of Commerce in Washington. NA, RG 46, box 2 of 2.

46. Quoted on the cover of the Motion Picture Herald, December 13, 1941, Media History Digital Library, http://www.archive.org/stream/motionpictureher145unse#page/n559/mode/2up/search/Pearl+Harbor.

47. Quigley, Martin, "Motion Pictures and the War," Motion Picture Herald, December 13, 1941, Media History Digital Library, http://www.archive.org/stream/motionpictureher145unse#page/n559/mode/2up/search/Pearl+Harbor.

48. "Newsreels Delayed by Censors," Motion Picture Herald, December 20, 1941, Media History Digital Library, http://www.archive.org/stream/motionpictureher145unse#page/n695/mode/2up/search/Pearl+Harbor.

49. "If an Air Raid Comes," Variety, December 17, 1941, Media History Digital Library, http://www.archive.org/stream/variety144-1941-12#page/n143/mode/2up/search/Pearl+Harbor

50. "Lose the Blackout Blues," Variety, December 24, 1941, Media History Digital Library, http://www.archive.org/stream/variety144-1941-12#page/n237/mode/2up/search/Pearl+Harbor

51. March of Time advertisement in the December 17 issue of Variety, 24, Media History Digital Library, http://www.archive.org/stream/variety144-1941-12#page/n143/mode/2up/search/Pearl+Harbor.

52. Crowther, Bosley, "NOW THAT WE'RE IN: The Actuality of War Should Compel Somber Restraint in Films," New York Times, December 14, 1941 (syndicated column, no publisher noted), Motion Picture World War II Files, Role of Motion Pictures in the War 1941–1944, 16.f-269, Margaret Herrick Library.

53. Crowther, Bosley, "NOW THAT WE'RE IN: The Actuality of War Should Compel Somber Restraint in Films."

54. Crowther, Bosley, "NOW THAT WE'RE IN: The Actuality of War Should Compel Somber Restraint in Films."

55. Several sources misreport this date, which perhaps stems back to an unfootnoted claim in Clayton R. Koppes and Gregory D. Black, Hollywood Goes to War: How Politics, Profits, and Propaganda Shaped World War II Movies (Los Angeles: University of California Press, 1987), 45.

56. Letter from Wheeler to Clark, National Archives, Washington, DC., RG 46, box 2 of 2.

57. Letter from Wheeler to Clark, National Archives, Washington, DC., RG 46, box 2 of 2.

58. Pryor, Thomas M., "Noting Some Major Battle Scars," New York Times, December 28, 1941, ProQuest Historical Newspapers, Library of Congress, Washington, DC.

59. Pryor, Thomas M., "Noting Some Major Battle Scars."

60. Rose, Billy, "Escapology Not the Answer; Showmen Must Sell Aggressive Americanism to Everybody," *Variety*, January 7, 1942, Motion Picture World War II Files, Role of Motion Pictures in the War 1941–1944, 16.f-269, Margaret Herrick Library.

61. Joseph, Robert, untitled column, *New York Herald Tribune*, April 5, 1942, Motion Picture World War II Files, Role of Motion Pictures in the War 1941–1944, 16.f-269, Margaret Herrick Library.

62. Wilkerson, W. R., "Tradeviews," *Hollywood Reporter*, September 18, 1942, and September 23, 1942, Motion Picture World War II Files, Role of Motion Pictures in the War 1941–1944, 16.f-269, Margaret Herrick Library.

63. Warner, Harry, "Patriotism in Pictures," *Variety*, January 7, 1942, Motion Picture World War II Files, 16.f-269, Role of Motion Pictures in the War 1941–1944, Margaret Herrick Library.

64. Warner, Harry, "Patriotism in Pictures."

65. Warner, Harry, "Patriotism in Pictures."

66. Walter Wanger Papers, speech files, Wisconsin Center for Film and Theater Research.

67. "Let's Begin to Win, Willkie's Academy Text," *Film Daily*, February 27, 1942, 4, Media History Digital Library.

68. "Let's Begin to Win, Willkie's Academy Text."

69. "Hollywood Goal $300,000 per Week," *Showmen's Trade Review*, May 9, 1942, 9.

70. "Hate Pictures Found Ineffective Propaganda," *Variety*, October 14, 1942, Motion Picture World War II Files, Role of Motion Pictures in the War 1941–1944, 16.f-269, Margaret Herrick Library.

71. "Hollywood's War Effort; Here Is the Overall Picture, Bureau of Motion Pictures, *Variety*, October 19, 1942, Motion Picture World War II Files, Role of Motion Pictures in the War 1941–1944, 16.f-269, Margaret Herrick Library.

72. Doherty, Thomas, "Frank Costello's Hands: Film, Television, and the Kefauver Crime Hearings," *Film History*, Volume 10, 1998, 368.

73. Elton McMillan Jr., James, *Ernest W. McFarland*, Sharlot Hall Museum Press, 2004, 91.

Epilogue

1. "C. S. Lewis Dead; Author, Critic, 64," *New York Times*, November 24, 1963, 18. http://www.nytimes.com/packages/html/books/lewis-obit.pdf.

2. "Aldous Huxley Dies of Cancer on Coast," *New York Times*, November 24, 1963, 1.https://www.nytimes.com/1963/11/24/archives/aldous-huxley-dies-of-cancer-on-coast-aldous-huxley-novelist-dead.html.

3. Doherty, Thomas, *Show Trial: Hollywood, HUAC, and the Birth of the Blacklist* (New York: Columbia University Press, 2018), 31.

4. Baum, Gary and Daniel Miller, "*The Hollywood Reporter*, After 65 Years, Addresses Role in Blacklist," November 19, 2012. https://www.hollywoodreporter.com/features/blacklist-thr-addresses-role-65-391931.

5. Collingwood, R. G., *The Idea of History* (New York: Oxford University Press, 1946), 366.

6. "4 in 10 Millennials Don't Know 6 Million Jews Were Killed in Holocaust, Study Shows," CBS News online, April 12, 2018. https://www.cbsnews.com/news/holocaust-study-millennials/

7. Chapman, Steve, "Why Young Americans Are Drawn to Socialism," *Reason*, May 21, 2018. https://reason.com/archives/2018/05/21/why-young-americans-are-drawn-to-sociali

8. Flaherty, Colleen, "The Vanishing History Major," *Inside Higher Ed*, November 27, 2018. https://www.insidehighered.com/news/2018/11/27/new-analysis-history-major-data-says -field-new-low-can-it-be-saved

9. "Anti-Semitic Incidents Surged Nearly 60% in 2017, According to New ADL Report," www.adl.org, February 27, 2018.

10. Churchwell, Sarah, *Behold America: The Entangled History of America First and the American Dream* (New York: Basic Books, 2018), 267–273.

Index

About the Author

Chris Yogerst is assistant professor of communication in the Department of Arts and Humanities at the University of Wisconsin–Milwaukee, where he teaches courses in film, media, and communication. Yogerst is a widely published author whose work can be found in books, journals, and the popular press. His first book, *From the Headlines to Hollywood: The Birth and Boom of Warner Bros* (2016), was published by Rowman & Littlefield. Additional essays can be found in the *Historical Journal of Film, Radio, and Television*, the *Journal of American Culture*, along with the *Washington Post* and *Los Angeles Review of Books*.

Printed in the United States
By Bookmasters